CW01659935

Constantin Brancusi

The essence of things

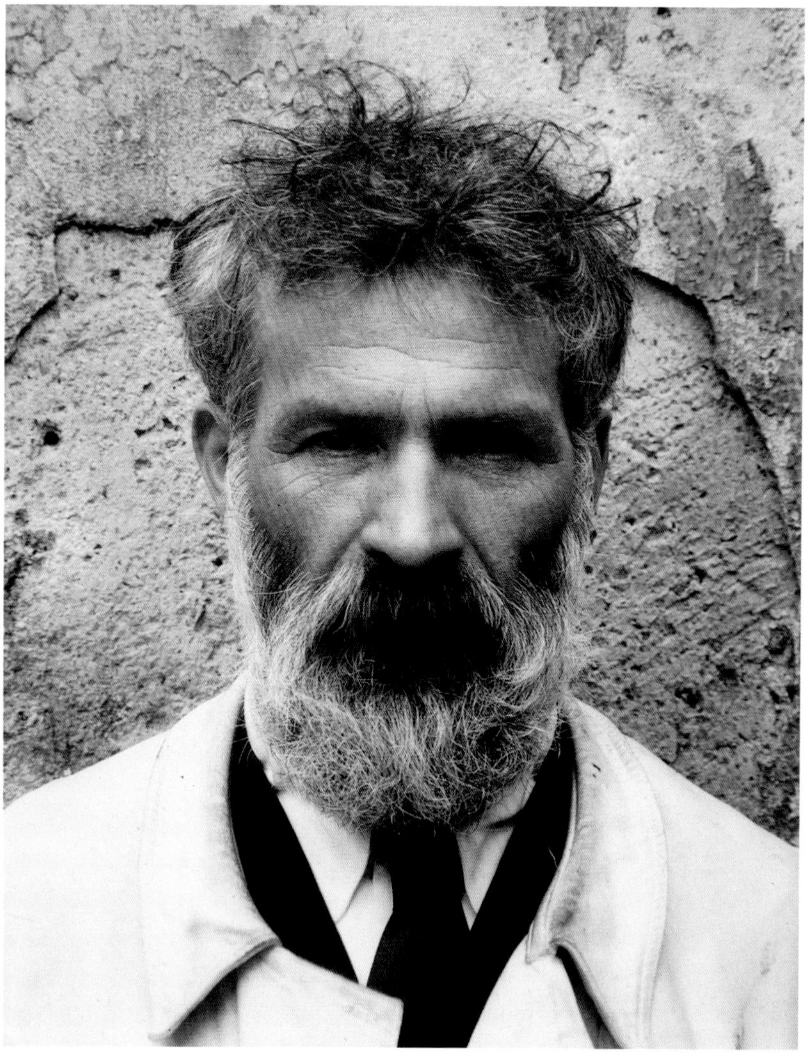

‘They are imbeciles who call my work abstract; that which they call abstract is the most realistic, because what is real is not the exterior form but the idea, the essence of things.’

Constantin Brancusi

The essence of things

EDITED BY
Carmen Giménez and Matthew Gale

WITH CONTRIBUTIONS BY
Sanda Miller, Alexandra Parigoris
and Jon Wood

Tate Publishing

Exhibition sponsored by

AVIVA

First published in 2004 by order of the Tate Trustees
by Tate Publishing, a division of Tate Enterprises Ltd,
Millbank, London SW1P 4RG
www.tate.org.uk
on the occasion of the exhibition jointly organised by

Tate Modern, London
29 January–23 May 2004

and

Solomon R. Guggenheim Museum, New York
10 June–19 September 2004

British Library Cataloguing in Publication Data
A catalogue record for this book is available
from the British Library

ISBN 1 85437 495 8 (pbk)
ISBN 1 85437 551 2 (hbk)

Distributed in the United States and Canada
by Harry N. Abrams, Inc., New York

Library of Congress Cataloging in Publication Data
Library of Congress Control Number: 2003113719

Designed by LewisHallam

Printed and bound in Belgium by
Snoeck-Ducaju & Zoon

All works are by Constantin Brancusi unless otherwise stated
Measurements of works of art are given in centimetres, height before width

FRONT COVER **Sleeping Muse I** (cat.20)
Hirshhorn Museum and Sculpture Garden, Smithsonian Institution
BACK COVER **Self-portrait** (Centre Pompidou, Paris, AM4002-717, PH709)
FRONTISPIECE Edward Steichen, **Portrait of Constantin Brancusi in Voulangis**
(Centre Pompidou, Paris, AM1988-1704, modern print)
For Brancusi's statement, see Selected Aphorisms, p.133
PAGE 6 **Studio view with marble Bird**, *c.*1922–3
(Centre Pompidou, Paris, AM4002-276(1), PH31A, modern print)
PAGE 10 **Studio view**, *c.*1943–6
(Centre Pompidou, Paris, AM4002-768, PH144, modern print)

Contents

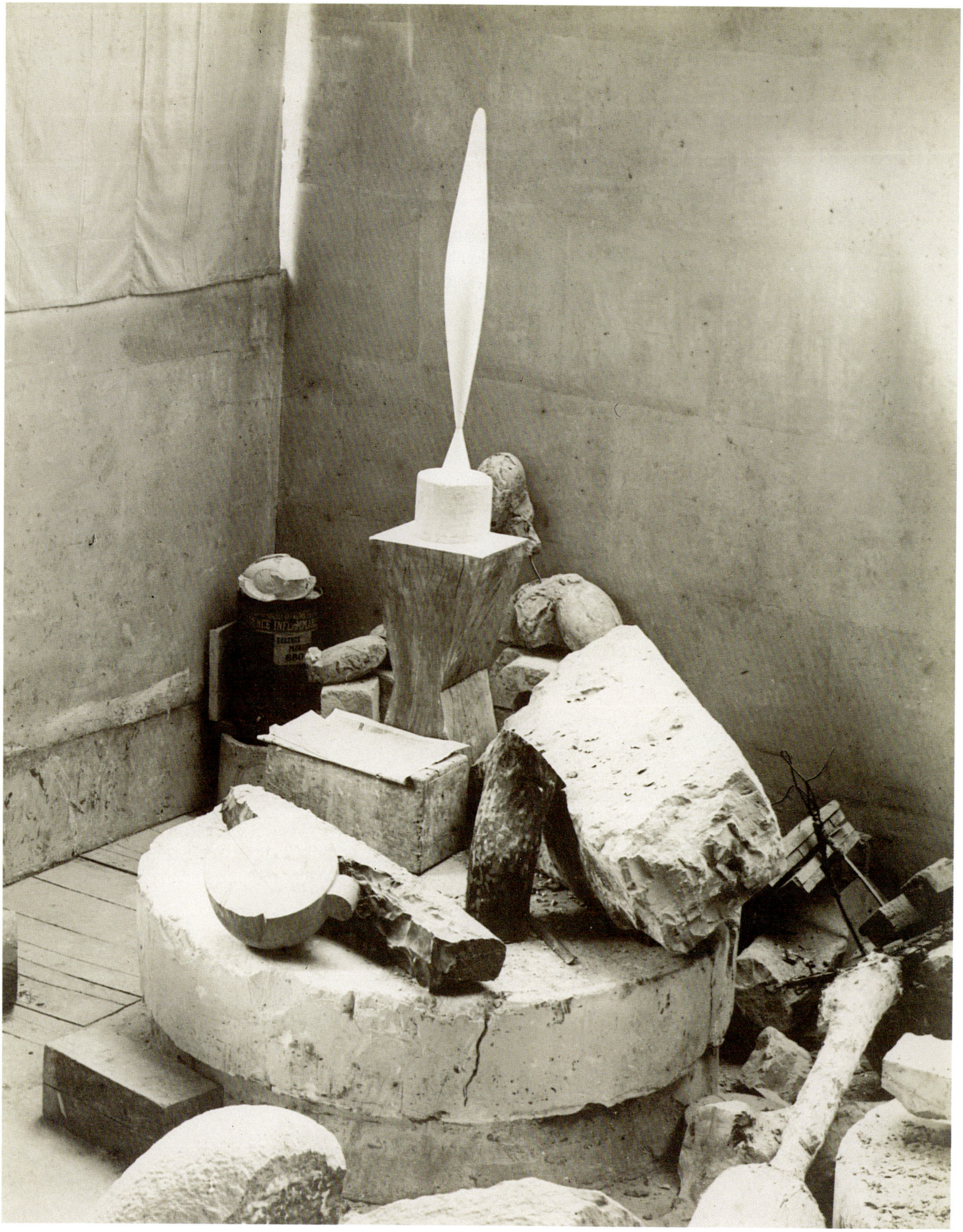

Sponsor's foreword

Aviva is pleased to partner Tate in this new exhibition of Constantin Brancusi's work. Brancusi is an iconic figure of twentieth-century modern art and his works grace collections the world over.

As an international financial services brand, Aviva operates in Romania, France, the USA, and over thirty other countries worldwide. Therefore this exhibition, with its associations with these countries, holds a special appeal for us.

I believe that it is our responsibility to support the arts and to ensure that the rare opportunity to view this collection of Brancusi's works is shared with the public.

I congratulate Tate on this great achievement and am delighted that Aviva is the sponsor of *Constantin Brancusi: The Essence of Things*.

Pehr G Gyllenhammar
CHAIRMAN, Aviva plc

Director's foreword

Constantin Brancusi occupies an almost unrivalled position as the quintessential modernist sculptor of the first half of the twentieth century. Romanian by birth, he spent fifty years in Paris – then at the highpoint of its artistic ferment – producing sculptures of extraordinary individuality, purity and luminosity. Central to his work was his practice of carving – whether in stone, marble or wood – and it is this that lies at the heart of our exhibition. For artists, both among his contemporaries and of succeeding generations, Brancusi represents an ideal of imaginative and tenacious creativity. Isamu Noguchi, who worked with him in 1927, believed that Brancusi's strength lay in sculpturally 'going back to beginnings'. For her part, Barbara Hepworth identified a 'humanism which seemed intrinsic in all the forms' that she found in his studio. Between these views of the technical and the conceptual lies the work.

It is now exactly one hundred years since Brancusi settled in Paris. His passage to an assured individuality was rapid. By 1913, he was contributing to exhibitions in London and in New York. It is appropriate that *Constantin Brancusi: The Essence of Things*, jointly organised by Tate Modern and the Solomon R. Guggenheim Museum, echoes those first steps on the international stage. Our exhibition seeks to capture the essential character of Brancusi's sculpture. The selection has been conceived by Carmen Giménez, Curator of 20th-Century Art at the Solomon R. Guggenheim Museum and Director of the Museo Picasso in Malaga, and she has developed it with Tate Curator Matthew Gale. It has been my pleasure to contribute to their deliberations at all stages along the way.

While some of Brancusi's most astonishing bronzes demanded inclusion, the selection concentrates on carvings in a way that is unprecedented for exhibitions of his work. The result is remarkable, even as this focus undoubtedly made the project more challenging. We are very grateful for the imaginative reception that our proposal met among collectors and museum colleagues alike, and thank them for lending so many of his finest sculptures that make this exhibition possible. As an institution which itself owns works by Brancusi, we can appreciate the difficulty inherent in agreeing to lend such fragile works and the degree of generosity and trust involved in the loan.

I should like to add to the curators' acknowledgements my own thanks to all those who have offered their advice, knowledge and support. It is fitting that in London such a challenging exhibition has benefited from the generous sponsorship of Aviva plc. Their support of Tate in recent years has been remarkable and we thank them for such wholehearted commitment to our work.

The catalogue, like the exhibition that it accompanies, draws upon a wide body of recent research. In their essays, the curators address the purity of the sculptures and consider the context of their making. Carmen Giménez explores how carving embodied Brancusi's practice and how the selection of the exhibition unveils his central concerns. Matthew Gale looks at the trajectory of the sculptor's career in relation to its public reception and the responses of his contemporaries. The other essays in this catalogue all reflect new thinking by specialists. In her essay, Sanda Miller examines the cultural climate in turn-of-the-century Romania that fostered the sculptor's ambitions. The challenge that Brancusi presented to sculptural conventions is addressed by Alexandra Parigoris in considering the importance of carving fragmented bodies. Finally, the artist's wit and playfulness are drawn out by Jon Wood in his discussion of the sculptures carved from reclaimed timber.

Despite his international reputation, Brancusi's work is only very rarely brought together. Astonishingly, *Constantin Brancusi: The Essence of Things* is the first major exhibition of his work in Britain, and in New York it will be the first for thirty-five years. It is a testament to the creative co-operation between the teams at Tate and the Solomon R. Guggenheim Museum, in consort with their colleagues around the world, that this joint venture has come to fruition. We believe that it is true to Brancusi's spirit: bold in conception but (seemingly) effortless in resolution.

Nicholas Serota
DIRECTOR, TATE

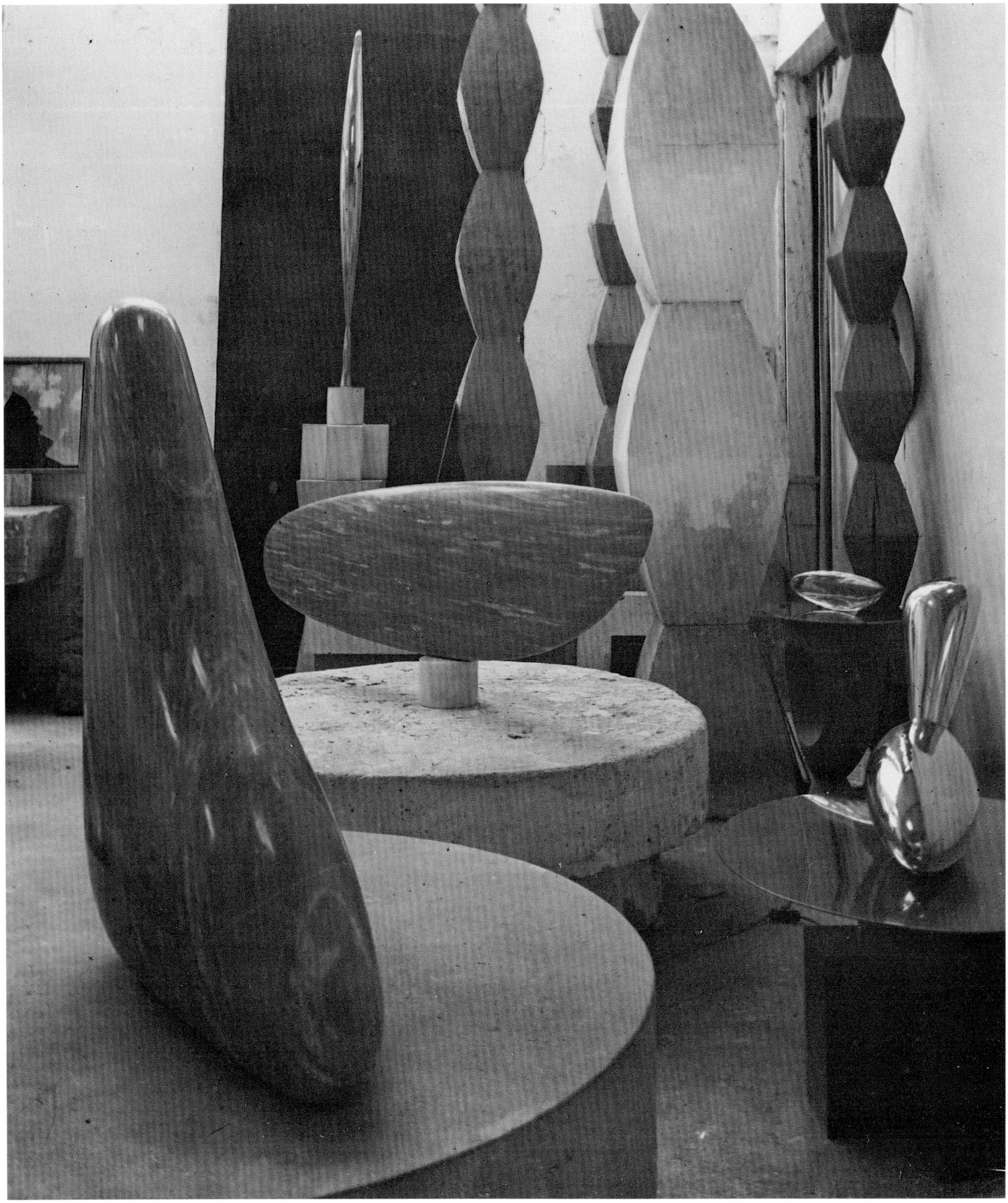

Curators' acknowledgements

The fact that Brancusi has had fewer major exhibitions than any other modern artist of his importance is a reflection of his small production of unique works and their delicacy. The mounting of an exhibition such as this, therefore, demanded a tremendous act of faith on the part of all the lenders. We have been fortunate to encounter enthusiasm and to receive advice from many people along the way. There would be no exhibition without this support and the generosity of the owners. We are very grateful to them for lending sculptures which, when brought together in this way, help us to experience Brancusi's work anew through our exhibition. As well as our colleagues in other institutions, we would like to thank those private lenders who would prefer to remain anonymous.

Any exhibition is something of an odyssey, in which the artist's travels and trials are distantly echoed. Our journey to Romania was eased by the kind offices of His Excellency Ambassador Dan Ghibernea and the Cultural Counsellor, Sinziana Dragos, in London and the Ministry of Foreign Affairs in Bucharest. We were greeted with great kindness by the Hon. Dr Razvan Theodorescu, Minister of Culture, and looked after with solicitude by Secretary of State Ioan Opris and their gracious staff. At the Muzeul National de Artă al României, Director General Roxana Theodorescu and Sculpture Curator Zoë Pop were generous with their time and offer of loans, as were Prof. Dr Paul Rezeanu, Director Muzeul de Artă Craiova and his staff in Craiova. It was a pleasure to discuss Brancusi with those who are so knowledgeable about his early life, and our visit to Târgu Jiu will live long in the memory.

In France, Brancusi's adopted homeland, we have consistently benefited from the reservoir of knowledge at the Centre Pompidou. Alfred Pacquement and Isabelle Monod-Fontaine greeted the project with enthusiasm and wisdom, and Marielle Tabart and Doïna Lemny have been tireless in offering advice and information. As custodians of the Atelier Brancusi, their support for the exhibition has been crucial. As well as those already mentioned, we would like to thank colleagues across Europe for their generous loans: Ernst Beyeler and Christof Vitali of the Fondation Beyeler; Prof. Dr Christian von Holst, Director, and Dr Karin von Maur of the Staatsgalerie Stuttgart; Lars Nittve, Director of the Moderna Museet, Stockholm; and Philip Rylands, Director of the Peggy Guggenheim Collection in Venice.

In the United States, where Brancusi's reputation was made, we should like to thank those at the lending institutions for all their help: James Cuno, former Director, and Marjorie B. Cohn, Acting Director, Harvard University Art Museums; Dr John R. Lane, Director, and Ellen J. Holdorf of Dallas Museum of Art; Janice Driesbach, Director of the Sheldon Memorial Gallery and Sculpture Gardens, University of Nebraska; Jock Reynolds, Director, Yale University Art Gallery; Kynaston McShine, former Acting Chief Curator and John Elderfield, Chief Curator, Museum of Modern Art, New York; Anne d'Harnoncourt, Director, Ann Temkin, former Curator, and Michael Taylor at the Philadelphia Museum of Art; Ned Rifkin, Director, Phyllis Rosenzweig and Brian Kavanagh, at the Hirshhorn Museum and Sculpture Garden, Smithsonian Institution.

Advice and help of many different sorts has come from the following: William Acquavella, Doris Ammann, Alexander Apsis, Francisco Calvo Serraller, Lisa Corrin, Patrick Elliott, Paul and Ellen Josefowitz, Jason McCoy, Nesha Mamod, Jacqueline Matisse Monnier, Patrick Noon, Susan Rosenberg, Eric Shanes, Esperanza Sobrino, Chris Stephens, Radu Varia, and Kenneth Wayne. So much of the research on Brancusi rests on the work of scholars such as Barbu Brezianu, Friedrich Teja Bach and, above all, Sidney Geist, that we – and the contributors to this catalogue, Sanda Miller, Alexandra Parigoris and Jon Wood – owe them a great debt.

In making this exhibition for Tate Modern and the Solomon R. Guggenheim Museum, we were very fortunate to have the unstinting support of both directors, Nicholas Serota and Thomas Krens. Vicente Todoli and Sheena Wagstaff, in London, and Lisa Dennison in New York have advised at crucial moments. At all stages, our colleagues in both London and New York have excelled in their calm efficiency. In London, the core team has been made up of Ben Borthwick, Nickos Gogolos and Stephen Mellor; Sophie Clark laid the groundwork and we have constantly been supported by Rebecca Lancaster and Paul McAree. In Madrid help has been offered at various times by Amaranta Ariño, Sofía Diez, Cecilia Gandarillas, Maria Gonzáles de Castejón, Bernardo Laniado-Romero and Maura Verastagui. The core team in New York has been made up of Tracey Bashkoff, Rosa Berland, Marion Kahan and Kara Vander Weg. They have benefited from the advice of Meryl Cohen and Marc Stieglitz.

With design by Juan Ariño and Marta Elorriaga, and lighting by John Johnson, the exhibition has been installed at Tate Modern by Phil Monk and the team headed by Glen Williams, under the watchful eye of Sculpture Conservator Elizabeth MacDonald. At various times and in a myriad of ways, we have benefited from the knowledge of our Tate colleagues in Development, Events, Interpretation, Press and Communications. Telling advice and support have been offered by: Dennis Ahern, Simon Bolitho, Stephen Dunn, Suzanne Freeman, Philippe Fouchard, Brian Gray, Adrian Hardwicke, Sophie Howarth, Adrian Jackson, J.J. Mitchell, Jemima Montagu, Lynn Murfitt, Caroline Priest, Derek Pullen, Jane Scherbaum, Calum Sutton, Nicky White, Liz Whiteley, Dominic Willsdon and Calvin Winner.

This catalogue has been guided through by Mary Richards as Project Editor and Emma Woodiwiss as Production Manager. We would particularly like to thank our designer Philip Lewis, as well as Melissa Larner, Caroline Mosedale and Alessandra Serri; Celia Clear, Roger Thorp and James Attlee have all been tremendously supportive. In New York the publication has been overseen by Anthony Calnek and Elizabeth Levy.

Such a major project would undoubtedly have been the poorer without the expertise of all these colleagues.

Carmen Giménez and Matthew Gale

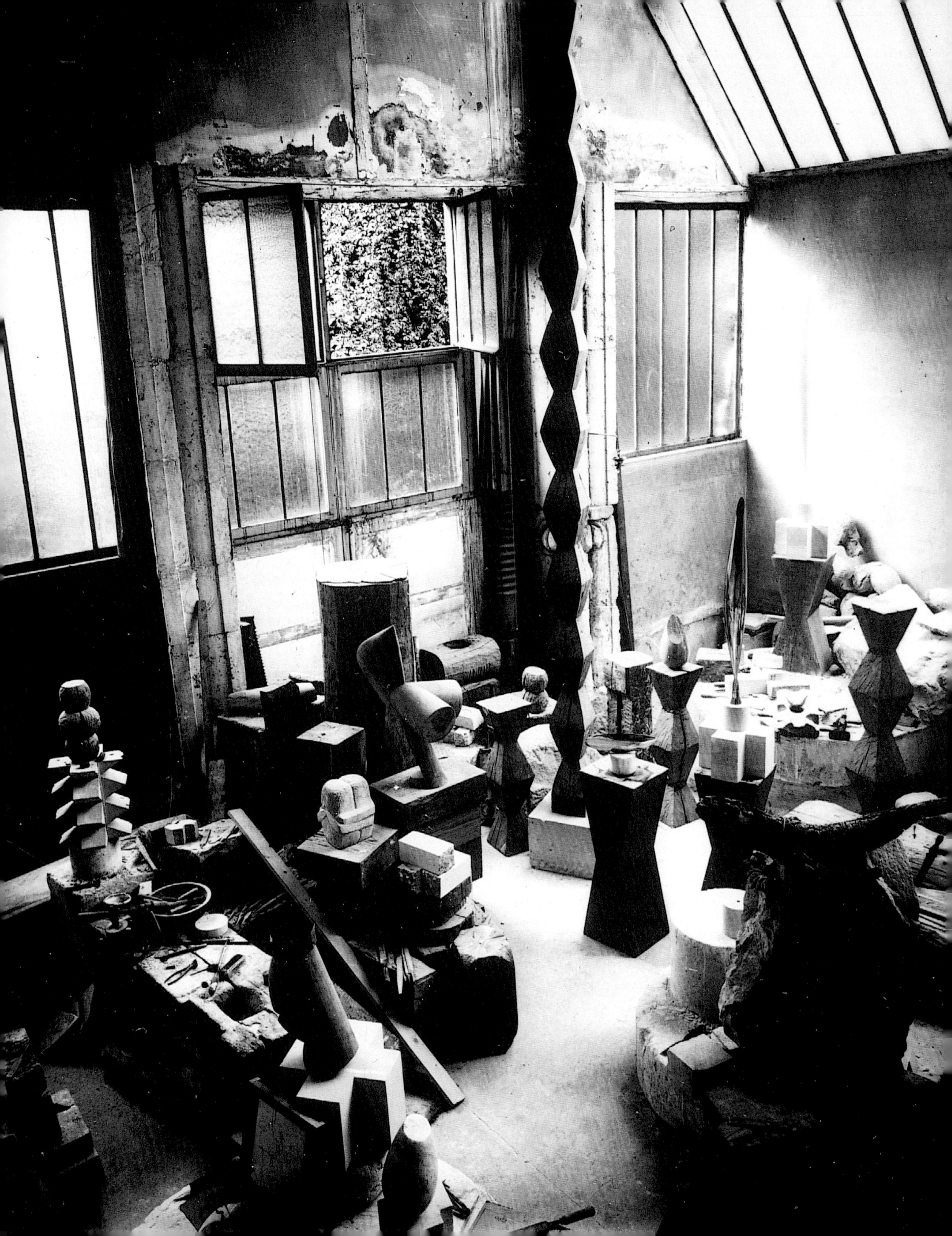

Endless Brancusi

CARMEN GIMÉNEZ

Fig.1 **Studio view with Crocodile**, 1925
Centre Pompidou, Paris (AM4002-3031, PH64, modern print)
8 impasse Ronsin, also showing **Torso of a Young Girl**, **Kiss**, **Sorceress** and **Endless Column**

Constantin Brancusi's career came to its inevitable conclusion on 16 March 1957, a month after his eighty-first birthday. But the work of great artists continues to appeal long after they are gone. While this may not constitute 'immortality', it certainly reaffirms the simple but absolute truth of Hippocrates's aphorism *Ars longa, vita brevis* (Art is long, life is fleeting). Now that almost fifty years have passed since Brancusi's death, few doubt that he was one of the greatest sculptors of the twentieth century. However, in today's highly complex art world, simply affirming this would constitute an empty rhetorical gesture if we didn't also ask ourselves each time we look at one of his sculptures just what the true reach of his work is. Simply affirming Brancusi's contemporary artistic importance is easy enough, but explaining exactly why he is important, and identifying the basis for that judgement, along with the precise source of our present admiration, is more difficult. This interrogative contemplation of Brancusi's artistic production will continue until there is no one left to engage in the intimate conversation to ask themselves, and ask of the work, what it is capable of communicating today.

While affirming Brancusi's artistic importance today, we could say virtually the same thing about the work of all the great artists of the twentieth century, since, irrespective of their greater or lesser fame, we are beginning to acquire a sufficiently critical distance from them to make a better appraisal of the reasons why they have survived. However, compared to his famous contemporaries – artists like Picasso or Modigliani, who were admittedly the subjects of public polemic before they received full recognition – Brancusi was not celebrated with quite the same resounding unanimity. His work has enjoyed the impassioned support of a small circle of admirers but, perhaps, has still to command an unquestioning critical consensus. It arouses, and continues to arouse, what we might call an endless critical debate.

Simply to allude to the fact that Brancusi was the creator of *Endless Column* in order to explain his importance would not necessarily be to lower the level of my discourse. The name of this essay plays on the title of that celebrated work because I believe that infinity is one of the basic creative impulses that give form to his sculpture, which is always marked by the unstable tension between two opposed points. For this reason, his work appears to hang in suspension, on the verge of taking flight. At the same time, it soars far above our reductive critical judgements, which cannot fix its infinite course with any certainty.

Critiques of Brancusi's sculpture have ranged from calling into question its modern value to suggesting that he fell into an abyss when he accommodated his initial innovating impetus to the formalistic refinement typical of Art Deco. Those who unreservedly admire his work have sometimes done so not because it marked new directions for sculpture, but because they saw him as the last dazzling voice in recent times of a declining classicism, almost as if, in a daring acrobatic feat, he had succeeded in reawakening the muffled voice of Antonio Canova, which we had long thought definitively silenced. Although it would be tempting to posit here a hypothetical,

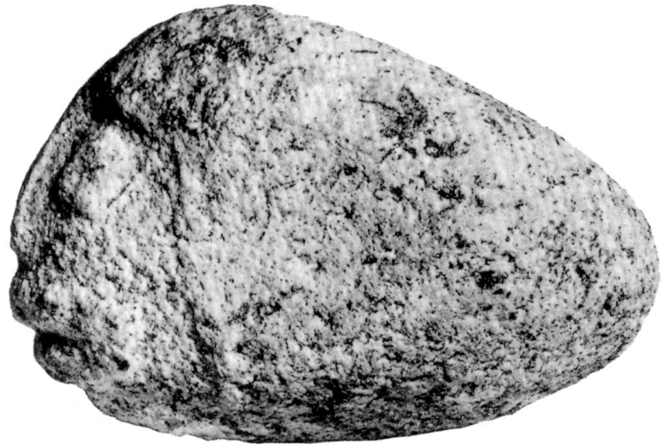

Fig.2 Neolithic egg or fish-shaped sandstone sculpture from Lepenski Vir in Iron Gates Gorge, present-day Serbia

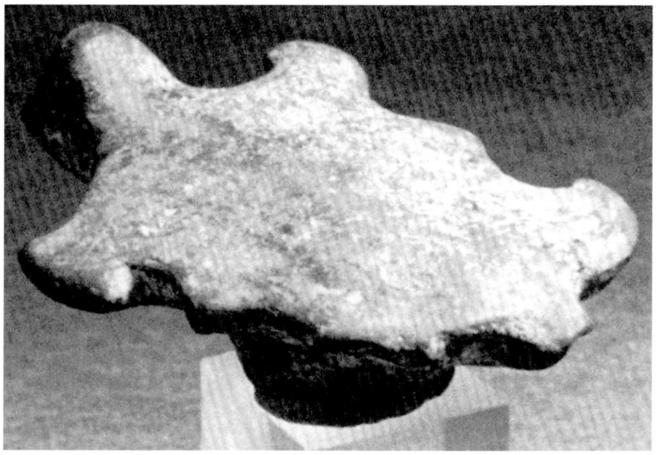

Fig.3 Neolithic terracotta figurine of a tortoise from Vinca, present-day Serbia

raucous rendezvous involving Canova, Brancusi and Jeff Koons, I refer to such critiques at random, and only to illustrate the reach and depth of the critical debates aroused by this Romanian sculptor, whose work is so charged with mystery. It is these doubts that we must face up to in addressing his work today. However, in my opinion they are not so much doubts *about* Brancusi as doubts that derive *from* him. If we start with the highly reasonable hypothesis that the possible confusion aroused by an artist is never, or very rarely, accidental, we might surmise that in the case of Brancusi the doubts he provoked correspond not only to the fact that he was someone who constantly questioned himself, but, above all, to the fact that he made doubting the principal source of his creative energy.

It is not necessary in this context to go into all the details of Brancusi's life and personality. It is worth mentioning, however, the traits that constitute his dualist, even duelist, identity as a creator: he was an artist trapped at the crossroads of two eras, two worlds, two cultures, two ways of seeing and (in his transition from modelling to carving) two artistic methods and styles. This experience can hardly be called exotic or unusual in our revolutionary and afflicted contemporary age, not even on the most elemental plane of mere anthropological experience, when a growing number of people are materially and spiritually displaced. However, Brancusi's was an extreme case, which he lived with great intensity. He came from a remote, rural environment in the Carpathian Mountains, deep in Eastern Europe, where his native language, Romanian, has Latin roots but is surrounded by Slavic or Germanic tongues. His family's religion, Orthodox Christianity, also existed in forced juxtaposition with other, very different credos. Additionally, his local artistic education, which was initially strongly determined by handmade crafts, and later by academic teaching in the French mode, was quite conventional. All of these factors must have amplified his initial perplexity when he moved to Paris, causing his Western artistic development to be marked by the same sign of the exotic that, centuries earlier, had made El Greco, a Cretan living in Spain,

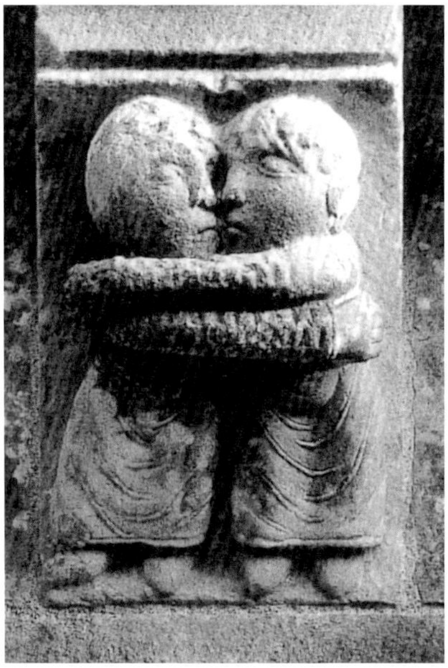
Fig.4 External modillion, façade of Saint-Pierre, Aulnay-de-Saintonge, France

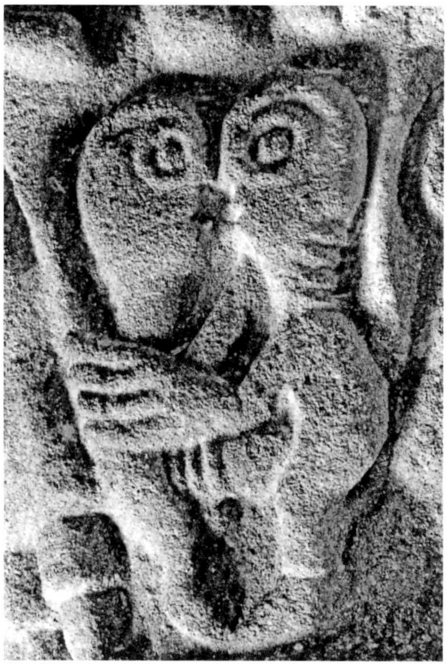
Fig.5 External modillion, façade of Saint-Hilarion, Perse, Commune d'Espalion, France

appear a peculiar being caught between two worlds that were moving further and further apart. One could add to this the heavy weight of his symbolic heritage and the extremely rich formal universe of his ancient local artistic tradition, reaching back to pre-history, whose effect on Brancusi has aroused many theories and whose study is far from complete. Without the slightest pretension to comprehensiveness, I have provided some illustrations that demonstrate a number of these connections.

It was not just these deep and singular ties, however, that kept Brancusi linked to a mythical past, a distant cultural memory whose indeterminate remoteness one could term 'the night of time'. We should also take into account his complex relationship with the tradition of artistic classicism that shaped him, and which considered sculpture the highest form of artistic expression. We only have to take a cursory look at Brancusi's first steps as a sculptor to confirm that he took this classical heritage very seriously, that he in no way undertook it simply as an academic exercise that had been imposed upon him. This can be appreciated if we study his intense reworkings of Hellenistic sculpture. A great deal has been written on this aspect as part of the search for the possible antecedents of Brancusi's first Parisian sculptures: *Sleeping Child* (1906–7), *Torment* (1907), *The Kiss* (1907–8, cat.1), *Sleep* (1908, fig.24), or *Torso* (1909–10, cat.4). Many models from the past, both recent and remote, have been proposed for these works, as well as the more evident contacts with the work of contemporaries like Auguste Rodin or Medardo Rosso. Sidney Geist, for example, suggested that *Torso* may possibly have been inspired by a similar element in a painting by Cézanne, a feasible hypothesis since Brancusi's attitude to classicism is very similar to Cézanne's. For both, modernism existed only by measuring itself against the classical heritage and not simply as a forward movement without any reference to the past. This chain of associations also leads backwards to connect late Cézanne with Ingres. To a degree one could say that Brancusi's 'abstract' sense took hold at this point of intersection, where

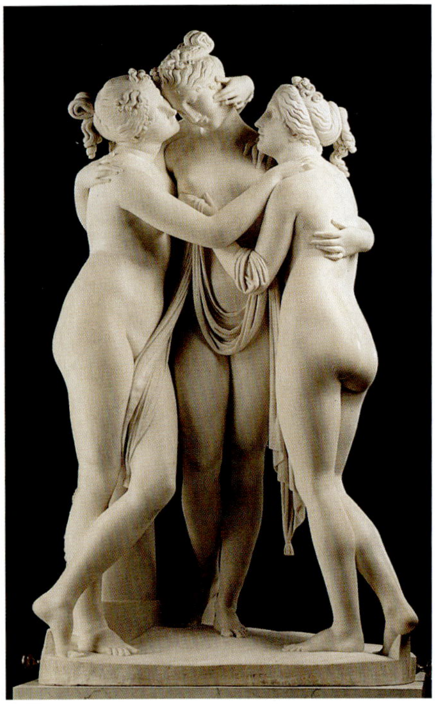

Fig.6 Antonio Canova **The Three Graces** 1814
Victoria & Albert Museum, London and National Gallery of Scotland, Edinburgh

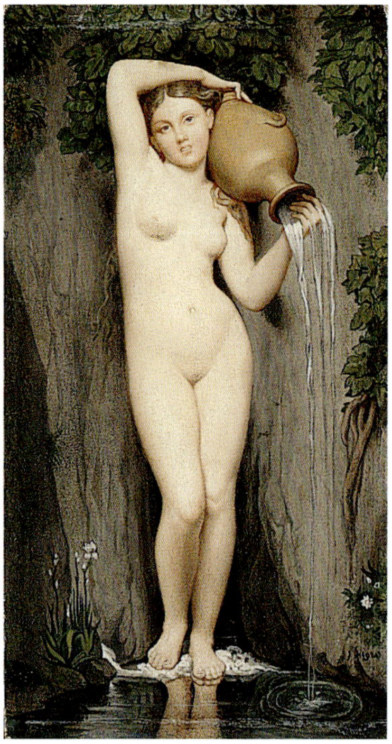

Fig.7 Jean-Dominique Ingres **The Source** 1856
Musée d'Orsay, Paris

we find not only the purity and synthesis that ultimately flourished with Cubism, but specifically the reduction of all forms to the melody of an endless line.

Brancusi's mythical and historical artistic heritage is as highly complex as the way in which he assimilated it. This should not detract from the importance of his contemporary dialogue, especially the way in which he was influenced by Rodin, whose approach he later rejected. But we should not passively accept the anecdotes that have accumulated around a relationship that at first encouraged Brancusi's plastic and pictorial sense. Instead we might focus on two crucial elements in Rodin's aesthetic: his way of fragmenting the human body, and his notorious suppression of the pedestal, which nullified the status of sculpture as statuary. Brancusi's response to both elements was highly original. On the one hand he gave a truly autonomous identity to the fragment, transforming it, in works like *Torso*, into a whole. At the same time he reinvented the base, converting it into an essential, integral part of the sculpture. This also symbolically enriches its meaning, establishing a vertical axis that provides an organic connection with the earth. And it is in proximity with the earth that the sculpture metamorphoses, materially and formally, anticipating the idea of the endless growth of the column.

Another powerfully original aspect of Brancusi's work is the elevation of his subtly tactile treatment of surface to an aesthetic category that calls attention to the material as something fragile, which is different from its mere plasticity or ductility. Brancusi not only took care that visitors to his crowded studio would not trip over his sculptures, but also made sure that they would not even brush against one. This reflected less his fear of potential accidents than his attunement to the 'spiritual' delicacy of his works. We can appreciate this in the exquisite refinement with which he caresses surfaces, as

OPPOSITE
Fig.8 **Studio view with Sorceress**, 1924–5
Centre Pompidou, Paris (AM4002-292, PH51, modern print)
8 impasse Ronsin, including bronze **Fish**, **Socrates**, **Timidity** and **Sorceress**

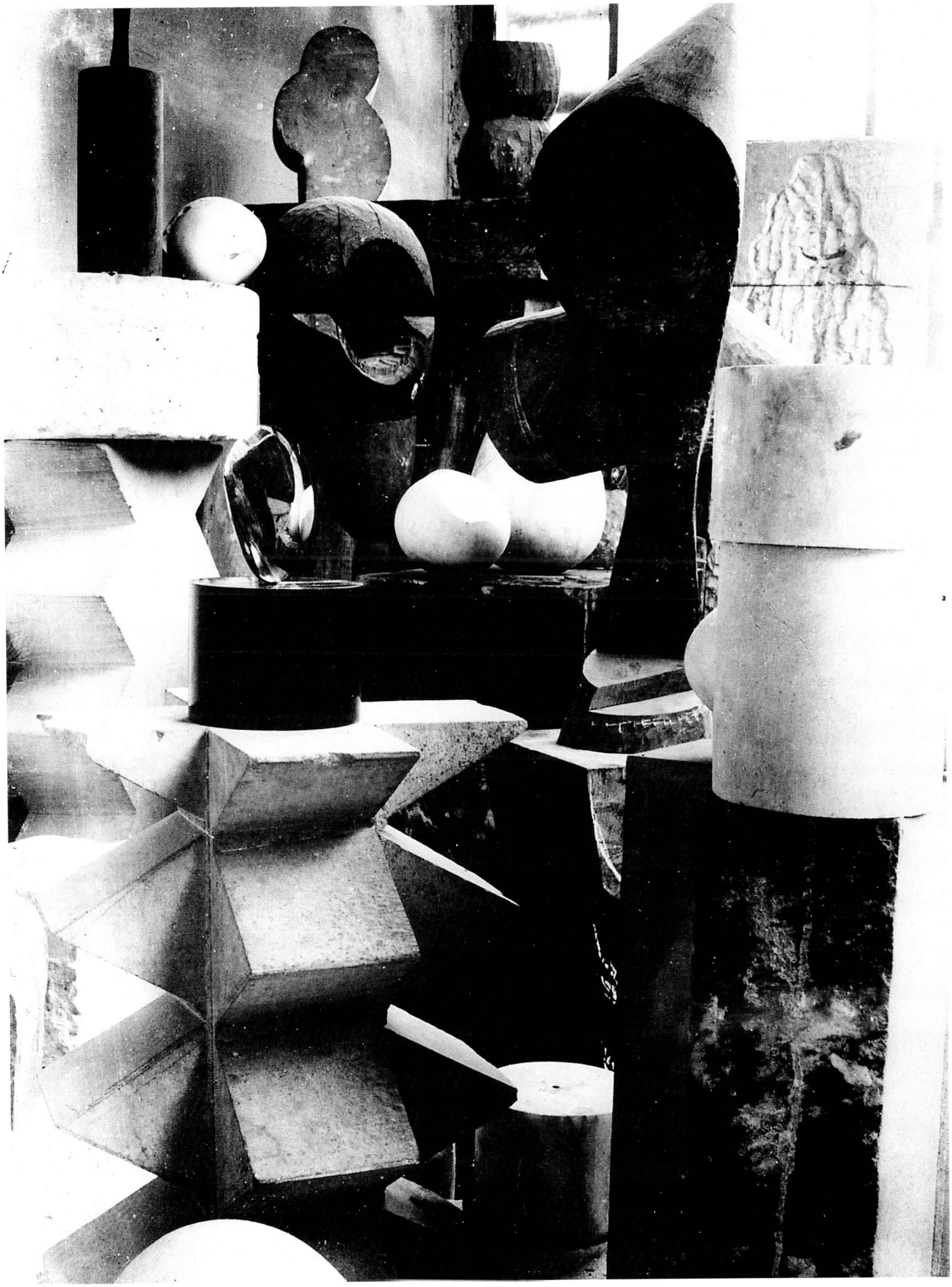

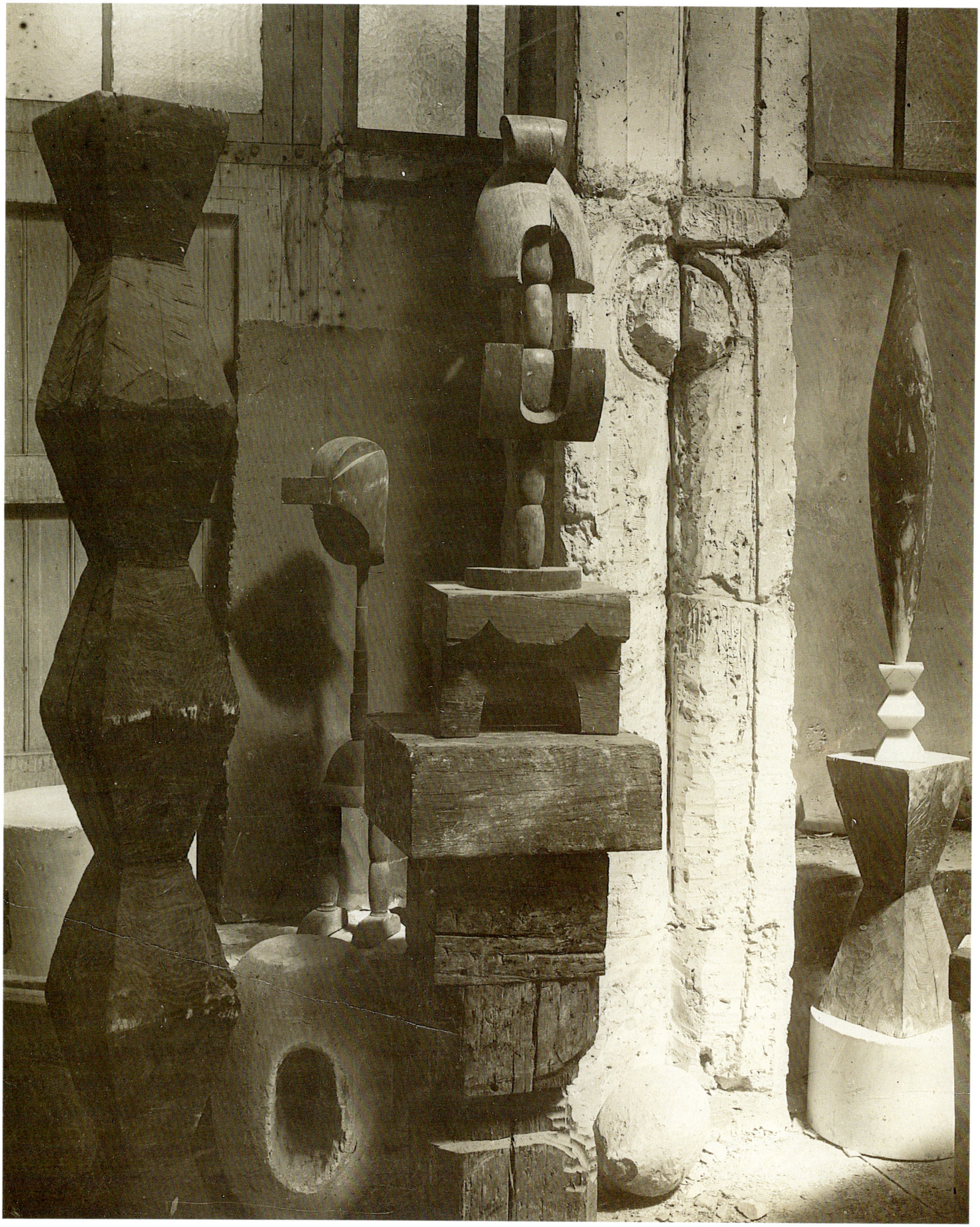

Fig.9 **Studio view with Portrait of Mme L.R.**, 1920
Centre Pompidou, Paris (AM4002–257(1), PH12A)
8 impasse Ronsin, including **Endless Column**, **Plato**, **Portrait of Mme L.R.** and **Bird**

well as in his obsession with capturing unique and instantaneous existential sensations and feelings. The fragility of material was for Brancusi central to its identity, but also a dramatic image of existence, a reinvention of the old tension between the body and soul of things.

Among the traits that can be said to determine the nature of a work of art – composition, sensibility and memory – the last bears the closest relationship to the soul of things and, therefore, to their fragility. Although Brancusi decisively demonstrated his mastery in all three of these areas, his achievement lies in an ability to balance the demands of innovation and memory in order to achieve an epic beauty. He believed that discoveries should never result in schisms, because he was convinced that while art changes it does not progress in a determined, preconceived, linear direction. This conviction constituted an aesthetic and moral accomplishment. His often-quoted affirmation that 'simplicity is resolved complexity', aside from providing a marvellous definition of composition and sensibility in art, may also be interpreted as a supreme effort of fragile memory. Materially and spiritually, Brancusi knew how to combine the fragility of the memorable, something compact, with the living tension of the contemporary, something for which elasticity is absolutely essential. Both fragile and elastic, his sculpture extends like an unending melodic line, where material and form are treated with such refined, aerodynamic purity that they seem about to take flight, free from the dead weight of inert memory, the ballast of contingency.

Few have surpassed Brancusi in his ability to compose such complex equations with such simplicity, using all kinds of materials from stone and wood to metal. Nor have many better understood the spatial potentiality of sculpture, the singular manner in which each piece occupies both its own place and projects itself by means of its aura as an animated 'ghost sonata'. This appears in the thousands of photographs taken by Brancusi of his work. These should not simply be considered as exceptional documents, but almost as other sculptures, since they show us new ways to see and feel the infinite malleability of space, which is lived physically and in reality but is also present as a spectral 'double'.

In a way, the difficulty in delineating, classifying and explaining Brancusi's work results from his prodigious artistic elasticity. Was he sculptor, architect, or photographer? Prehistoric or classical? Modern or traditional? Abstract or figurative? His work cannot be approached in its full dynamic dimension unless one understands that it is conceived and established as a complex, infinite dialectical tension. It is to be hoped that it is possible to achieve this understanding through the intimate and mute direct contemplation of his work offered by this exhibition. The show places an unprecedented concentration upon Brancusi's carvings, but beyond this it does not illustrate any thesis, in the academic sense. As neither a Brancusi specialist nor an academic I would not be the right person to carry out such a project. What did inspire me was a certain 'intuition' based on a life of impassioned contemplation of his work. I conceived the show as an anthology of *morceaux choisis*, denoting the emphatic selection of the best elements and the most dynamic axes of Brancusi's production. Taken in their totality the works selected form the endless creative line that weaves its way through his career and make it possible to hear the subtle, delicate, and refined and infinite musicality of Brancusi's work.

Translated from the Spanish by Alfred MacAdam

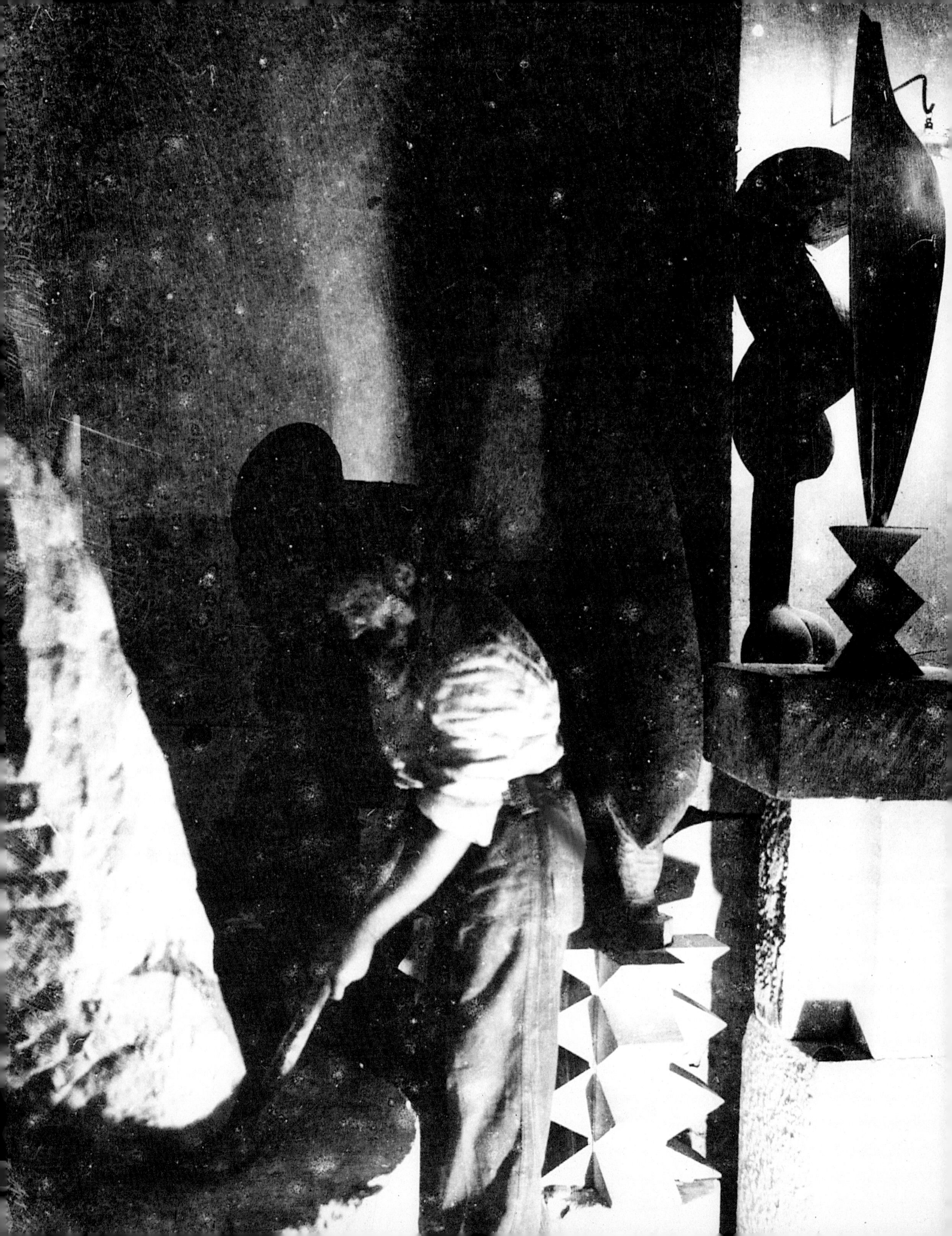

Brancusi: An equal among rocks, trees, people, beasts and plants

MATTHEW GALE

When the modernist critic and poet André Salmon published a survey of French sculpture in 1919, Constantin Brancusi's name did not even merit a mention. [1] Yet, by 1937, Carola Giedion-Welcker considered him the 'greatest modern sculptor living'.[2] This contrast exposes a striking transformation in Brancusi's fortunes during the interwar years, and provides a glimpse of some more general concerns that marked the period. Through a combination of determination and opportunism he became one of the towering modernist sculptors of the early part of the twentieth century. Soon after arriving in Paris in 1904 he transformed himself from a would-be academic sculptor into a radical equipped to challenge the dominance of Auguste Rodin. Unlike the intermediate generation who had sought to emerge from Rodin's shadow – such as the 'Independent' sculptors Antoine Bourdelle and Aristide Maillol, who made recourse to classical restraint – Brancusi undertook a transformation of sculptural means, methods and ambitions.[3] He replaced the academic preference for anthropomorphic monumentality with intimacy and calm, developing a private art that was, paradoxically, in continual public demand. Gradually, he was able to adapt its elements to a new understanding of the monumental in the memorial ensemble at Târgu Jiu in Romania (1937–8), one of the most startling achievements of sculptural form of the last hundred years (figs.15, 17–18). What concerns us here is the public position that Brancusi achieved during the interwar years and how this is traceable through a series of encounters with contemporaries.

One of our most beloved

Much is habitually made (and was made by the sculptor himself in later years) of Brancusi's peasant roots. He was born in Hobiţa, in the foothills of the Romanian Carpathians in 1876. As well as being an overseer for the lands of the local monastery, his father was a small-scale landowner and he left Brancusi a plot on his death, the sale of which helped finance his studies.[4] This makes the artist's background somewhat more privileged than has come to be acknowledged. His later espousal of a simple life in Paris was entangled with a recapturing of his origins, a desire for the essential values of the land in an increasingly unstable world. Of course, this required some theatrical touches, from the rural calm maintained in the studio that he occupied at impasse Ronsin within the hurly-burly of Montparnasse, to his chosen attire of white garments, clogs and beard. Some of this seems to have been fuelled by nostalgia as he aged, so that, despite the fact that for most of his life he lived in an international community, his art was constructed around a sense of Romanian identity heightened by exile.

Brancusi grew up on the margins of the new country of Romania. The border with Austria-Hungary, nearby in the mountains, introduced an aspect of *realpolitik* that broadened his local concerns. Identity, language and culture, nationality and nationhood did not coincide precisely. However, if Brancusi's youth could be characterised in a single generalisation, it would be as a rebellion against these origins. He was so anxious to get away from Hobiţa as a boy (or so the myth goes) that he ran away from his family

Fig.10 **Self-portrait in the studio** *c.*1922
Centre Pompidou, Paris (PH712, modern print)

more than once. Certainly his travels as a young man took him progressively further: to the local town Târgu Jiu, the provincial capital Craiova, and on to Bucharest.[5] In these gradual moves towards the capital, Brancusi turned his back on his rural environment as if he sought to breathe deeply the animated modernity of the city. Already in the Şcoala de Meserii (School of Arts and Crafts) in Craiova he secured sponsorship and scholarships from local dignitaries and charities. In Bucharest, at the Şcoala Naţională de Arte Frumoase (National School of Fine Arts), he was marked out as a sculptor of potential who, by implication, could continue the burgeoning national line of monumental sculptors. He carried this advantage and burden of expectation with him.[6]

The same ambition was behind Brancusi's supposed visit to Vienna (perhaps in 1896 or 1897), his application to study in Italy in 1902 and his eventual, and fabled, walk to Paris in 1904.[7] Whether or not he did cross Europe entirely on foot, the very idea shows a telling combination of single-mindedness and self-mythologising. Once established in Paris, at 16 place Dauphine in 1905, he found himself in a close-knit artistic milieu.[8] Among his Romanian neighbours was Otilia Cosmutza, who was notable for her links both to Rodin and to Anatole France, the towering figures of French sculpture and literature respectively.[9] He secured a recommendation from another neighbour, Louis Herbette, a state councillor, who wrote to Antonin Mercié, a leading sculptor and teacher at the Ecole des Beaux-Arts. Although florid, the terms in which this letter is couched confirm the perceived primacy of French culture at that moment (which had drawn Brancusi to Paris in the first place) and the slightly condescending benevolence with which the strivings of a Balkan artist were viewed. 'Is it not natural,' Herbette wrote, 'that the Romanians look towards the eminent author of a monument that graces their country?'[10] This secured Brancusi a position in Mercié's studio, with funding from the Romanian Ministry of Education, within a matter of days. Though he remained at the Ecole des Beaux-Arts for a relatively brief period, he received a diploma that could open the way for participating in French government competitions and securing commissions. Both of these opportunities were highly sought-after, and he appeared to be set on course for academic success.[11] That Brancusi was asked to make a bust of Anatole France provided confirmation of his rising status, as did his acceptance into Rodin's studio (both secured through Cosmutza). That he declined both opportunities – working with Rodin for only a month in 1907 – may be an indication that success was riven with doubt.[12]

Brancusi's move to Paris reinforced his potential to contribute to Romania's cultural awakening, and he continued to send works for exhibition in Bucharest. The cultural fluidity between the two countries is indicated by the fact that the 1907 contract for his first major commission, the *Stanescu Monument* (fig.22), though the work was to be erected in Buzau, was signed in Paris.[13] Brancusi did not set up the monument until May 1914 but, in the intervening period, used this commission and others to fund his move to a substantial studio at 54 rue du Montparnasse, where he stayed from 1908 to 1916. He exhibited in Bucharest and at the Paris Salons, and extended his international connections as his reputation grew. By 1910 a Bucharest critic was already calling him 'one of our most beloved'.[14] In 1913, as well as exhibiting at the renowned *Armory Show* in New York, he was among six artists officially representing Romania at the *Kunstausstellung* in Munich.[15]

While keeping one eye on Romania, Brancusi was involved with various artistic allies in Paris. Not only was he associated with the Symbolists who gathered around Paul Fort's periodical *Vers et Prose*, but he also exhibited, in 1907, with the Abbaye de Créteil group of artists and poets. Among their number were the painter Albert Gleizes and the writer Alexandre Mercereau, both of whom would pass into Cubist circles.[16] On the one hand, this group was deeply influenced by the aesthetics and metaphysics of Henri Bergson, who argued that the perception of reality was in flux. Bergson's position was explicitly anti-positivist and fitted with a pervasive post-symbolist aesthetic.[17] On the other hand, over the following five years members of the Abbaye became associated with the Celtic League, which stressed the primacy of Celtic roots in French culture over Germanic and Latin interlopers.[18] The former was rejected because of the current animosity to the growing threat from Germany, and the latter due to the appropriation of Latin culture – conjoined with a Cartesian rationalism – by the Action française and monarchist parties of the extreme right. Celtism represented a return to the 'true' stock of the country; it suggested that manual labour and an attunement to the seasons and the land lay at the heart of Frenchness, and could provide a platform for a political and philosophical renewal. In art, the point of comparison was the Gothic.

Brancusi called upon different cultural sources from those delimited by his friends, as the rhetoric of Romanian national identity, formed around language, was closely bound up with Latinity.[19] However, he did temporarily reject the stylistic devices of classicism (as handed down by the academies in which he had been trained) and it is possible to see the emergence of the rough-hewn forms in his work of 1907–8 in the light of the widespread interest in French Gothic art. Inevitably, in later years his practice was compared with that of Medieval carvers.[20] The ideal combination of community, collaborative work, spirituality and dedication infused the received idea of medieval culture. For the sculptor, a devotional art born of a direct encounter with stone – as it were, hewn from the land but raised up by the spirit – was also comparable with folk art. It was the untutored but traditional and individual nature that distinguished such work from the official culture, a divide that had become especially marked in the recent cultural modernisation of Romania.[21] Brancusi appears to have rediscovered this more ancient allegiance at this time. Furthermore, this identification with those working on the land may have been given a sharper contemporary relevance by the political unrest among Romanian peasants that led to an uprising in 1907.[22] Whatever the case, it is in this realm – of carving and honesty, craftsmanship and rootedness – that Brancusi's concerns appear to coincide with those promoted at the Abbaye. In this sense it is possible to see the emergence of carving in his practice as impelled both by a reconsideration of sculptural means and by a rhetoric of community and meaning. His curious *Caryatids* (Museum of Modern Art, New York, *c.*1908) that form the base for the first *Maiastra*, may be seen in the light of Gothic portal sculpture; even *The Kiss* series (cat.1–3) reflect this return to a direct confrontation with material that was the experience of the cathedral builders.

The true road to sculpture

The practice of 'direct carving', cutting into the block and responding to its qualities in resolving the work, has long been central to discussions of Brancusi's work.[23] It became an important issue because it was connected with modernist notions of honesty, with a rejection of modelling for casting and with the status of bronze as the medium of monuments. Brancusi's craft-based sensibility and insistence on self-reliance seem to have made it natural for him to carve the block himself: only he could find the image, through co-operation with the material.

In fact, the situation is rather more complex. As with most sculptors, Brancusi's idea coincided closely with his choice of stone, selected from those kept in his studio. The ability to envisage the form within the block, rather than impose it, came with practice, though quite when this experience was achieved is unclear. When he joined Rodin's studio for a month in early 1907, it was in the capacity of a *metteur à pointe*, that is to say a carver transferring an image from a clay original to marble, using a pointing machine.[24] Whether or not he was already skilled in this capacity, it seems possible that it was through this brief contact with the other craftsmen who worked for Rodin that Brancusi made this shift.

The precise chronology of his ensuing works remains somewhat hazy, and their stylistic inconsistency provides few clues. Twenty years later he identified the, now lost, *Head of a Young Girl* as his 'first direct stone, 190' leaving the date incomplete.[25] This is generally dated to 1907 and the surviving photograph suggests that Brancusi was already subsuming primitivising influences in this work. The prime extant examples of his earliest direct carving from 1907–8 are *The Kiss*, now in Craiova (cat.1), first shown in Bucharest in 1910, and the full-length version of the same motif (fig.25) raised on the tomb of Tatiana Rachewsky in Montparnasse Cemetery in early 1911 (and still there). To these versions may be added another, made around 1908 (cat.2), on which the incision is deeper. What they all demonstrate is the choice of a relatively coarse stone, granular rather than veined, cut into planes. These allow for the interlocking of the two bodies – one slightly overlapping the other in the embrace – in which verisimilitude plays little part.[26] Taken together, they reflect the exploration of the possibilities of an increasingly expressive technique. In cutting his signature into the only un-dressed face of the plain monolith supporting the Montparnasse version, Brancusi also seems to proffer confirmation of his position on carving.[27]

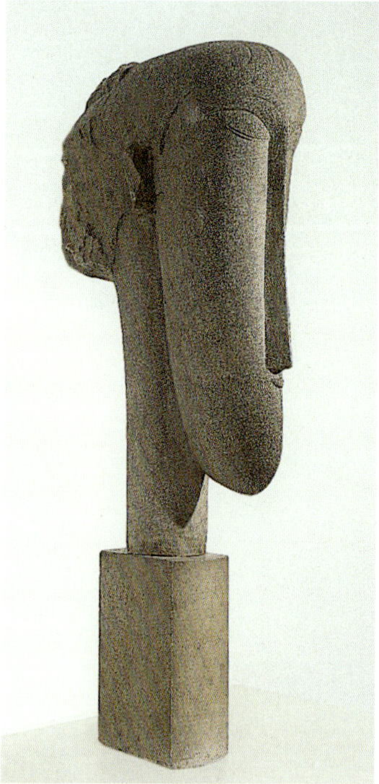

Fig.11 Amedeo Modigliani
Head *c.*1911–12
Tate

While stone carving was not taught in Mercié's studio at the Ecole des Beaux-Arts in Paris,[28] it is striking that Maurice Drouard, Brancusi's (now almost unknown) friend and fellow-student, who was later killed in the First World War, began to carve at about the same time. Their supporter Paul Alexandre is reported as saying that they both 'modelled in clay as well as making carvings', and a surviving photograph of Drouard's work indicates that they explored the carving of heads in a similar way.[29] Their circle included Amedeo Modigliani, whose surviving sculptures, such as *Head* (fig.11) date from 1911–12. Drouard and Brancusi are said to have advised Modigliani about carving, and the works of all three display an openness to influences from Medieval and non-Western art with strong carving traditions. This suggests that the practice of direct carving was more widespread than is generally acknowledged in the period before the war. The possibility that such an exploration was undertaken with friends, rather than through formal instruction, may help to explain the uneven development of Brancusi's early style.

However, the debate about direct carving centres not around this pre-war period, but around the rhetorical position associated with the period immediately following the death of Rodin in 1917. At that time, Rodin's practice of making clay models and ordering (sometimes multiple) copies to be carved by marble craftsmen emerged to public scrutiny through a court case against one of the technicians.[30] In a climate of a booming art market, public sensibilities were offended by the shadow of doubt that lingered over the role of the artist and the uniqueness of the artwork. The controversy exposed the fact that sculptors were neither trained nor generally aspired to work as carvers; all academic marbles were cut by craftsmen. It is in this context that the ideology of direct carving was established as a modernist response to the decayed practices of the Academy and the official Salon. Those who had already experimented with carving, for whatever reason, came to represent this technical honesty. It is in this context, too, that the most famous of Brancusi's 1925 aphorisms may be read: 'Direct cutting is the true road to sculpture.'[31] Summarising a position achieved over nearly twenty years, this reads like a manifesto statement. Brancusi was encouraging a retrospective reading

OPPOSITE
Fig.12 **Studio view**, *c.*1923–4
Centre Pompidou, Paris (AM4002-281(1), PH36)
8 impasse Ronsin, including **Sorceress**, **Plato**, **Blonde Negress**, **Socrates**, **Bird in Space** and bronze **Princess X**

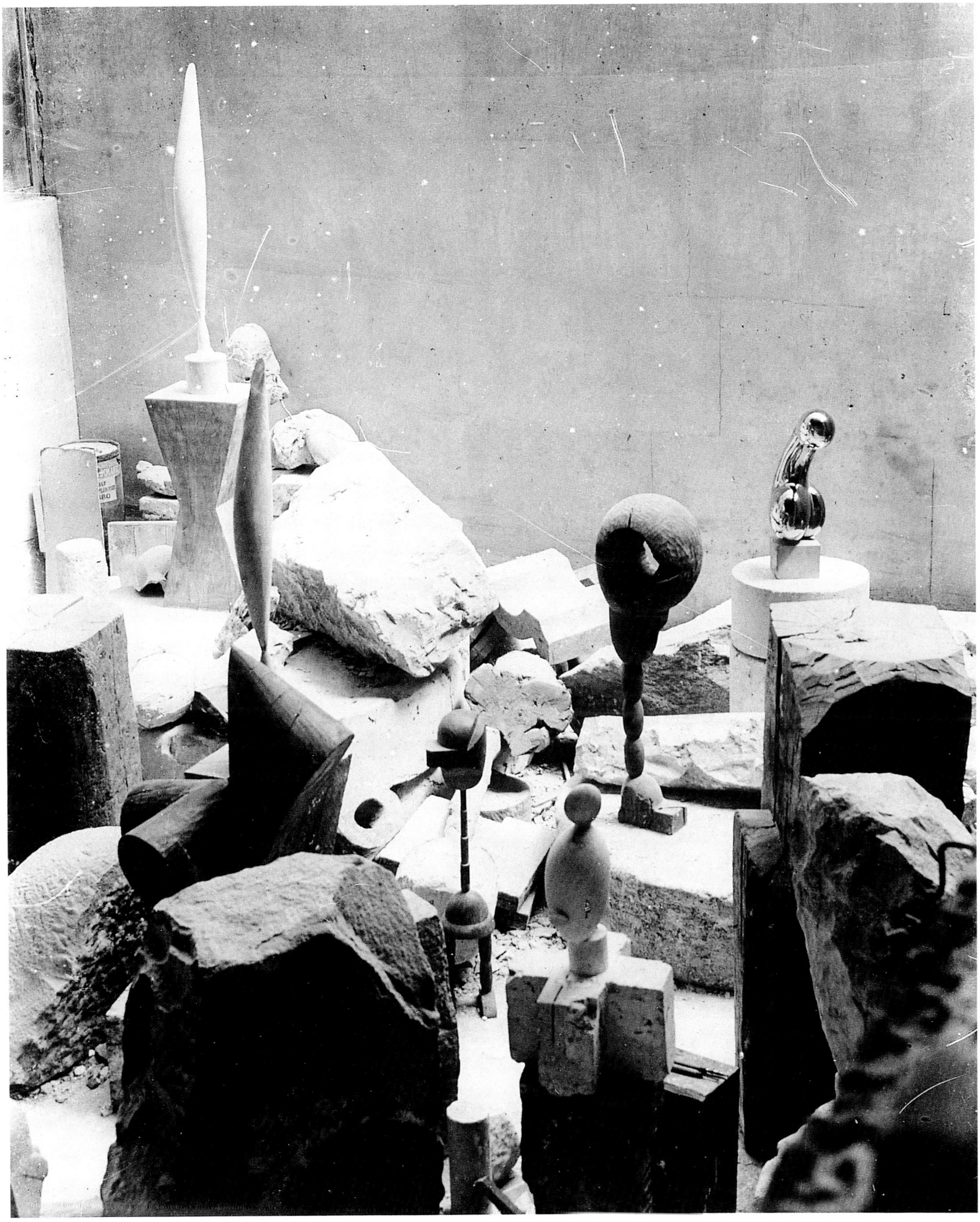

of his practice that would render his early experiments the epitome of modernist individualism and struggle.

In art, there are no foreigners

During the First World War the cultural liberalism and internationalism epitomised in Montparnasse was swiftly replaced by an atmosphere of xenophobia and a strengthening of official French culture, so that patriotism became a cover for anti-modernism. None other than Antonin Mercié distinguished himself in a newspaper interview in early 1916 in which he equated Cubism with German culture. As reported by the Italian writer Alberto Savinio, Mercié concluded: 'I do not understand why we have not undertaken the same prudent defence provisions against [Cubists] that we have against spies and traitors. Anti-German committees have been established, perhaps we should constitute anti-Cubist committees.'[32]

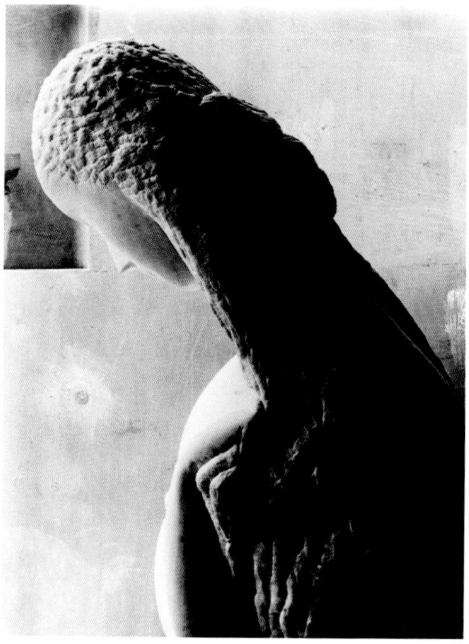

Fig.13 **Woman Looking at Herself in a Mirror**, 1909
Centre Pompidou, Paris (AM4002-524, PH407A, modern print)

In such circumstances even neutrality was a precarious situation in Paris. It is telling that when Romania joined the fray on the side of the allies in 1916, Brancusi expressed relief: 'I was found unfit for military duty, but I am glad that my country has gone into the war.'[33] Perhaps this development liberated him. In September 1917 he supported the establishment of the group *Art et Liberté*, set up specifically in response to a sustained and xenophobic press campaign by the newspaper *La Renaissance* against the designer Paul Poiret, which accused him of promoting an unpatriotic and Germanic *style munichois* (Munich style).[34] This was the period in which Brancusi was experimenting with wooden pieces that fuse non-classical sources from Africa and Romania.[35] As a co-signatory of the founding document of *Art et Liberté*, he publicly committed himself to a position of tolerance and cultural pluralism exactly opposed to that of Mercié in the previous year.

Although such statements suggest an emboldened attitude, the situation hardly became more straightforward after the war. Salmon's book *Le Jeune sculpture français* (Young French Sculpture) of 1919 focused, as the title indicates, on the national school, even though its author was a knowledgeable supporter of modernism, who predicted that: 'The most revolutionary art will be accepted tomorrow by the most bourgeois.'[36] The absence of Brancusi has already been mentioned, but a year later he became the subject of unwelcome attention when his 1916 bronze *Princess X* caused a scandal at the 1920 *Salon des Indépendants*. From Brancusi's point of view, the controversy grew out of a misunderstanding of his personal practice of stylistic reduction. The marble of *Princess X* (cat.16) originated in a sculpture known as *Woman Looking at Herself in a Mirror* (fig.13). However, the process of refinement resulted in an incontrovertibly phallic form.

The sculpture was removed by the police as an offence to public decency, but it may reasonably be assumed that the artist's connections made the Salon authorities suspicious. Francis Picabia was a close friend at that moment, and was also in the process of inventively challenging the censorship imposed by the avant-garde salons. In his letter of protest to the Salon president, the sculptor cited Picabia's support,[37] a move that probably gave the impression that he was playing a Dada-inspired game of challenging convention. This suspicion, reinforced by the echoes of the scandal around Marcel Duchamp's *Fountain* in New York in 1917, has since gained ground.[38] The report in Picabia's own periodical unsurprisingly took a defiant tone.[39] Gratifyingly, a swathe of modernist figures signed the public statement 'Pour l'indépendance de l'art' (For the Independence of Art) in Brancusi's defence. This brazenly acknowledged the sexual nature of the work while staking a claim for art unfettered by censorship.[40] For his own part the sculptor is said to have resolved never to show again in Paris (though it is not strictly the case).

Two years later, on 17 February 1922, a comparable cross-section of Parisian artists gathered at the Closerie des Lilas café in Montparnasse in order to mount a defence of the Dada poet Tristan Tzara; Brancusi was among them.[41] This time it was not the authorities who were their target, but the poet André Breton, who had described Tzara as 'come from Zurich', a phrase specifically interpreted as xenophobic. This charge remained a sensitive subject. Brancusi, signing the resolution in Tzara's defence, pin-pointed his position by adding: 'In art, there are no foreigners.'[42] At every stage Brancusi was vulnerable to attack because he was a foreigner. His only defence was the idealism of this resonant phrase.

Between these controversies the sculptor found himself in another difficulty that was all the more acute because it revolved around sculptural aesthetics. Despite his support for Brancusi's right to exhibit *Princess X*, Salmon, in his review of the controversial 1920 Salon, criticised the sculptor for 'stylisation'. He claimed that Brancusi was 'elevated, dominated, devastated by a passion for pure forms. He is damned, exalted by a mathematics that reduces mathematical perfection to the purity of zero, 0. This is one sort of perfection. Alas!'[43] Salmon specifically pitched Brancusi, maker of pure forms, against the Cubist sculptor Jacques Lipchitz (until 1916, Brancusi's immediate neighbour at 54 rue du Montparnasse). This criticism was taken up later in 1920 and given more programmatic form in an article by Paul Dermée on Lipchitz in the new periodical *L'Esprit nouveau*.[44] To Salmon's earlier equation of 'stylisation' and mathematical reduction, was added the danger that distillation would lead to superficiality. In promoting Lipchitz's Cubism as born of intellectual rigour, Dermée characterised his 'deductive' sculptural method in which the initial formal volumes evolved into recognisable forms. 'At the first stage of artistic creation,' Dermée claimed of the Cubist constructor, 'he only has pure plastic intentions . . . then comes the discovery of the motif.'[45] Although not named in Dermée's dismissal of 'stylisation', as a subscriber to *L'Esprit nouveau* Brancusi was surely alive to the implied criticism of his practice.[46]

A disdain for theory may have inured Brancusi against such criticism, and a statement among his papers locates a sense of liberation from constraint a month after Salmon's review of the scandalous Salon: '1920 March 5: Today I am cutting the towline and casting myself adrift on the vast ocean toward the unknown, with joy to steer me.'[47] Whether this relates to the Salon or the debate around purity is unclear. However, if he was to weather the criticism coming from such a modernist as Salmon, the need for a theoretical position may have appeared necessary. Brancusi's views, reported three years later by (the still unidentified) 'M.M.', open with the claim: 'The work of Constantin Brancusi is the expression of a cosmogonic conception.'[48] Here, in contrast to the purity that Dermée had attributed to 'Lipchitz the Constructor', the aspiration of modern sculpture is: 'To create an object that gives by its own organism that which nature gives by its eternal organisation . . . and to do that it must enter into the universal spirit of things.'

Perhaps Brancusi's most persuasive counter-weight to Salmon's criticism lay in his sculptures themselves. During 1920 he made *Beginning of the World*, in many ways a reprise of the earlier *Sculpture for the Blind* (cat.22 & 21), that bears microcosmic/macrocosmic implications. Both present pure but not reductive forms. In terms of Cubist claims to 'plastic form', Brancusi's resolution became the motif itself. This may also be said of the *Endless Column*, a two-metre-high version of which he had completed by 1918. He would carve the five-and-a-half-metre version for Edward Steichen's garden during 1926, and make a thirty-metre version for Târgu Jiu in 1938 (fig.14–15). In the *Endless Column* the reference to the cosmic is made on his own terms, and with pan-cultural resonances.[49] In the early versions, Brancusi ensured that the proportional harmony

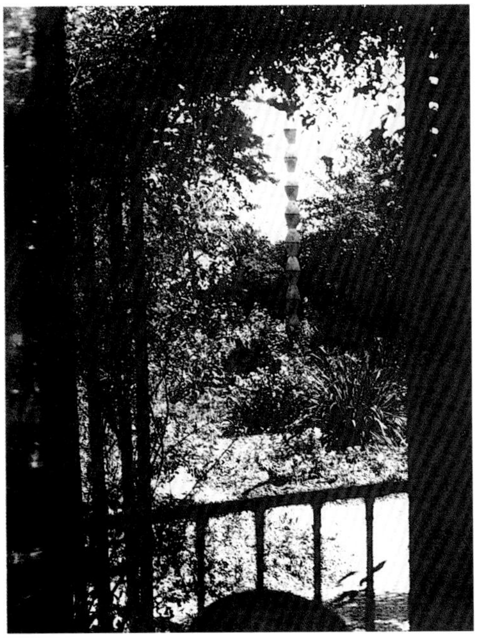

Fig.14 **Endless Column at Voulangis**, 1926
Centre Pompidou, Paris (AM4002-609, PH539)

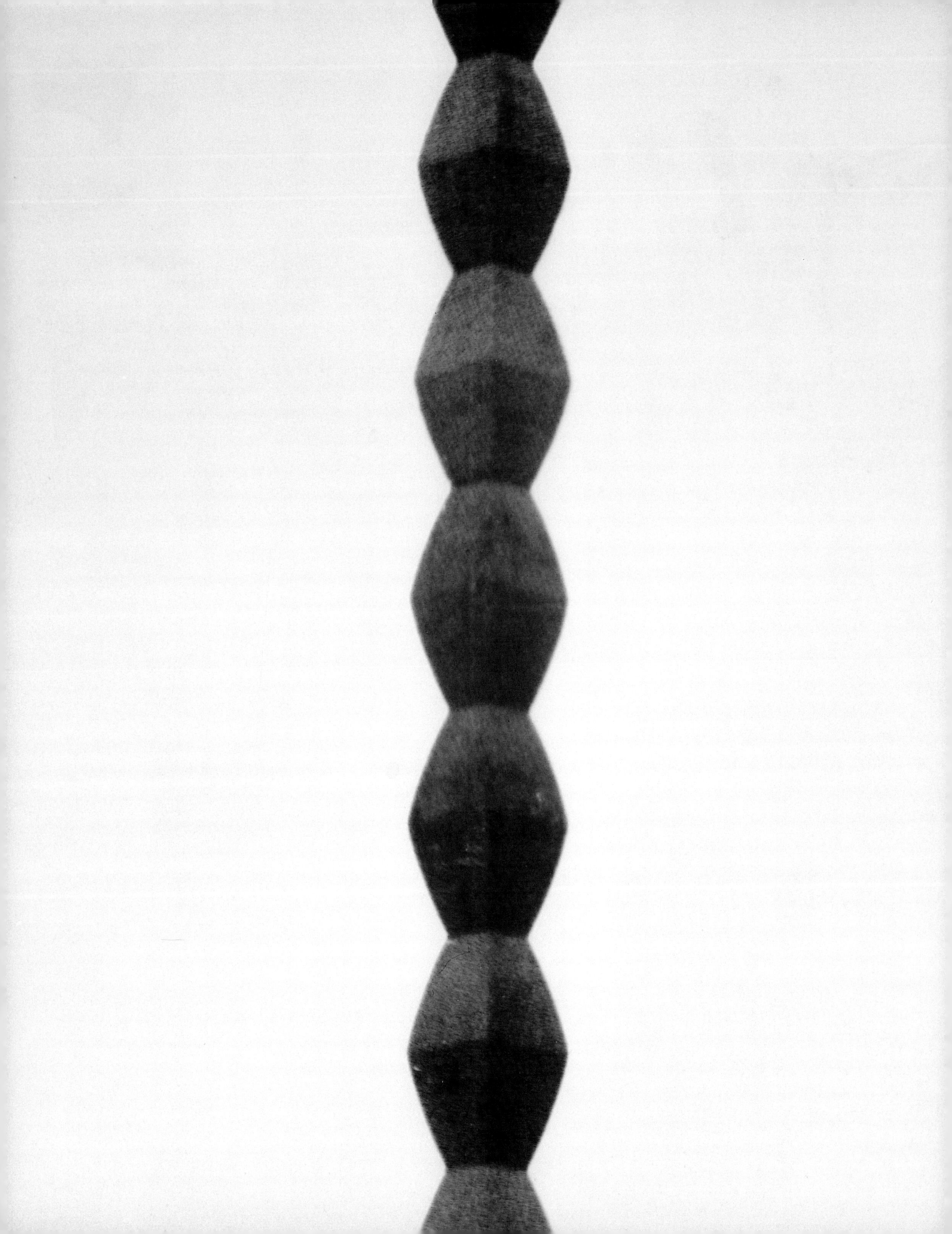

governing the unitary repetition was mediated by the variability arising from the hand-carving of each plane. Further, the very notion of endlessness (the title, *Colonne sans fin*, embraces both 'infinite' and 'unfinished') goes some way to substantiate the sculptor's cosmic aspirations.

My own special creation

It has long been acknowledged that the theme of the *Bird* held a special place in Brancusi's work.[50] He began to capture a form through which to imply flight in 1910, and continued to elaborate on the theme into the 1940s. In the white marble *Maiastra* of 1910 and the immediately ensuing bronzes, movement is suggested synaesthetically through the evocation of sound. Whatever the specific source of inspiration, long and inconclusively debated, the abiding association is with a mythic bird. The allusion indicates the sculptor's bedding-down in his rural heritage, although the sleek form is significantly different from the rough-hewn carvings that had previously been associated with this concern. Indeed, the only point of conjunction between the *Birds* and the earlier carvings is the physical placement of the earliest *Maiastras* on carved bases (cat.34), where the contrast in handling emphasises the difference between the avian and the earth-bound.[51]

In producing the bronze *Maiastras* Brancusi had already begun to shift towards the vertical, but a leap in scale came with the *Bird* series proper. In the astonishing yellow *Bird* of 1919 (cat.36), the features of the earlier pieces are subsumed into an aspiring upward movement. The choice of coloured marble lends an air of exoticism, while a slight notch at the summit condenses head and beak into an embodiment of sound. Up-ended, the whole form is stream-lined but not insubstantial. Again Brancusi followed this marble with bronzes, a transfer that resulted in a further refinement, partly because of the natural strength of the metal and partly through its highly reflective surface. In her 1922 poem on one of these *Golden Birds*,[52] Mina Loy wrote:

> the ultimate rhythm
> has lopped the extremities
> of crest and claw
> from
> the nucleus of flight

Perhaps it was the realisation of the bronzes that prompted Brancusi to even greater daring in the *Bird in Space* series (cat.37). Beginning around 1924 and extending into the 1940s, he pushed the materials – marble and bronze – to new extremes of etiolation. The ratio of height to girth is at the limits of the physical capabilities of the materials. Brancusi dramatised this effect by setting the sculptures up in a shaft of light in his studio, providing a moment of revelation for awe-struck visitors as well as recording it for posterity in his photographs.

The *Bird in Space* belonging to Edward Steichen became the subject of the most famous of the controversies associated with Brancusi. In 1926, the remarkably busy year of his fiftieth birthday, Brancusi held two exhibitions in New York, crossing the Atlantic for each. It was in relation to the second of these, at the Brummer Gallery, that the intervention of customs officials would result in the famous trial of the *Bird in Space*. The legal position was relatively clear: no import duty was payable if an item was defined as art, but if it was considered functional or, crucially, decorative, New York customs officials imposed a levy of 40 per cent of its value. Unable to fathom the nature of *Bird in Space*, the authorities deemed that duty was payable. Together with Duchamp, who had

Fig.15 **Endless Column at Târgu Jiu**, *c.*1938
Centre Pompidou, Paris (AM4002–922, PH581)

travelled with the works and acted as Brancusi's agent in America, Steichen decided to challenge this decision, and a trial about the definition of modern abstract art ensued in 1927–8.[53] The story and the positive resolution for Brancusi have been retold a number of times, and it is possible to see Duchamp's encouragement as indicative of an elaborate subversion of authority by forcing an absurd legal debate. Among all the distractions before he eventually won the case, the deposition that Brancusi made at the American consulate in Paris on 22 November 1927 offers a revealing clarification of his methods:

> I conceived the first idea of this bronze as long ago as nineteen hundred and ten, since when I gave it much thought and study. I conceived it to be created in bronze and I made a plaster model of it. This I gave to the founder, together with the formula for the bronze alloy and other necessary indications. When the roughcast was delivered to me, I had to stop up the air holes and the core hole, to correct the various defects, and to polish the bronze with files and very fine emery. All this I did myself, by hand; this artistic finishing takes a very long time and is equivalent to beginning the whole work over again. I did not allow anybody else to do any of this finishing work, as the subject of the bronze was my own special creation and nobody but myself could have carried it out to my satisfaction.[54]

The tone is naturally defensive, as if Brancusi were loath to divulge the details but felt bound to stress the importance of each stage. Governed by the context of the trial, uniqueness and originality underpin the statement, although the reference to the original conception of the idea in 1910 touches on the notion of seriality. On both counts he must have been aware that he was on slightly dangerous ground. In answer to a further question, he made the confusing claim that the bronze was 'the original production as it is the only one I have made of this subject, and its first replica is not yet finished'.[55] Furthermore, his claims to total control overlooked the presence of his assistants, who had included Isamu Noguchi since April 1927.[56] A fine distinction is drawn between a sequence of unique works and hand-finished casts of an edition. With such assertions, the sculptor formulated an aesthetic of serial uniqueness that was both admirable and ambiguous.

Withdrawn without reason

The tenacity with which Brancusi pursued his technical experiments is embodied in his insistence on using stone for many of the *Birds in Space*. The structure would have been realised with fewer difficulties in wood. Perhaps his belief that materials gave rise to their own forms explains why, when he did make two birds in wood, the lost *Cock* of 1922 and the cherry-wood version of 1924 (cat.30), they had quite individual formal qualities. *Cock* is jagged, its form tallying with the rhythm of the bird's crow. It stands for domestication – a reflection of the human ordering of the world and an attunement to a diurnal and seasonal ruralism. This fits with its ancient use as a symbol of the republican French working-class with which, as we have seen, Brancusi already seems to have formed sympathies. That he was alluding to this symbolism, which had seen a patriotic revival during the war, is confirmed in the first title of the 1922 version: *Le Coq Gaulois* (Gallic Cock).[57]

There were various projects to enlarge these sculptures but they foundered on the technical problems encountered by those trying to fabricate them to Brancusi's standards. He began to make larger versions of *Cock* himself, in a series of increasingly monumental stages, starting with two in 1930 and working on a further version through-

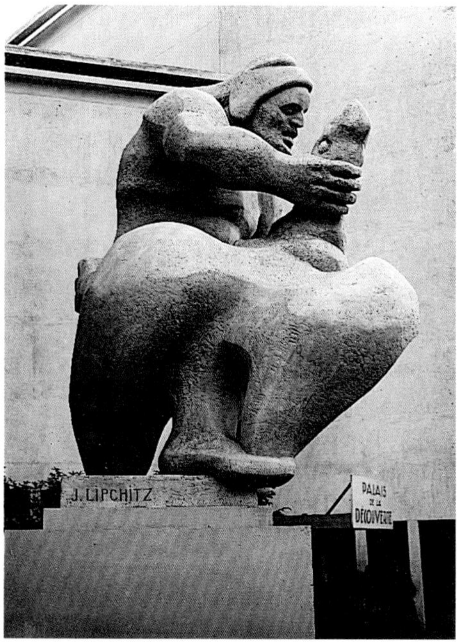

Fig.16 Jacques Lipchitz **Prometheus Strangling the Vulture** 1937 (destroyed 1938)
Lipchitz Papers, Tate Gallery Archive

out the 1940s. Their size necessitated a return to plaster. The results dominate the late photographs of the studio as uplifting and, at times, slightly ominous presences (fig.39). The leap in scale from the wooden version gives rise to works of entirely different proportions and the change in material means that they have textured surfaces not used since his youth.

The series bears comparison with the gigantic plaster *Prometheus Strangling the Vulture* that Lipchitz made for the Paris *Exposition Internationale* of 1937 (fig.16). Lipchitz's sculpture was explicitly anti-Fascist, with the mythical Titan as a man of the people rising up against the tyrannous oppression represented by Zeus's vulture. He placed himself within the tradition of nineteenth-century political art, even if, formally, the result was seen as modernist.[58] Chillingly, the sculpture was quickly destroyed in the spring of 1938, as a result of a campaign mounted in the right-wing press; one account considered it 'little in line with contemporary French sculpture and its traditions', another simply proclaimed against 'Bolshevik influence'.[59] Brancusi was invited to contribute to the major international survey exhibition, entitled *Origines et développement de l'art international indépendant,* that accompanied the *Exposition.*[60] He is often said to have done so, although a review in *Cahiers d'Art* suggests otherwise. 'Among the artists who do not belong to any particular tendency,' wrote the reviewer, 'we cite: the Romanian Brancusi who, after having promised M. Dezarois a large contribution for his exhibition, has withdrawn without reason in his usual way.'[61] Nevertheless, Brancusi would certainly have been aware of the publicity that accompanied the making of Lipchitz's work and the later controversy surrounding its destruction. It may even be that he took an interest in the theme, having long before concerned himself with the suffering Prometheus. Though not submitted to public judgement, Brancusi's *Cock*, with its use of traditional working-class connotations, had similar resonances to Lipchitz's monument. As foreign artists long resident in Paris they expressed a coincident faith in the civilising message of (French) culture, an international medium representing freedom in the context of 1930s political polarisation.

At the time Brancusi was also bringing to fruition his scheme for Târgu Jiu. This was a culminatory period for the sculptor, in which he felt equipped to carry his work to a grand scale. It is as if he conceived this three-part monument in a traditional sense, as a constant within the slippage of time. The extreme political uncertainty of the period lends their public position an acute relevance. The Ligei Naţionale a Femelior Gorgene (National Women's League of Gorj) commissioned the monument in 1935 in memory of those who fell in the battle for the valley in the First World War. They anticipated a relatively orthodox monument until Militia Patrascu withdrew in favour of Brancusi. He devised the tripartite urban scheme located in two public parks, which helps to secure the idea of local martyrdom in the everyday life of the city. As the basis for a national myth of resistance the works needed to evoke and memorialise the dead in the presence of the living. The *Table of Silence* (fig.17) and the *Gate of the Kiss* (fig.18) occupy positions on the river near the site of the battle, while the thirty-metre-high steel *Endless Column* stands on a bluff above the town. There are subtle degrees of participation for local people, from the integration of the *Gate* and the *Table* into the heart of the town to the more distant symbolism of the *Column*, shielded by a church from the simple vista along the newly laid out street.[62]

Beyond the local significance of the monument lies a greater sense of the role of art as it was currently debated in Paris. The tradition of grand gestures gained renewed impetus when artists sought a means to use art as a bulwark against the rising tide of Fascism. An art of engagement was the substance of the 1936–7 debates known as the 'Querelle du réalisme' (the realism dispute). Like Picasso's *Guernica* or Miró's *Reaper* in the Spanish Republican Pavilion of the 1937 *Exposition*, Brancusi's work is an act of protest. Lacking the anger of the Spaniards in the throes of the Civil War, it is melancholic in its memorialisation of the violent sacrifice of ordinary people. Perhaps too, Brancusi saw his urban scheme as one of healing at a time of intolerance. He could hardly have been unaware of Corneliu Codreanu's nationalist Iron Guard and Romania's own inclination towards Fascism at this time.[63] As well as memory the *Gate* suggests understanding, and the *Table* comradeship. The *Column*, in keeping with the universality of its plastic form, is physically and conceptually distant.

An 'equal among rocks, trees, people, beasts, and plants'

Brancusi's daily activities over the forty years from 1916 were enclosed within the studio complex at impasse Ronsin. Even the address suggests that he had gone to ground in a cul-de-sac, and it seems appropriate that he was described, in 1927, as 'One on the inside of things, who stands on the ground an equal among rocks, trees, people, beasts and plants, never above or apart from them'.[64] However, he must have been a noisy neighbour, constantly sawing, hammering, chipping and polishing. Huge beams of wood and blocks of stone arrived by strenuous means into the tight, steep courtyard. There must have been regular deliveries to the foundry and the reciprocal arrival of plaster and materials for armatures. Within this curious place, which he preferred to a projected (but never built) studio, he conceived works tempered to its scale.[65] He tested and dramatised them, and the studio itself, through his carefully conceived and controlled photographs, which fixed momentary juxtapositions and mediated his work for his public. They were his calling cards to the world, given to friends and interested collectors who wandered into his seclusion.

After the intensely productive interwar years, Brancusi's seeming withdrawal became actual. In 1946 he was seventy and far from the dynamic creator that Picasso

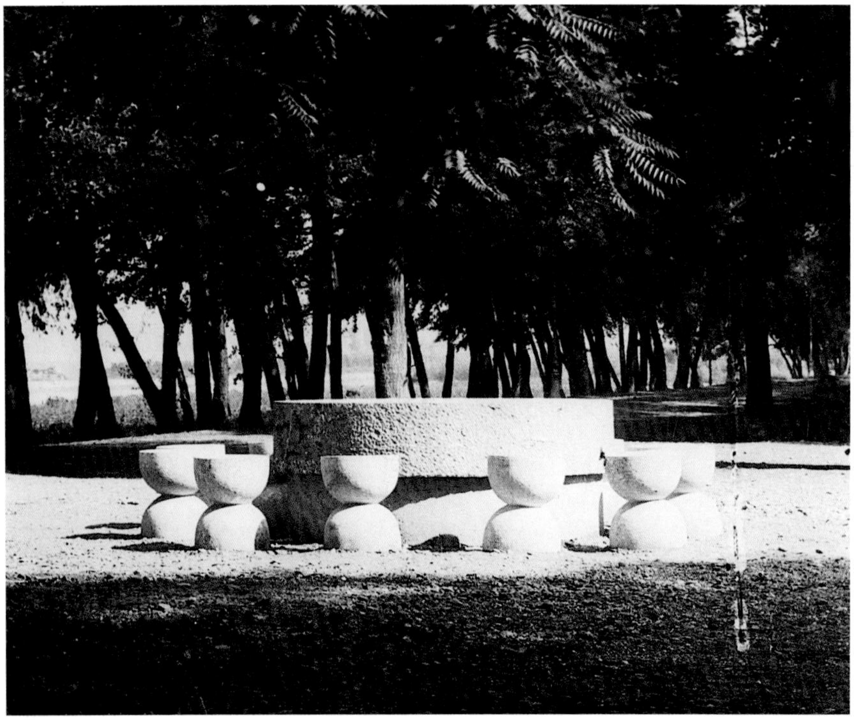

Fig.17 **The Table of Silence at Târgu Jiu**, *c.*1938
Centre Pompidou, Paris (AM4002–926)

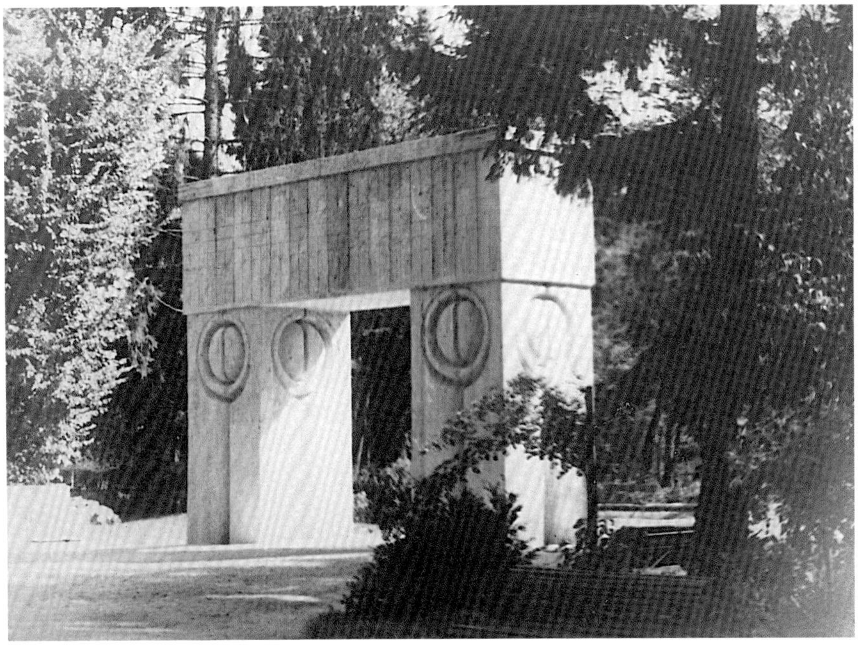

Fig.18 **The Gate of the Kiss**, 1938
Centre Pompidou, Paris (AM4002–805, PH231)

would be at the same age. Isolation may have started as a means of weathering the war years in Paris, but it became normality. The studio, constantly visited by admirers, achieved an aura and its adjustment and maintenance became his sole preoccupation.

Brancusi's impact on his contemporaries – from Modigliani to Hepworth – has now been outshone by his influence on the generation that came to maturity shortly after his death in 1957: Carl Andre, Donald Judd, Robert Morris and other Minimalist sculptors. At the same time there were those for whom the purity and mysticism of the white studio were too far withdrawn from the contemporary world. On 12 February 1961, four years after Brancusi's death, the courtyard of impasse Ronsin was the site of a reinvention of art seemingly opposed to every aspect of Brancusi's activity.[66] With a violence that chimed with the times, Niki de Saint-Phalle produced her first *Tirs* or *Shooting Paintings* there. Firing a gun at plaster-encrusted compositions, Saint-Phalle punctured hidden reservoirs of paint that bled bright colour down the pure white surface. This gesture may be seen as an assassination of Brancusi's aesthetics, indeed of the structure of modernism of which his work was exemplary. At the same time, Saint-Phalle's violent plunge into chaos serves to affirm by contrast the compelling power that Brancusi captured through his universal forms.

1 André Salmon, *Le Jeune sculpture français*, Paris 1919.

2 Carola Giedion-Welcker, *Moderne Plastik: Elemente der Wirklichkeit, Masse und Auflockerung*, Zurich 1937.

3 His conceptual and formal experiments may be set alongside those of Picasso, Tatlin, Duchamp and others. For the Independent sculptors, see Patrick Elliott, 'Sculpture in France and Classicism, 1910–1939', in Elizabeth Cowling and Jennifer Mundy (eds.), *On Classic Ground: Picasso, Léger, de Chirico and the New Classicism, 1910–1930*, exh. cat., Tate Gallery, London 1990, p.284.

4 Benjamin Fondane called him 'this peasant from the Danube', in 'Brancusi', *Cahiers de l'Etoile*, no.11, Sept.–Oct. 1929. For early family life see Hulten, Dumitresco and Istrati 1988, pp.56–7, and Brezianu 1998, p.17. For the abbreviations used in the notes, see Selected Reading.

5 For the early years see Hulten, Dumitresco and Istrati 1988, pp.57–63; Brezianu 1998, pp.16–19; and Paul Rezeanu, *Brâncuşi la Craiova*, Bucharest 2002, pp.51–3. See also Sanda Miller's essay and the Chronology in this catalogue.

6 The Hungarian sculptor Joseph Csáky secured local scholarships under similar terms; see Edith Balas, *Joseph Csâky: A Pioneer of Modern Sculpture*, Philadelphia 1998, p.4.

7 Hulten, Dumitresco and Istrati 1988 (p.58) places the Vienna trip in the summer of 1896 but Brezianu 1998 (p.17) places it in the following year. Both specify work with the cabinet-maker Roth. The chronology in Tabart and Lemny 1997 (p.264) places it in 1897 and mentions an apprenticeship to Thonet. Brancusi applied to the Madona Dudu Charity for study in Italy, and was turned down (Brezianu 1998, p.18). He is said to have arrived in Paris on 14 July 1904.

8 Hulten, Dumitresco and Istrati 1988, pp.65–6.

9 Cosmutza was trained as a sculptor and was Anatole France's secretary; see Tabart and Lemny 2003, pp.207 n.4, 220 n.3.

10 Louis Herbette to Antonin Mercié, 19 June 1905, letter kept by Brancusi and reproduced in Hulten, Dumitresco and Istrati 1988, p.65. For the link to Herbette, see Brezianu 1998, p.287.

11 According to Tabart and Lemny 1997 (p.266), he joined Mercié's studio on 23 June 1905 and remained there until 19 January 1906; the certificate is reproduced in Hulten, Dumitresco and Istrati 1988, p.66. For the progression from Ecole des Beaux-Arts to official commissions see Elliott 1990, pp.284–5; for the difficulties of those outside this system securing commissions see Christopher Green, *Art in France 1900–1940*, New Haven and London 2000, p.45.

12 The bust of Anatole France proposed *c.*1909 is cited by Brezianu 1998, p.24 and Marielle Tabart, 'L'Atelier comme lieu de mémoire', in Tabart and Lemny 1997, p.102. Brancusi worked with Rodin at Meudon from 24 March–27 April 1907 (Tabart and Lemny 1997, p.267).

13 On 18 April 1907, see Hulten, Dumitresco and Istrati 1988, p.69 for the full text. For *The Prayer* see Bach 1987, p.420, no.72.

14 Theodor Cornel, 'Indrumări in artă' ('New Guidelines in Art'), *Viața socială*, vol.1, no.4, May 1910, trans. Julian Semilian in Timothy O. Benson and Eva Forgás (eds.), *Between Worlds: A Sourcebook of Central European Avant-gardes, 1910–1930*, Cambridge (Mass.) and London 2002, p.137.

15 *Kunstausstellung*, Munich, June–Oct. 1913. The other representatives were Grigorescu, Luchian, Paciurea, Steriadi and G.D. Mirea (director of Şcoala Națională de Arte Frumoase in Bucharest when Brancusi was there).

16 Brancusi had a full run of *Vers et Prose*, 1905–14 (see Tabart and Lemny 1997, p.249, P45), and is said to have attended the regular soirées that Fort held at the Cloiseries de Lilas. Mercereau included Brancusi in his *Vystava Moderniho Umeni* (Modern French Artists) exhibition in Prague in 1914; see Hulten, Dumitresco and Istrati 1988, p.94 and Kristina Passuth, *Les Avant-gardes de l'Europe centrale, 1907–1927*, Paris 1988, p.14.

17 On Brancusi's Bergsonianism see Geist 1968, p.147.

18 As revealed by Mark Antliff, *Inventing Bergson: Cultural Politics and the Parisian Avant-Garde*, Princeton 1993, pp.125–7, whose argument I follow here.

19 See See Alexandra Parigoris, 'Brancusi: "En art il n'y a pas d'étrangers"', in André Kaspi and Antoine Marès (eds.), *le Paris des étrangers depuis un siècle*, Paris 1989, p.214 and Miller in this catalogue.

20 Notably in M.M., 'Constantin Brancusi. A Summary of Many Conversations', *The Arts*, vol.4, no.1, July 1923, reprinted in Bach 1987, pp.316–19.

21 See Parigoris 1989, p.215.

22 Ibid., p.216, n.24. See also John Buchan (ed.), *The Nations of Today: Bulgaria and Romania*, London 1924, p.300 and, more widely, Misha Glenny, *The Balkans 1804–1999: Nationalism, War and the Great Powers*, London 1999, pp.57–69, 444–5.

23 See Alexandra Parigoris's essay in this catalogue, and Margit Rowell, 'Brancusi: Timelessness in a Modern Mode' in Bach, Rowell and Temkin 1995, pp.38–48.

24 Rowell ibid., p.39, citing Remus Niculescu, 'Bourdelle et Anastase Simu', *Revue Roumaine d'Historie de l'Art*, vol.3, 1966.

25 Inscription in *This Quarter*, 1925, p.42, see Bach 1987, p.422, no.78.

26 Geist 1978, pp.9–16.

27 For the story of the tomb see Barbu Brezianu, 'Le secret du Baiser de Montparnasse', republished in Sidney Geist, Barbu Brezianu and S.L.F., *Les carnets de l'Atelier Brancusi: Le Baiser*, Paris 1999, pp.50–5.

28 It has been assumed that Brancusi studied architectural stone carving in Craiova, but this is not among the craft skills listed by Brezianu 1998 (pp.16–17), who notes him specialising in wood carving from 1895; Miller 1995 (p.14, n.35) gives a detailed account of surviving wooden furnishings. See also Parigoris in this catalogue.

29 See Noël Alexandre, *The Unknown Modigliani, Drawings from the Collection of Paul Alexandre*, exh. cat., Royal Academy, London 1994, pp.59, 44. For Modigliani see Kenneth Wayne, *Modigliani and the Artists of Montparnasse*, exh. cat., Albright-Knox Art Gallery, Buffalo 2002 and Marc Restellini, *Amedeo Modigliani*, exh. cat., Musée du Luxembourg, Paris 2002.

30 As Patrick Elliott has shown in 'La Sculpture en taille directe en France Durant le vingtième siècle: practique et théorie' in *La Sculpture en taille directe en France de 1900 à 1950*, exh. cat., Fondation de Coubertin, Saint-Rémy-les-Chevreuse 1988.

31 See Selected Aphorisms in this catalogue.

32 Cited (in Italian, my translation), as having been in *Liberté*, in Alberto Savinio, 'La Realtà dorata: Arte e Storia moderna – Guerra – conseguenze', *La Voce*, VIII, no.2, 29 Feb. 1916, p.79. Mercié died that same year.

33 Brancusi to Walter Pach (by whom translated for the collector John Quinn), 4 Oct. 1916, John Quinn Memorial Collection, New York Public Library, transcribed in Ina Klein, *Brancusi: Natur, Struktur, Skulptur, Architektur*, Cologne 1994, vol.2, p.403.

34 See Kenneth Silver, *Esprit de Corps: The Art of the Parisian Avant-Garde and the First World War, 1914–1925*, London 1989, pp.167–85. The issue was resolved on 15 September 1917 by both sides publishing the letters of support that they had received – both for the attack on modernism and in support of Poiret as a true patriot.

35 See Jon Wood's essay in this catalogue.

36 Salmon 1919, p.16. For the polarisation of the Parisian art world see Romy Golan, 'The "Ecole Français" vs. the "Ecole de Paris": The Debate about the Status of Jewish Artists in Paris between the Wars', in Kenneth Silver (ed.), *The Circle of Montparnasse: Jewish Artists in Paris 1905–1945*, exh. cat., Jewish Museum, New York 1985, pp.81–7.

37 See Chave 1993, p.93. Picabia had included Brancusi's name alongside his own in *Mouvement Dada*, a diagrammatic illustration in the periodical *Dada 4–5*, 1919.

38 See William A. Camfield, *Marcel Duchamp: Fountain*, Houston 1989, pp.54–6.

39 *Cannibale I*, 25 Apr. 1920, p.7, reprinted in Michel Sanouillet, *Francis Picabia et 391*, II, Paris 1966, p.187.

40 See 'Pour l'indépendance de l'art', *Le Journal du peuple*, 25 Feb. 1920, reproduced in Anna C. Chave, '*Princess X/Prince's Sex*: le diomorphisme sexuel dans la sculpture de Brancusi', in Marielle Tabard (ed.), *Les carnets de l'Atelier Brancusi: Princesse X*, Paris 1999, p.34, fig.1.

41 The meeting's 'Résolution' and the list of signatories are given in Michel Sanouillet, *Dada à Paris*, Paris 1965, pp.334–5.

42 'En art, il n'y a pas d'étrangers.' A revised version of the 'Résolution' was drawn up by Tzara the same evening, with this and other manuscript additions; 'Dossier du "Congrès de Paris"', item 144 in the Bibliothèque Nationale (Mss. N.A.F. 14316) quoted in ibid., p.335 n.1.

43 André Salmon, 'Aux Indépendants (II) – Le Bonnat du Cercle Volnay', *L'Europe Nouvelle*, 7 Feb. 1920, pp.232–3, my translation from the French quoted in Christopher Green, 'Lipchitz and Gris: the Cubisms of a Sculptor and a Painter', in J.B. Yvars (ed.), *Lipchitz: Un mundo sorprendido en el espacio*, exh. cat., Museo Nacional Centro de Arte Reina Sofía, Madrid and IVAM, Valencia 1997, p.206.

44 Paul Dermée, 'Lipchitz', *L'Esprit nouveau*, no.2, Nov. 1920, p.171, as discussed in Christopher Green, *Cubism and its Enemies: Modern*

Movements and Reaction in French Art, 1916–1928, New Haven and London 1987, p.81, whose argument is followed here.

45 Dermée, ibid., my translation; see also Green 1997, p.205.

46 *L'Esprit nouveau* is listed in Brancusi's library, Tabart and Lemny 1997, p. 248, P16.

47 Hulten, Dumitresco and Istrati 1988, p.128.

48 M.M., 'Constantin Brancusi. A Summary of Many Conversations', *The Arts*, vol.4, no.1, July 1923, reprinted in Bach 1987, p.316. For the mystery of M.M. and the French manuscript, see Tabart and Lemny 2003, pp.95–8.

49 See Mircea Eliade, 'Brancusi et les Mythologies', in Petru Comarnescu, Mircea Eliade and Ionel Jianou, *Témoignages sur Brancusi*, Paris 1967, pp.9–19.

50 See, above all, Anthea T. Spear, *Brancusi's Birds*, New York 1969 and Marielle Tabart (ed.), *Les carnets de l'Atelier Brancusi: L'Oiseau dans l'espace*, Paris 2001.

51 This marks the beginning of the artist's complex choice of materials for the bases, the quality and significance of which has been much debated, notably by Chave 1993, pp.225–47 and Friedrich Teja Bach, 'Brancusi: The Reality of Sculpture' in Bach, Rowell and Temkin 1995, pp.22–37.

52 Mina Loy, 'Brancusi's "Golden Bird"', *The Dial*, Nov. 1922, republished by Jon Wood in *Shine: Sculpture and Surface in the 1920s and 1930s*, exh. cat., Henry Moore Institute, Leeds 2002, p.2.

53 See Margit Rowell, 'Preface', *Brancusi vs. United States: The Historic Trial, 1928*, Paris 1999, pp.7–11, and Doïna Lemny, 'Maurice et Morice: chronique d'une amitié', in Marielle Tabart (ed.), *Les carnets de l'Atelier Brancusi: Brancusi & Duchamp*, Paris 2000, pp.21–62.

54 Transcript published in *Brancusi vs. United States: The Historic Trial, 1928*, Paris 1999, p.48.

55 Ibid., p.49.

56 See 'Noguchi on Brancusi', 1976 in Diane Apostolos-Cappadona and Bruce Altshuler (eds.), *Isamu Noguchi: Essays and Conversations*, New York 1994; Bach 1987, p.284; and the 1975 interview with Friedrich Teja Bach, in Bach 1987, pp.287–93.

57 Bach, Rowell and Temkin 1995, pp.220–1; see Antliff 1993 (p.118) for the currency of *Le Coq Gaulois* symbol.

58 As such Lipchitz was part of the wider debate around how to use art to respond to the threat of Fascism, for which the militant nineteenth-century tradition became a model.

59 *Mercure de France*, 15 Nov. 1937, press-cutting in Lipchitz Papers, Tate Gallery Archive. See Pascal Ory, 'L'affaire Lipchitz, ou Prométhée fracassé' in *Face à l'histoire: L'Artiste moderne devant l'événement historique*, exh. cat., Centre Georges Pompidou, Paris 1996, pp.152–3.

60 *Origines et développement de l'art international indépendant*, Jeu de Paume, July–Nov. 1937; a 'copper' *Bird* by Brancusi is listed in the catalogue on loan from Helena Rubenstein.

61 Anon (Christian Zervos?), 'Les expositions: Origines et développement de l'art international indépendant, Musée du jeu de paume, July–November 1937', *Cahiers d'Art*, 1937, no.4–5, p.164.

62 A document from October 1937 indicates that the street was laid out as a result of expropriations of land funded by the League, see Brezianu 1998, pp.252–3, document 43.

63 For the Iron Guard, see Glenny 1999, pp.455–60, and the Chronology in this catalogue. For the contention that the scheme at Târgu Jiu threatens the absorption of the individual by the state, see Chave 1993, p.270.

64 Dorothy Dudley, 'Brancusi', *Dial*, Feb. 1927, reprinted in Bach 1987, p.322.

65 See Tabart and Lemny 2003, pp.74–7.

66 Pierre Restany, 'An Immense Oeuvre to Challenge the New Century', in *Niki de Saint Phalle: Monographie/Monograph; Peintures, Tirs, Assemblages, Reliefs, 1949–2000*, Lausanne 2001, pp.117–18.

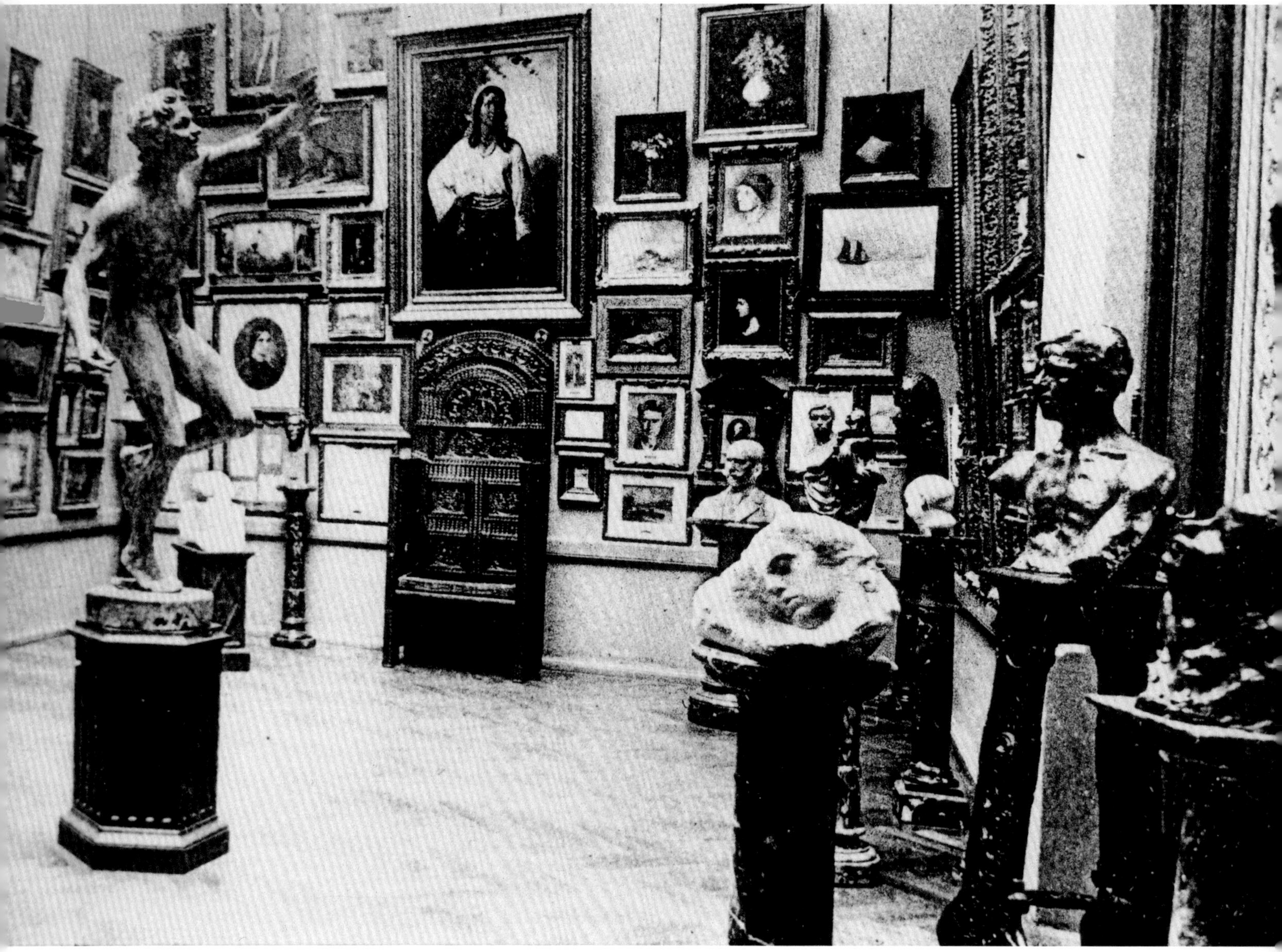

Reconfiguring Brancusi's formative years: Hobița – Craiova – Bucharest

SANDA MILLER

'In the history of the Romanian people we do not find sculpture. In the artistic patrimony of the past we have Byzantine frescoes and the art of the peasant.' Thus wrote the Romanian sculptor Oscar Han in 1935, in a monograph dedicated to Dimitrie Paciurea, one of Romania's most original sculptors.[1] Paciurea's early development mirrored that of his famous contemporary and friend, Constantin Brancusi.[2] Both studied in Paris, but while the latter settled there, Paciurea returned to Bucharest around 1900.[3] There, he battled with poverty, lack of recognition, artistic isolation and, late in life, alcoholism, dying a broken man in 1932. His oeuvre, completely unknown in the West,[4] remains insufficiently researched. Yet he deserves recognition, not least for his series of eerie sculptures entitled *Chimeras*, on which he started work around 1919.[5]

It would be futile to speculate on whether or not an analogous fate would have awaited Brancusi had he too abandoned Paris and returned to Bucharest. It is worth noting, however, that the prevailing notion that during the nineteenth century Romania was an underdeveloped Balkan country, and thus unable to nurture its artists, is misleading. Though nineteenth-century Romania was a rural society whose peasant population outnumbered town dwellers, inevitably political changes towards the end of the century affected its superstructure and a process of Westernisation began, induced by the monarch Carol I and by the emerging Romanian intelligentsia. The quest for 'Latin roots' prompted them to turn to France, whose political interests conveniently coincided with such idealistic aspirations. Practical steps were taken to aid Romania's emancipation and this is reflected in the proliferation of political institutions, cultural developments and the education system. Thus, although Han was correct to observe that there was no real sculptural tradition in Romania, aspiring artists such as Brancusi received a thoroughly French academic training during the 1880s and 1890s.

Fig.19 Muzeul Simu, Bucharest. In the foreground to the left is Oscar Spaethe's **Dancing Faun**. In the centre is Brancusi's marble **Sleep**, and on the right is **Portrait of the Painter Darascu**

The achievements of Carol I are not acknowledged in post-World War II accounts: after the Communist takeover in 1947, the royal family was obliterated from Romanian histories.[6] A similar fate awaited the Romanian diaspora – including Brancusi – who did not comply with the Socialist–Realist doctrines dominant during the Cold War in the Soviet Union and its satellite countries. A little-known exception exists in the form of V.G. Paleolog's book on the sculptor, published in Bucharest in 1947 in French, of which 150 copies financed by the author were printed.[7] During the 1960s, after Brancusi's death in 1957, Romanian scholars were able to start publishing their research on the artist, but they were still obliged to avoid contextual analysis and to pay lip-service to Marxist–Leninist ideology. Among the first of these scholarly books to incorporate Brancusi's Romanian years, albeit summarily, was a monograph by the art historian Ionel Jianou, published in Paris in 1963.[8]

It is now possible to throw new light on Brancusi's Romanian context, with the help of previously untapped contemporary sources. Following a brief account of Romania's history, this essay will present the three formative stepping-stones in his career: his childhood in Hobița from 1876 to 1888, his apprenticeship in Craiova in 1888–98, and his student years in Bucharest from 1898 until his departure for Paris in 1904.

A brief history

Brancusi's Romania was very different from the modern state, which acquired its present boundaries in 1918. Until the mid-nineteenth century, it consisted of two independent principalities, Wallachia and Moldavia. In 1856 the Treaty of Paris made the Danubian principalities independent of Russian influence, though they remained under the suzerainty of the Ottoman Empire whilst securing the protection of Western powers. It has been observed that the 'freeing of the Danubian principalities, which led ultimately to an independent Romania, was the real achievement of the Treaty of Paris'.[9] In 1858 the Paris convention – which became the official constitution of the Danubian principalities – decreed that Wallachia and Moldavia would 'receive the name of United principalities' – leading eventually to the emergence of modern Romania.[10]

In 1866, Prince Carol de Hohenzollern-Singmaringen (1838–1914), a foreigner, became the ruler of the Danubian principalities.[11] Romania's quest for national identity was achieved when it fought as a Russian ally in the war against Turkey (1877–8), culminating in the decisive battle of Plevna.[12] The Treaty of Berlin in 1878 finally brought Romania full independence, and Prince Carol was crowned King in 1881.

The final stage in Romania's historical development took place in 1918 in the aftermath of World War I, when the dismembered Austro-Hungarian Empire ceded Transylvania and the Banat to Romania. Bessarabia (lost to the Russians in 1877), and part of Dobrudja (which had been under Bulgarian occupation), were also returned.[13] Thus modern Romania was politically engineered as a consequence of historical events and, as Martyn Rady wrote in 1996: 'although the Romanians comprise one of Europe's oldest nations, their state is a modern creation . . . essentially a product of this century's diplomacy. In a sense the Romanian nation has been left a political orphan by the vicissitudes and experience of the past.'[14]

1876–88

A Romanian village: Hobița

The grim economic situation in late nineteenth-century rural Romania is amply corroborated by the contemporary accounts of foreign travellers. In his book *Moldo-Wallachia*, published in 1867, G. Le Cler paints a sorry picture: towns were in a 'bad state' and Bucharest appeared to be 'an endless village' where cattle were slaughtered in the street. What filled his soul with despair was 'the peasants' deplorable state of poverty' – that there was so much deprivation and misery, whilst other sectors of society lived in luxury. Some urban homes were filled with 'Aubusson and Smirna carpets, furniture from Vienna, things from Paris, porcelain from China, Hungary, Sèvres'. Meanwhile, in the country, 'the sick die without help, with a touching resignation, stretched on some mat or even on the bare earth. The peasant is thin, pale, drained, in rags, old before his time; his gaze is sad and withered, his body bent.'[15]

Two decades later, in rural 1885, another book entitled *Grèce, Turquie, Danube*, written by Charles Bizot, painted a different picture. Here, Bucharest was transformed from an 'endless village' into an elegant metropolis with terraced houses, tramways circulating in every direction, bad-tempered carriage drivers, beautiful theatres, abundant stores, luxurious coffee houses and many new buildings, some barely finished, some in progress. In the countryside he found the 'corn to be weak, but admirable maize'. Little had improved in the life of the peasants however: 'everywhere in the countryside women in the fields; an industrious people, but what a hard life. The poor folk in the country eat only badly cooked maize porridge with onions.'[16]

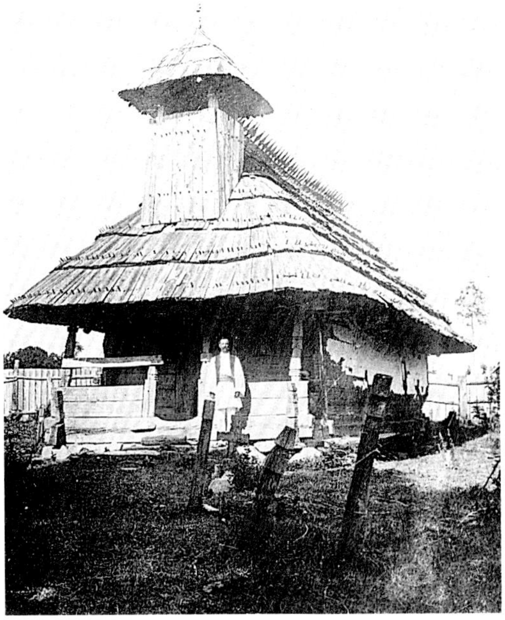

Fig.20 Wooden church in the cemetery at Glodeni in Wallachia, *c.*1900

The weekly *Tribuna Familiei*, subtitled 'Magazine of literature, arts and popular sciences' and first published in 1898, identified another problem:

> The peasant is pushed into alcoholism because, besides his miserable condition, he lacks a proper drinking place as well as work during the winter months. Drink produces these miserable consequences because the body, weakened by poverty, has no resistance to the destructive effect of alcohol, which is more intensely manifest in the country due to a pronounced physical, moral and economic degradation.[17]

The pioneering weekly publication *Noua Revistă Română Pentru Politică, Literatură, Ştiinţă şi Artă*, launched in 1900, was the first to introduce a regular feature dealing with rural issues, entitled 'Literature and Folklore'. In an article about the wedding ritual in Brancusi's native region of Oltenia, Anton Eliade quotes a lovely oration based on Genesis, giving the following rendition of the creation of Eve:

> Do not fear, Adam
> because she is
> from your bones
> and flesh from your flesh
> and she is to you a wife
> and you will be one body
> and God's will is that the young man and his maiden
> will leave his father and his mother
> and he will be joined to his woman and they will be one body[18]

Brancusi would have been familiar with such wedding orations and the *Kiss* series (begun around 1907, cat.1–3) could be interpreted as the embodiment in stone of these tender verses and perhaps justify the bold use of the full-length version of the sculpture as a funerary monument (fig.25). Born in 1876, he grew up in this environment, epitomised by these two opposing poles of rich creativity and physical poverty, whose fortunate corollary was a popular culture whose beauty was aptly summed up by Brancusi's future friend Marie Bengesco, as 'resembling a poem'.[19]

In one of the first scholarly books on peasant art, published in Romania in 1923 and soon after in Britain entitled *Peasant Art in Roumania*, George Oprescu emphasises the importance of the correlation between rites of passage central to village life and artistic production. As an example of this, and directly evocative of the graveyard at Hobiţa where Brancusi's family are buried, his analysis of the cemetery is worth quoting in full:

> the cemetery is not a gay, cheerful place, as with the Turks, nor a staid trim garden in which tombstones half overgrown with moss induce a mood of sad and tranquil meditation, as with the English. It is a grim place, reflecting the soul of the peasant. A Christianity dealing sternly with man, tainted with a good deal of paganism, determines its appearance and its architecture. Frequently, especially in the district of Oltenia, wooden crosses of imposing size are set out in lines, raising to heaven their powerful arms covered with a medley of vivid colours, with figures and symbols carved with knives, and taking us right back to the style of the catacomb. Squat figures with enormous eyes, expressive to the pitch of grimacing, remind the living that they tread the soil of the dead. The crosses, single, double or triple, are all covered with a conical or pyramidal

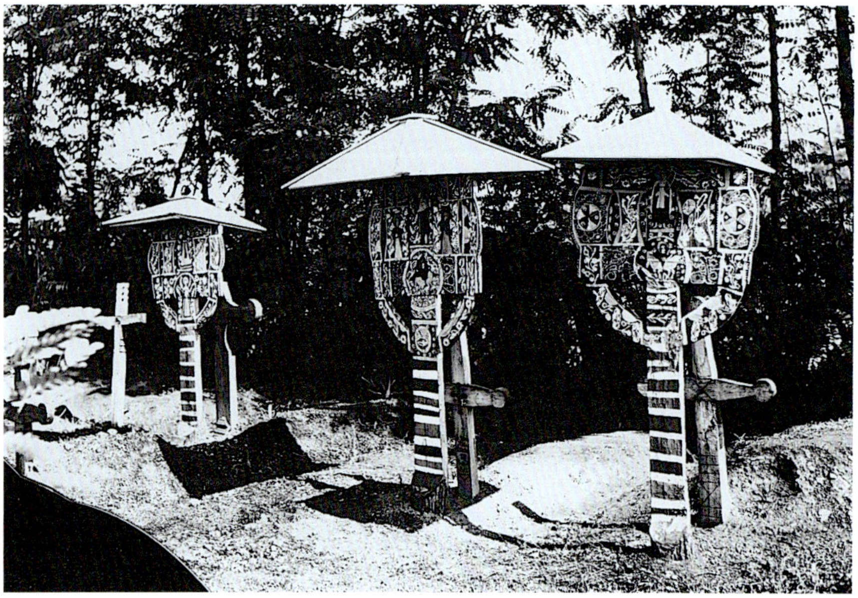

Fig.21 Roadside crosses in East Wallachia

> roof of shingle boarding [fig.21]. These strange silhouettes are visible from afar. They are crowded round the churchyard or aligned along the highway to commemorate some accident or important event, or merely to remind the wayfarer of the presence of the Holy Trinity.[20]

Brancusi's childhood was brief and, from what we can glean from the available material, unhappy. One source of information about this period comes from his schoolmate Vasile Blendea, nicknamed Trifu:

> We started school together in Peștișani . . . he remained there for two years. The teacher's name was Zaharia. Once he scratched something on his desk with his pocket knife and the teacher punished him by locking him up in a dirty cupboard. He ran away and never came back. He started in Brediceni where the teacher was Petre Brâncuși and there he finished the remaining years of his primary school. I did not finish mine. He was clever, understood quickly and liked to know everything.[21]

Brancusi had repeatedly run away from his parental home, finally leaving for good around 1888, when he escaped to Slatina and then to Craiova.[22] His short childhood in Hobița had provided him with his earliest visual stimuli, whose importance to his subsequent development cannot be overestimated. The next stepping-stone was Craiova.

1888–98

A Romanian provincial town: Craiova

In an article dealing with Romania's geography signed by S. Mehedinti, Craiova was referred to as the 'former residence of the *bani* [the old aristocracy] of Oltenia', whilst its peasant population was described as 'fruit and vegetable merchants, one of the characteristic features of the capital'. The article continued: 'Craiova, like almost all the other urban centres in the country, through its multitude of gardens, gives the traveller an impression of joyousness and semi-rural life. Nevertheless, several monumental buildings elevate the ancient town of the *bani* beyond the rank of a simple regional capital and give it a more modernist character.'[23]

These buildings were a testimony to the process of Westernisation under way in Craiova when Brancusi arrived there in 1888. Apart from various permutations of Western European classicism, romanticism and eclecticism, represented in different degrees of concentration in Romania's cities, a national style was also emerging. Among its major exponents were Ion Mincu – who, after studying from 1877–84 at the Ecole des Beaux-Arts in Paris, embarked on a distinguished career in Bucharest – and Petre Antonescu, responsible for the imposing Administrative Palace in Craiova, built between 1912 and 1913.[24]

Thus Brancusi's first intimations of Western European art in Craiova came from witnessing the erection of public edifices and private residences inspired by French and Italian architecture, and built by the new generation of Romanian architects. It is likely that he watched work in progress on the Palace of Justice (at present the University of Craiova) built from 1893–5 after plans by the Bucharest-based architect I.N. Socolescu. Its grandiose classical façade and central Corinthian portico would have been a revelation for the country boy. Also from Bucharest, Toma Dobrescu – assisted by two local architects, Costa and Nedelcu – provided plans for the Carol I Lyceum (still functioning today as a school) and for the imposing Geblescu and Minerva hotels, dating from 1895–6 and 1898–1903 respectively. The French architect A. Galeron designed a number of *hotels particuliers* (town houses), including that owned by Brancusi's future friend and patron Victor N. Popp in 1895.[25]

Brancusi's first job in Craiova was as a waiter at a rough railway buffet. After two years he progressed to an upmarket grocery shop situated in the commercial heart of Craiova, specialising in 'colonial goods and delicatessen' and 'fine wines and spirits'. Its owner, Dan Zamfirescu, was a rich merchant with political aspirations.[26] Whilst the fabric of Craiova's society was changing to accommodate the new bourgeoisie exemplified by Brancusi's employer, the majority of its community was still living in poverty. This is illustrated by an account of life in suburbia left by the painter Francis Sirato (1875–1935), who spent his childhood in Craiova:

> the inhabitants lived in wooden houses, like those in villages, with big, carved wooden gates; the cattle were kept in the court, which had a barn and weaving looms. They wore Oltenian blouses with a wide leather belt. I spent my childhood playing on the dusty roads, near a fountain, like all the poor children of that time, for no one bothered about our education.[27]

In 1894 Brancusi enrolled as a student of sculpture at the Şcoala de Meserii (School of Arts and Crafts). Founded in 1871 as the Şcoala Industrială de Meserii (Industrial School for Mechanical Arts),[28] it became one of the pioneering institutions with an industrial profile. As the concept of 'industrial design' did not exist, those specialising in these emerging fields were still regarded as craftsmen. The existence of comparable schools elsewhere in the country enabled Romania to take part in the Universal Exhibitions that were being organised in Paris and elsewhere. In 1901 *Noua Revistă Română* looked back on Romania's enthusiastic participation in the Great Exhibition in London of 1851 – albeit in the Turkish pavilion, since it was still under Turkish rule – recording that it exhibited 'silk, amber, cotton, costumes, etc'.[29] The 1889 *Exposition Universelle* in Paris saw the participation of eight Romanian schools of arts and crafts, including that from Craiova. Its contribution was 'a walnut bureau' as well as 'various tools made by the students'. Bucharest was more generously represented by twenty-four artefacts including several portrait busts in marble, bronze and plaster alongside domestic appliances and objects more readily associated with industry.[30] By 1906 a comprehensive

Expozițiunea Generală Română (General Romanian Exhibition), complete with extensive catalogue, replicating its European counterparts, was held in Bucharest.

In Craiova, where the thriving *nouveaux riches* clientele favoured 'Biedermeyer armchairs, Louis XV and hideous Napoleon III style furniture',[31] Brancusi was acquiring multiple skills, including joinery and ironmongery. According to an American painter whom he later met in Paris, Brancusi even volunteered to make 'dustpans to help his poor and less versatile friends'.[32] He also studied painting and sculpture, and acquired the skill of decorative carving, which was deemed 'artistic' since it served a non-functional purpose in the manufacturing of furniture. Thus he was taught to carve decorative elements such as acanthus or vine leaves copied from models, sketchbooks and drawings. Neither invention nor the direct imitation of nature was encouraged. During this period Brancusi is believed to have produced several functional objects including two lime-wood frames, a loom, a walnut casket and an ornate walnut chair, all now displayed in the school's museum.[33] He also executed a plaster bust, now lost, of the politician and teacher Gheorghe Chitu (1828–97), exhibited in 1898 at the Expozițiuneă Regionâlă (Regional Exhibition) held in the Bibescu Park, where it was given pride of place in the entrance to the school's pavilion.

Brancusi graduated with a diploma in sculpture. The path was now open for him to continue his studies at the Scoala Națională de Arte Frumoase (National School of Fine Arts) in Bucharest.

1898–1904

The Romanian capital: Bucharest

In 1898 Bucharest was undergoing an unprecedented process of modernisation, and in less than a decade nothing would remain of 'the semi-Oriental town of half a century ago'.[34] Nevertheless, the capital did not succumb totally to the brutalising effects of capitalism. According to Mehedinti, writing in 1906, 'Bucharest does not yet convey the oppressive feeling of the great commercial and industrial cities . . . Apart from the centre, the capital of Romania can be said to be more a city of villas . . . the houses are rare and the gardens not a luxury but a habit that helps hygiene. Seen from above, the capital gives the impression of a park adorned by villas.'[35] This description is found in the same geographical section as that of Craiova in the catalogue of the General Romanian Exhibition. It appeared alongside a history of Romania by Dimitrie Onciul. In it he stressed the contribution of Carol I to its speedy modernisation, quoting from the speech that the King delivered on 14 December 1869 at the inauguration of the newly founded University of Bucharest: 'The power of a modern state is measured especially by the level of its intellectual culture.' His intention was to turn Romania into 'a centre of light in the Orient'.[36] During the same year, the first Regulations for the National Schools of Fine Arts in Romania were published, whereby 'two schools of Fine Arts, one in Bucharest and another in Iassy [the Moldovan capital], each with an attached *pinacotheca* were founded'.[37] The elaborate curriculum of the Academy gives an idea of their rigorous academic requirements. Until the nineteenth century Romania did not have a tradition in the secular arts. Onciul notes: 'the arts in the principalities were cultivated almost exclusively as religious arts (church architecture and sculpture, metal work and filigree, gold and silk thread embroidery). The profane arts emerged only during the nineteenth century.'[38] This explains why the first teachers of sculpture in the Bucharest Academy were foreigners. The schools of painting and sculpture were inaugurated in 1864 and 1866 respectively. However, a secular Romanian school of painting was already emerging, represented by Theodor Aman (1831–91) and Gheorghe Tăttărescu (1820–94),

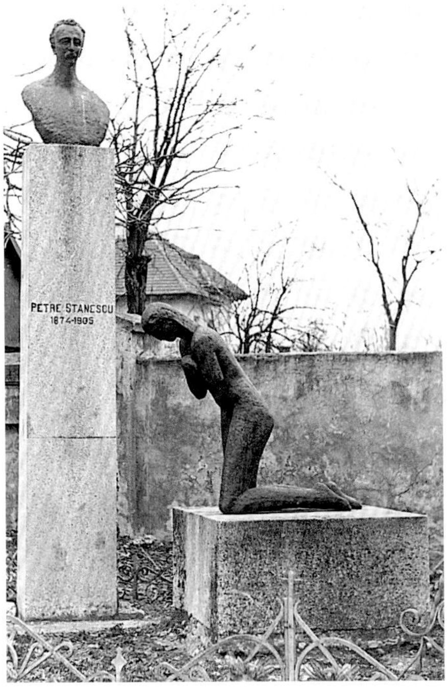

Fig.22 Stanescu Monument in Dumbrava Cemetery, Buzau, comprising **Portrait of Petre Stanescu** and **The Prayer**

its founders and first professors,[39] and Nicolae Grigorescu (1838–1907), who was enjoying an international reputation. Meanwhile sculpture lagged behind, leaving the German-born sculptor Karl Storck (1828–98), who had settled in Bucharest after the 1848 revolution, to become the Academy's first professor and the founder of modern sculpture in Romania. Among the first important Romanian sculptors, both trained in Paris, were Ion Georgescu (1856–98), who was professor at the Academy from 1887 until his tragic death at the age of thirty-two, and Ştefan Ionescu-Valbudea (1856–1918). The Polish-born sculptor Wladimir C. Hegel (1839–1918) arrived in 1885, and in 1891 became professor of sculpture at the Bucharest Şcoala de Meserii (School of Arts and Crafts). Finally, Karl Storck's son, Carol (1854–1926), who studied painting with Thomas Eakins in Philadelphia, returned to Bucharest and dedicated himself to sculpture. Their pioneering contributions included the first public monuments.[40]

Apart from teaching, the main source of income for sculptors was funerary sculpture, emerging at the moment when 'the Romanian people were awakened to life in a modern state'. Successive generations of 'conscientious artists . . . followed the prescribed requirements to represent a portrait bust of the deceased in full regalia, whether military uniform or jewels and silk finery'.[41] The standard accompaniments for these portraits were 'marble angels and *pleureses* imported ready-made from abroad according to the law of supply and demand'.[42] Most important was the inclusion of an allegorical figure, customarily 'a woman fallen on the steps of the pedestal in a calligraphic gesture of despair, with an arm outstretched towards the bust and depositing a bouquet of flowers'.[43] Just such a commission for a funerary monument came to Brancusi in 1907 from the widow of Petre Stanescu. Apart from the portrait bust of the deceased, to be executed from a photograph, the contract stipulated a 2 to 2.5-metre stone pedestal and an allegorical figure of a woman. A faded photograph reveals the initial idea to represent a veiled woman prostrated on the lid of a three-stepped tomb.[44] Brancusi later turned this figure into his sculpture *The Prayer* (1907, fig.22).

The ambitious curriculum awaiting Brancusi in Bucharest encompassed painting, sculpture and architecture. It also included aesthetics, history of art, perspective and anatomy. Whilst we are familiar with his practical endeavours, his early intellectual development has been overlooked, and the aim here is to provide fresh insight into the context in which he was maturing. Primary printed sources – newspapers, magazines and books – give an idea of the general texture of intellectual life in Bucharest at this time. Important exhibitions and related public events demonstrate significant artistic developments, while a brief consideration of collectors and collections reveals the cultural underpinning of Brancusi's emerging intellectual life.

Publications

The wide range of information found in the press both at a national and international level proves that Carol I was on course in achieving his ambition of providing 'a culture of light in the Orient'. The introduction of relatively new academic subjects such as aesthetics and art history on the syllabus of the Academies can be regarded as symptomatic of this process. Aesthetics had emerged as an independent branch of philosophy during the Enlightenment, when Alexander Baumgarten coined the term, defining it as 'the science of sensory cognition'.[45] A century later Heinrich Wölfflin published his pioneering books *Renaissance and Baroque* and *Classical Art* in 1888 and 1899 respectively, proposing an art history based on Hegelian dialectics. During the same period an obscure Romanian professor of history, N.E. Idieru, published the first art history in the Romanian language, entitled *Istoria Artelor Frumoase* (The History of Fine Arts). In the introduction, the author stated that he had been inspired to write this book due to 'the total lack of such a work in the Romanian language' and that it had taken him fourteen years of scouring the libraries, museums and art collections of Europe and attending university lectures to amass the necessary material. Conversant with Hegel's writings on art, he proposed to write 'a philosophy of art history' because 'writing just a history of art without aesthetics would be a simple catalogue of human names and works of art . . . without any relevance for the spirit'.[46]

Among the impressive number of newspapers and magazines on offer, *Tribuna Familiei* and *Noua Revistă Română* are seminal examples. The former, pitched as a family entertainment, dealt with issues of lifestyle, fashion and topical debate. Alongside translations from Charles Dickens, Guy de Maupassant, Jules Verne (whose novel *Five Weeks in a Balloon* of 1862 was serialised), the visual arts were also well represented. Thus engravings reproducing famous paintings from European collections (such as Murillo's *Madonna and Child* in The Hague) can be found alongside illustrations of works by contemporary Romanian artists (like the analysis of a sketch for a proposed commemorative monument to the recently deceased sculptor Ion Georgescu). Important political events such as the Dreyfus affair and a weekly bulletin about the Boer War were reported side by side with the latest medical and scientific discoveries. Lighter topics such as fashion were equally prominent. Thus we find a fascinating debate regarding the abolition of the corset, which pitted the couturiers and the medical world against each other.[47] More notable is the introduction of a regular column dedicated to the feminist movement in Europe, in which issues regarding higher education, professional careers and social status are discussed. A report about a club for divorced women in Vienna appears on the same page as an appraisal, shortly after her death, of Queen Victoria as a role model for womankind: 'Today, when women conduct such lively campaigns to win political and civil rights, here is a glorious figure who could be an example and support.' Apart from being a mother and wife for sixty-three years, Queen Victoria was the head 'of the largest empire in the world'.[48]

Noua Revistă Română was edited by the right-wing philosopher C. Rădulescu-Motru. It gathered together some of the finest intellectuals, such as the historian Nicolae Iorga and the literary critic Ovid Densușianu. Notwithstanding its right-wing tendencies, it maintained a comprehensive intellectual profile and, as its editor wrote in the inaugural issue published on 1 January 1900, it aimed 'to embrace all issues of general interest as well as . . . reports about all important artistic, scientific and literary publications'. Apart from the pioneering column on 'Folklore and Popular Art' mentioned previously, European developments were also prominent. Thus an obituary of John Ruskin accompanied by an article entitled 'Ruskin's Aestheticism', by the splendid symbolist poet Ștefan Petică, reveals his impressive knowledge of English aesthetic and artistic debates, with discussions of the Pre-Raphaelite Brotherhood and Oscar Wilde's Aesthetic Movement.[49]

In *Noua Revistă Română's* review of the 1900 *Exposition Universelle* in Paris, the well-known critic Nicolae Vasehide, who signed himself Kean, deplored the mediocrity of the Romanian paintings on view, in his opinion not helped by the conspicuous absence of 'our great Grigorescu'. He was even more scathing about the sculpture section, deeming Wladimir Hegel's portrait busts 'not nationally representative, just salon busts', eclipsed by the works of art on display in the Grand Hall of the Palais des Beaux-Arts. Dimitrie Mirea and Constantin Bălăcescu are mentioned, but the sole artist of whom he approved was Oscar Spaethe whose *Dancing Faun* (fig.19) 'gives the impression of a sculptor who will not limit himself to making busts of ladies with *décolletages*, the rich bourgeois with their decorations, and the powerful politicians whose banal and conventional expressions appear puzzled that a fine block of marble should have been ruined for the preservation of their mediocre personalities'.[50]

As the catalogue of the *Exposition Universelle* reveals, the competition in the Palais des Beaux-Arts – in the form of Bourdelle, Barias, Rodin (*The Burghers of Calais*) and Brancusi's future professor in Paris, Antonin Mercié – proved too stiff for the mediocre Romanian contingent. Romania's presence did not go unnoticed, however; even if its visual arts were still in their infancy, special emphasis was placed on its production of fine wines and spirits: 'in the Romanian lowlands a grain-based aquavit is made [while] in the mountains a plum brandy or *tsouica* is most common' and testimony to the high quality of the produce were 'the prizes won at various expositions'. Equally admired were artisanal products such as carpets, tapestries and, above all, folk costumes: 'The Romanian section, with a very seductive appearance with popular costumes, harnesses, fabrics and embroidery in startling colours, presents one exhibitor Mme Lucescu (Ecaterine).' The reward was five gold medals, seven silver, four bronze and nine honourable mentions.[51]

Exhibitions and collectors

An important development at the turn of the century in Bucharest was in the field of contemporary visual arts, manifest not only through the number of exhibitions organised at home and abroad, but also through the founding of institutions and venues dedicated to supporting them.

In 1896 a document entitled 'Regulations for Exhibitions of Works by Living Artists' was published.[52] It contained twenty clauses that established the criteria for the selection as well as the rights and duties of artists in the *Expozițiunea Artiștilor in Viață* (Exhibition of Living Artists). Held in the Athenaeum, and tantamount to Bucharest's official salon, this exhibition had been an intermittent event in the city since at least 1870.[53] In 1896 its primacy was challenged by the *Expozițiunea Artiștilor Independenți* (Exhibition of Independent Artists), an alternative show held in a building opposite the Athenaeum. As a result of this exhibition's success, the Societate Pentru Dezvoltarea Artelor in România (Society for the Development of the Arts in Romania) was inaugurated two years later. It was named Ileana after a fairytale heroine.[54] Among the committee members were the symbolist painter Ștefan Luchian, the art critic Leo Bachelin and the colourful writer, collector and Rosicrucian Alexander Bogdan-Pitești, who – having been mysteriously expelled from Paris in 1897 – returned to Romania to begin his career in the arts. He invited his friend and Rosicrucian leader Sâr Joséphin Péladan to Bucharest in 1898 to deliver the second lecture organised by Ileana, whose title was 'The Genius of the Latin Race'. When Bogdan-Pitești died in 1922, his collection of some 967 art objects was auctioned and dispersed. It included four works by Brancusi: a stone *Kiss* and white marble *Head of a Child* (1907 and 1907–8 respectively, both now lost), *Head of a Japanese Woman* (also known as *Danaide*, 1907–9, cat.12) and a bronze *Head of a Woman* (now known as *Sleeping Muse*, 1910).[55]

An impressive culture of collecting was emerging in Romania. One of the pioneers was the distinguished politician and writer Mihai Kogălniceanu. As a diplomat he was in a position to scour the European markets acquiring paintings by van Dyck, Poussin, Rembrandt, Reni, Rubens, Fragonard, whilst following contemporary developments with great interest. The earliest information about his collection dates from 1870; by 1887 he was forced to part with it. Comprising 185 paintings it was auctioned by J. M. Heberle in Cologne.[56]

By the turn of the century, Bucharest could boast of collectors on the scale of Moscow's Sergei Shchukin and Ivan Morozov – rich industrialists who built magnificent museums and donated them to the state. One such collector was Krikor H. Zambaccian (1889–1962), who initially favoured Romanian artists but after 1933 turned his attention to France, acquiring works by Delacroix, Corot, Renoir, Sisley and Matisse. During World War II he opened his house to the public and in 1947 bequeathed the collection, totalling about 240 works, to the state. At the inauguration of the new museum, the poet Tudor Arghezi announced:

> Starting with the Aman Museum dedicated to Theodor Aman's own paintings, we have witnessed, through the efforts of collectors of beautiful things, the emergence of several fine arts centres: the Kalinderu Museum, the Simu Museum; the Toma Stelian Museum. Mr Zambaccian is parting with his treasure trove of precious objects, which he is donating to the state together with the building – the temple in which he displays these icons of a life of ardent devotion.[57]

The most important Romanian collector was Anastase Simu (1854–1935), who became heir to a huge fortune at the age of nineteen. In 1907 he began construction on a grandiose neo-classical building (fig.23), reminiscent of the Maison Carée in Nîmes, to house his collection. Twenty years later it was donated to the nation. When he died, his house also became state property and a museum. A comprehensive catalogue of the museum was published in 1937, followed by the inventory of the house in 1944, from which we learn that the museum contained 1,330 works, with a further 285 in its stores, while the house held 287 works. In 1943 its director Marius Bunescu paid public homage to Simu's contribution to the cultural life of the capital: 'At the time when . . . the Simu Museum was established, the capital did not possess another public art institution other than the state *pinacotheca*, housed very inconveniently in two annexes of the Romanian Athenaeum.'[58]

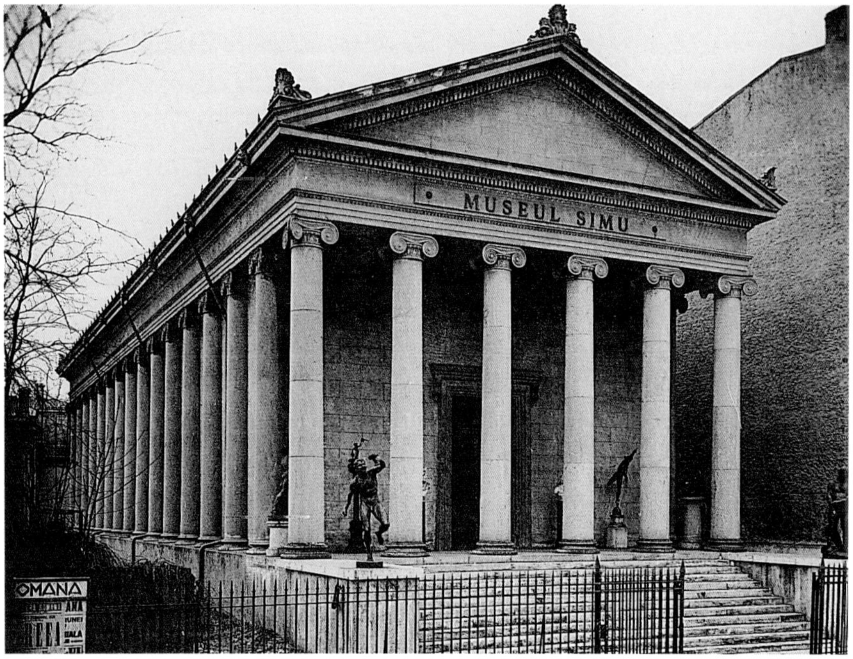

Fig.23 Muzeul Simu, Bucharest

Fig.24 **Sleep** 1908
Muzeul National de Artă, Bucharest

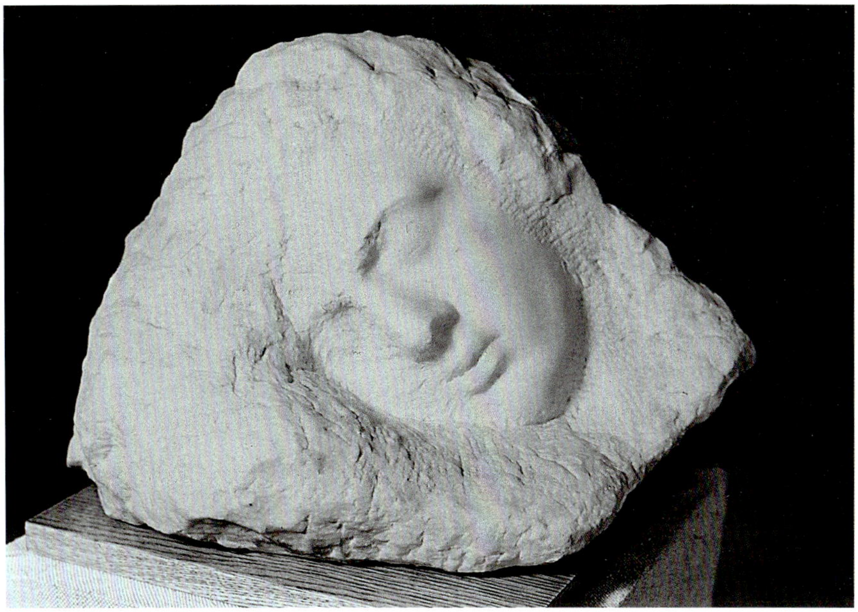

A discerning collector of European art and antiques, Simu was a generous patron and friend of artists such as Antoine Bourdelle, who executed his bust portrait and that of his wife Elena. He was also one of Brancusi's earliest patrons. His first commission was the beautiful marble entitled *Sleep* (fig.24). Later, on hearing that Brancusi was hard up, he paid 1,000 francs for the bronze *Portrait of the Painter Darascu*, after having admired the plaster version in Brancusi's Paris atelier. Both sculptures are visible in the surviving photographs of Simu's museum (fig.19).

This was the Bucharest that Brancusi encountered when he arrived as a penniless immigrant in 1898. He later reminisced: 'Those were times of frightful want through which I would not wish to pass again.'[59] Four works survive from his student years: the plaster bust of the emperor *Vitellius*, *The Flayed Man*, *Portrait of Ion Georgescu-Gorjan* and *Bust of General Carol Davila*.[60] These early works do not suggest an outstanding talent. On the contrary, Brancusi appeared to be primarily concerned with the requirements of the curriculum. With the *Portrait of Ion Georgescu-Gorjan*, for example, he complied *ad litteram* to the requirement for realism in his 'Life Study' course by measuring his sitter's face with callipers.[61] Twelve works are known only from photographs.[62] Among them are two anatomical life studies,[63] while his 'Antique Studies' *Head of Laocoon* and *Mars Borghese*, a full-length relief, testify to Brancusi's instruction in classical sculpture.

Brancusi's efforts were rewarded when he graduated with two bronze medals and several honourable mentions for practical as well as theoretical work, including the study of anatomy, perspective, aesthetics and history of art.[64] Although we do not know the specific reason, the long-standing cultural exchange with France made it natural for him to choose Paris as the next stepping-stone in his career. Once he had taken the decision, he set out with characteristic determination (according to the artist's, possibly romanticised, account, he walked the entire way) to achieve his aim: 'Ultimately, because I wanted to, I arrived in Paris.'[65]

1 Oscar Han, *Sculptorul Dimitrie Paciurea: Fundaţia Pentru Literatură şi Artă, Regele Carol II*, Bucharest 1935, p.12.
2 See Miller 1995, pp.29, 32, n.106, pp.46–7. See Selected Reading for the abbreviations used in the notes.
3 Ion Frunzetti, *Dimitrie Paciurea*, Bucharest 1971; p.18 states that Paciurea returned to Romania 'before the end of 1900'. Mircea Deac, *Paciurea*, Bucharest 2000, p.16 specifies 'towards the end of 1899'.
4 See Sanda Miller, 'Paciurea's Chimeras', *Apollo*, Oct. 2003.
5 See Ion Frunzetti, 'Sculptorul Dimitrie Paciurea', in *Studii şi Cercetări de Istoria Artei (SCIA), Academia Română*, July–Dec. 1955, pp.229–30.
6 See Dinu Giurescu, *Istoria Ilustrată a Românilor*, Bucharest 1981. On p.565 we find the last mention of the royal family in the book: 'On 30 December 1947, King Michael I abdicates and leaves the country, accompanied by his mother, Elena, and a retinue of twenty-eight persons . . . On 30 December the Chamber of Deputies ratifies law no.363, which proclaims the Popular Republic of Romania.'
7 V.G. Paleolog, *C. Brâncuşi*, Bucharest 1947.
8 Ionel Jianou, *Brancusi*, Paris 1963.
9 A.J.P. Taylor, *The Struggle for Mastery in Europe*, Oxford 1971, p.85.
10 Giurescu 1981, p.345.
11 See Radu Olteanu, *Bucureşti în Date şi Întâmplări*, Bucharest 2002, pp.99–100, 279, 340.
12 Taylor 1971, p.245.
13 See Olteanu 2002, pp.377–80.
14 Martyn Rady, *Romania in Turmoil*, London and New York 1996, p.6.
15 Cited in Nicolae Iorga, *Istoria Românilor Prin Călătorii*, Bucharest 1981, p.661.
16 Cited in ibid., p.677.
17 Dr Felix, 'Alcoolismul la ţară şi la oraş' in *Tribuna Familiei (Revistă Pentru Literatură, Artă şi Ştiinţă Populară)*, 20 Nov.–1 Dec. 1902, pp.83–5.
18 Anton Eliade, 'Nuntă Ţărănească în Partea Olteniei', in *Noua Revistă Română Pentru Politică, Literatură, Ştiinţă şi Artă*, no. 39, 1 Sept. 1901, pp.115–26.
19 Marie Bengesco, 'L'art en Roumanie', in *La Roumanie en Images*, vol.I, Paris 1919, p.25.
20 George Oprescu, *Peasant Art in Roumania*, London 1929, pp.14–15.
21 Petre Comarnescu, *Mit şi Metamorfoză în Sculptura Contemporană*, Bucharest 1972, p.30, quoting the critic Vasile Drăguţ who interviewed Vasile Blendea 'Trifu' in 1958.
22 See V.G.Paleolog, 'Prima şi a Doua Fugă a lui Brâncuşi din Hobiţa', in *Inaintea*, 5 July 1964, pp.36–7; *Tinereţea lui Brâncuşi*, Bucharest 1967, pp.36–7. Paleolog dates Brancusi's first departure from Hobiţa as 1887, while Ionel Jianou, 1963, p.23, states that he left his father's house aged nine (1885) to seek his fortune in Târgu Jiu, 'the nearest city'. Both Paleolog and Jianou date his second departure from Hobiţa as 1887, but Petre Comarnescu dates it a year later (Comarnescu 1972, p.54).
23 S. Mehedinti, 'România: Schiţă Geografică', *Expoziţiunea Generală Română, 1906. Călăuză Oficială şi Catalogul Expoziţiunei*, Bucharest 1906, pp.1–25.
24 See Grigore Ionescu, *Arhitectura pe Teritoriul României de a Lungul Veacurilor*, Bucharest 1982, pp.496–568.
25 See Paul Rezeanu, *Artele Plastice în Oltenia 1821–1944*, Craiova 1980, pp.56–7.
26 See Paleolog 1967, pp.43–54.
27 Quoted in Ion Biberi, 'Lumea de Mâine: Francis Şirato', 1945, in Jianou 1963, pp.23–4, n.40, p.73.
28 See *The Industrial Agricultural Mechanical Lyceum, Craiova, One Hundred Years: 1871–1971*, Craiova 1971, catalogue published on the centenary of the School of Arts and Crafts, today the Industrial Mechanicăl Lyceum.
29 F. Robin, 'Expoziţia Universala din Paris', in *Noua Revistă Română Pentru Politică, Literatură, Ştiinţă şi Artă*, no.1, Jan. 1901, pp.7–11.
30 'Section Roumaine de Exposition Universelle de Paris', *Exposition Universelle Internationale de 1889 à Paris*, Paris 1889, pp.10–14.
31 Petre Pandrea, *Brâncuşi: Amintiri şi Exegeze*, Bucharest 1967, pp.159–61.
32 Ibid.
33 Barbu Brezianu, 'Lucrări Artizanale', in Brezianu 1998, pp.202–5.
34 Mehedinti, 1906, pp.1–25.
35 Ibid.
36 Dimitrie Onciul, 'Din Istoria României', in ibid., p.99.
37 *Regulamentul Pentru Şcolele Naţionale de Belle-Arte*, Bucharest 1869.
38 Onciul 1906, pp.102–3.
39 On Theodor Aman and Gheorghe Tăttărescu as professors at the Academy, see Vasile Florea, 'Pictura in Secolul al XIX-lea', in Vasile Drăguţ et al, *Pictura Românească*, Bucharest 1976, pp.127–213; Miller 1995, pp.16–19.
40 See Miller 1995, pp.16–24; George Oprescu, *Sculptura Românească*, Bucharest 1965, pp.29–80.
41 Han 1935, p.13.
42 Ibid.
43 Ibid., p.18.
44 See Brezianu 1998, pp.130–3.
45 Monroe C. Beardsley, *Aesthetics from Classical Greece to the Present*, New York 1966, p.156.
46 N.E. Idieru, *Istoria Artelor Frumoase (Arhitectură, Sculptură, Pictură, Muzică – din Toate Timpurile şi din Toate Ţerile – Incluzînd România)*, Bucharest 1898, pp.9–13.
47 *Tribuna Familiei*, Oct. 1898, p.11.
48 Ibid., Jan. 1901, p.167.
49 *Noua Revista Română*, 1 Feb. 1900, pp.42–5.
50 Ibid., 1 March 1901, pp.210–11.
51 *La Roumanie à l'Exposition Universelle de 1900*, Paris 1900, pp.127, 258.
52 *Regulament Pentru Expoziţunea Operelor Artiştilor în Viaţă*, Bucharest 1896.
53 Teodor Enescu, *Scrieri Despre Artă*, Bucharest 2000, pp.101–17, states that the first Romanian artist to show at the 'Exhibition of Living Artists' was Nicolae Grigorescu in 1870.
54 See *Ileana: Societate Pentru Dezvoltarea Artelor in România. Regulamentul Pentru Întâia Expoziţune de Artă*, Bucharest 1898 (unpag.).

55 See I.L. Georgescu, 'Colecţia Alexandru Bogdan-Piteşti. Imagine a Unui Moment Plastic Românesc', in *Arta*, no.1, 1971, pp.12–13.

56 See 'Academia Republicii Populare Române: Mihai Kogălniceanu, Collecţionar de Artă', in P. Constantinescu, *Omagiu lui P. Constantinescu–iaşi*, Bucharest 1965, pp.670–2.

57 *Muzeul Zambaccian*, Bucharest 1947.

58 Marius Bunescu, *Actele Fundaţiei Anastase Simu*, Bucharest 1944.

59 Constantin Brancusi quoted in Carola Giedion-Welcker, *Constantin Brancusi*, New York 1959, p.197.

60 See Brezianu 1998, pp.208–16, figs.46–57.

61 See Ştefan Georgescu-Gorjan, 'Mărturii despre Brâncuşi', in *Studii şi Cercetări de Istoria Artelor (SCIA), Seria Artă Plastică*, vol.12, no.1, Bucharest 1965, pp.65–74.

62 See Brezianu 1998.

63 Ibid., p.210, fig.48 and p.212, fig.51.

64 See Comarnescu 1972, p.91.

65 Brancusi quoted in ibid., p.106.

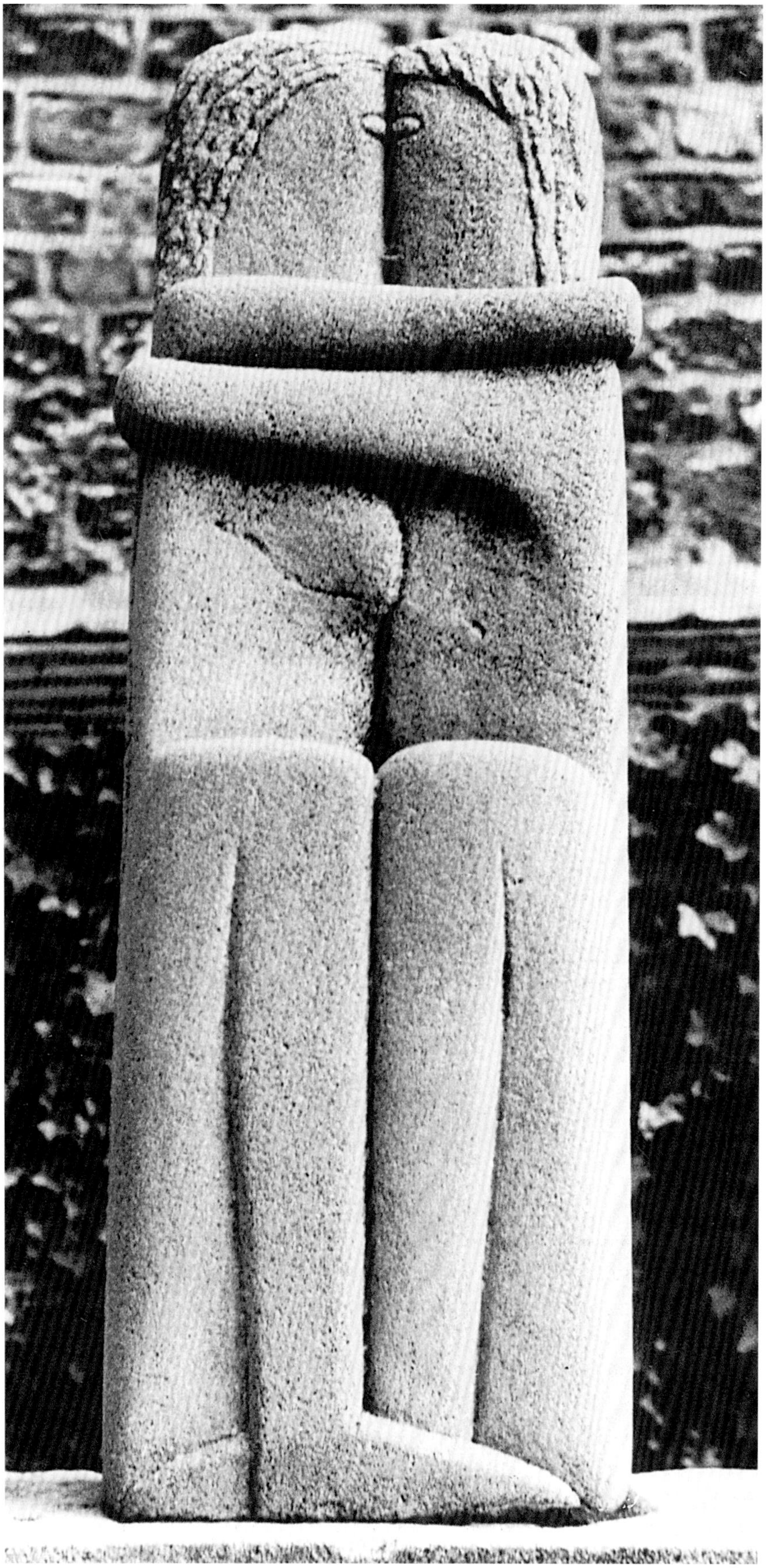

Fig.25 **The Kiss** (1909–10) in Montparnasse Cemetery, Paris

The road to Damascus

ALEXANDRA PARIGORIS

Henri-Pierre Roché recounted in his funeral oration for Brancusi how the sculptor referred to the Montparnasse *Kiss* (1909–10, fig.25) as his 'Road to Damascus'.[1] The sculpture that Brancusi felt marked a watershed in his career is part of a series of works which he always carved in stone. Although this was quite an appropriate material for modest funerary monuments, like the one for which the Montparnasse *Kiss* was created, in the period 1907 to 1910 stone was still an unusual choice for sculpture that aspired to the status of fine art and might be exhibited in salons, like his Craiova *Kiss* (1907–8, cat.1). But stone was also being explored by other young artists of his generation – artists like André Derain, whose stone *Crouching Figure* (1907, fig.26) precedes and is usually compared to the Craiova *Kiss*.[2]

Nowadays such works are generally deemed to share the concerns about art that were being articulated in the advanced art circles of the time and given visual expression through the works of Gauguin and Cézanne, in posthumous retrospective exhibitions.[3] These ideas were given a number of formulations but all contained a call for a renewed concept of art and its relationship to life that rejected any notion that art's role was merely to imitate the visible world. The new art was to provide a catalyst for thought and experience, in a form that reflected the subjective nature of this experience. What especially concerns us here is that many of these ideas were already widely recognised in Auguste Rodin's day and could also justly be said to form part of that artist's creative constitution and outlook.[4]

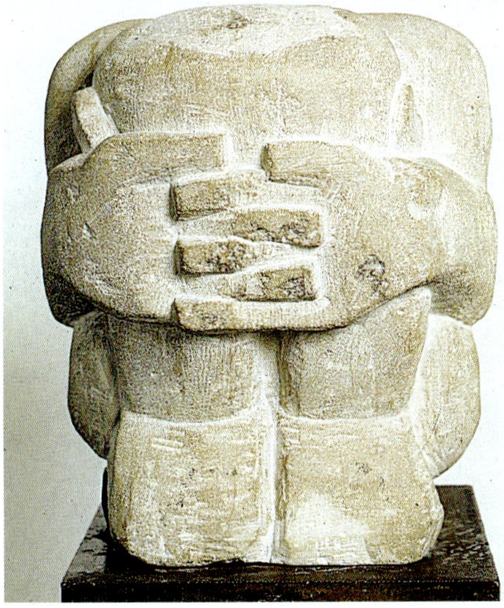

Fig.26 André Derain **Crouching Figure** 1907
Museum Moderner Kunst Stiftung Ludwig, Vienna

It is therefore worth reassessing the traditional claim that works like those of Derain and Brancusi challenge the sculptural language embodied in a work such as Rodin's *Kiss* (1898, fig.27): a brilliantly executed marble group, representing a nude couple embracing on a rock. The work was hailed in its day for the sensation of life that the sculptor had succeeded in imparting to the material through the illusionist depiction of textures, in particular 'trembling, palpitating flesh'.[5] Such effects, we know today, were rendered in marble by a number of talented studio assistants, whose exclusive role was to translate into marble Rodin's plaster compositions, often using mechanical devices like pointing machines.[6] According to this view, the figures of Brancusi and Derain, which were carved by the artists themselves, were more 'honest', even if the results were less sophisticated.

What is also always pointed out is that Derain's *Crouching Figure*, like his *Standing Nude* of the same year, represents the work of a gifted amateur – a painter trying his hand at a different medium. For Brancusi, however, working *directly* in stone on the Craiova *Kiss* is unlikely to have posed a technical challenge given the fact that he was among the best-trained sculptors as well as the best-trained craftsmen of his generation and had, by 1907, produced virtuoso carvings like the marble *Sleep* (fig.24), as well as the exquisitely modelled bronze *Heads of Children*.[7] Although when working in marble or stone Brancusi never renounced the technical subtleties of the art of carving to the extent he did when working on his first wood sculptures,[8] carving the stone of the Craiova *Kiss*, a material far less luminous than marble, might have induced him to conceive a simpler approach to imagery. It may even have helped him to rein-in his natural virtuosity as a carver, which was noticed by critics very early on and regarded with suspicion by some. Roger Fry, for example, writing in 1913, noted that the most remarkable works 'show a technical skill which is almost disquieting, a skill which might lead him, in default of any overpowering imaginative purpose, to become a brilliant *pasticheur*'.[9]

The traditional account referred to above chooses to understand the so-called sculptural revolution solely in terms of technique and practice, and accordingly gives pre-eminence to 'direct carving'. However, it fails to take into consideration the fact that this concern was hardly ever mentioned in the artistic discourse of the day, let alone evidenced in the work of Brancusi at this time. The most obvious material evidence of Brancusi's disregard for the exclusivity of 'direct carving' lies in the fact that so many of his carved or bronze works were reproduced as plaster casts and offered for sale or given away to friends.[10] This was also the customary commercial exhibiting practice in the period, as indicated in catalogues from the salons and from the 1913 *Armory Show*, where Brancusi not only sent but sold plaster casts of his works.[11] Furthermore, it is now accepted that the concern with direct carving really only gained currency after the First World War.[12] In fact, even when asked for an interview in *This Quarter* in 1925 to give his views on sculpture and direct carving, which had become the dominant issue of the day, Brancusi's response remained unequivocal in its defence of a sculptor's right to be free from any constraint: 'Direct cutting is the true road to sculpture, but also the most dangerous for those who don't know how to walk. And in the end, direct or indirect, cutting means nothing, it is the complete thing that counts.'[13]

So, if not because it was a feat of direct carving, why did Brancusi see the *Kiss* as marking a turning point in his career? With the Montparnasse *Kiss*, Brancusi was striking at the one element that critics admired above all in Rodin's marble work: the illusionist *non finito* aspect of the material, that allowed the marble figure and its rocklike base to blend into each other in a seamless unity. What had been the distinguishing feature of Michelangelo's late sculpture, the unfinished figure embedded in the marble and appearing to emerge from the rock, had become a conceit in Rodin's marble sculpture, where the illusionist, *non finito* rock-effect was fabricated and laboriously carved by his *praticiens* so that the same piece of marble could look like flesh *and* like rock, as required by the representational content of the piece.[14] Thus what was really at stake in the Montparnasse *Kiss* was the fact that the work and its image were one and the same, entirely contained within the stone block. This was to be the dominant feature of all of Brancusi's carved work, and would eventually result in the sculptor forsaking modelling in clay entirely, having devised a means of casting his bronzes directly from carved models.

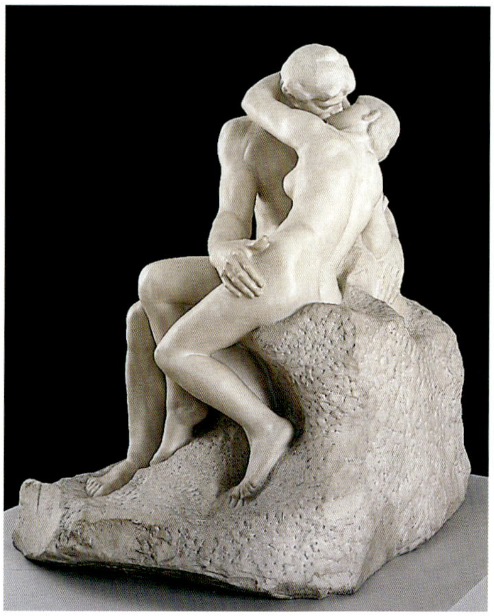

Fig.27 Auguste Rodin **The Kiss** 1901–4
Tate

But the Craiova *Kiss* takes up another feature of Rodin's art, that is hinted at in the original title of the work, as found in the catalogue of its first exhibition, the 1910 *Tinerimea artisticà* in Bucharest, where it was entitled *Fragment of a Capital*. The title, *The Kiss*, only appears two years later, when a version was exhibited at the Salon des Indépendants.[15] It would appear that the 'road to Damascus' leads to what was arguably the most important new conceptual approach to affect the practice of sculpture at the beginning of the twentieth century: the partial figure or 'fragment', as it was termed at the time. This revolutionary break had originated in the work of Rodin and was also being taken up by the younger generation of sculptors, including Maillol, Matisse, Duchamp-Villon and Lehmbruck.[16] But what distinguishes Brancusi's approach may well have been his ability to respond not only technically but conceptually to Rodin's *Kiss*, to rethink that popular group in terms of a fragment. Perhaps it is this that he believed marked the watershed in his career.

Reading the partial figure

In 1966, the Minimalist sculptor Robert Morris insightfully noted that in Brancusi's work 'the other ultimate, phenomenological term besides surfaces in objects is the edge', be it 'curved, straight, joined at an angle'.[17] This realisation determines our perception of the works as objects. And we shall examine now how this essentially sculptural feature, what another sculptor, Louis Slobodkin, writing in the late 1940s, called 'the aesthetic reason for the work',[18] was again and again given an anecdotal, psychoanalytical or narrative interpretation.

There is evidence to suggest that, as early as 1914, Brancusi was aware of the kind of reception his works were getting in the American tabloid press and accordingly (as though 'in advance of a broken arm', to quote Marcel Duchamp) was taking precautions to ensure that his work was viewed according to his intentions, particularly when dealing with new collectors. Only thus can we possibly appreciate the meaning of the extraordinary advice Brancusi sent back to John Quinn in 1916, when asked by the latter to provide a base for the recently acquired *Kiss*. Brancusi replied that it should be placed 'just as it is, on something separate; for any kind of arrangement will have the look of an amputation.'[19] Terms like these were used by critics at the time, as Anna Chave has argued. The French poet Roger Vitrac had written in the 1920s about 'the peril of wandering into the world of Brancusi' and finding the 'decapitation' and 'mutilations' that the sculptor inflicts upon his imagery. In the light of these observations Chave puts forward a psychoanalytically informed interpretation.[20] However, when we return to Vitrac's text we find that he uses these terms in order to describe an oeuvre that has 'shed' its realistic appearance and escaped the confines of the everyday world.[21] Vitrac's essay is essentially trying to address the difficulty that 'language', in other words everyday language, has in coming to terms with this kind of imagery, which involves 'the highest of faculties without the mediation of intelligence'. He argues that 'language' is limited by having 'poor means' at its disposal and is thus 'incapable of accounting for that precise and demanding activity [Brancusi's art] that reaches to the invisible frontiers where a bird or a female torso reigns'.[22] Vitrac closes his defence with the optimistic assertion that Brancusi does not interpose intelligence or knowledge between the viewer and the work, declaring he 'has thrown a great bridge between the senses and the mind, which we cross at the speed of lightning while attention adopts the passive attitude of the Sphinx.'[23] However, it is clear from the scandals that arose when some of his works were exhibited in public – like the bronze *Princess X* at the 1920 Salon des Indépendants in Paris, which was forcibly removed because judged obscene,[24] or the court case involving the abstract *Bird in Space* (1926)[25] – that there was a deep gulf between Brancusi's supportive circle of critics, who were mostly poets and able to find words to articulate the works' difficult imagery, and less enlightened members of the public as represented by officialdom.

In the case of the *Bird in Space*, the U.S. customs officials, faced with a work divorced from naturalist representation, found only a resemblance to the ordinary and the familiar manufactured object. *Princess X*, on the other hand, made full use of the flesh-like qualities inherent in translucent polished marble (cat.16). But instead of being presented with a female bust, as its first title *Buste de Femme* would suggest, viewers were confronted with a fragment whose suggestive curves made unavoidable references and confirmed their instinctive response that they were indeed in the presence of a phallus, when in fact they were in the presence of an abstracted work of art that reflected the conceptual perceptions of an artist[26] – something Brancusi always insisted upon, presenting as evidence a photograph of the more naturalistic figure with which he had begun (fig.13).[27]

Vitrac, writing again on Brancusi in 1933, five years after the famous New York trial, summed up the sculptor's predicament perfectly, showing how early on the reception of Brancusi's work was subject to rival and contradictory theoretical positions: 'Brancusi participates in the modern spirit that the pre-war period did not bother to define; that the war left temporarily undefined, but that our post-war critics have, alas, undertaken to kill by trying to give it a thousand different meanings.'[28] It is all too clear that the substance of most of these different meanings – the currency of particular concepts or the range of metaphors available to artists and poets, many of whom continued to be art critics well into the twentieth century – are lost to us today.[29] The thinking that informed the pre-war 'modern spirit' was balanced between the still dominant culture of late nineteenth-century symbolism and its attempt to come to terms with the new concerns brought about by the experience of modern life. Thus, in spite of the fact that this period was witness to the birth of psychoanalysis, attempts to interpret Brancusi's partial figures simply as symptoms of castration just because they look like amputations seem far too reductive. A more sophisticated application of psychoanalytic concerns would be to make sense of the meaning of the term 'fragment', as it was used at the time, when speaking of the revelation of the unconscious as fragmentary.

Furthermore, it is important to distinguish the notion of symbolist *mind-set* from that of symbolist *motif*; in other words to understand what was part and parcel of a culture, and what was part of its iconography. The poets of the period were perhaps best placed to articulate what the aesthetic engagement with the fragment involved. Rainer Maria Rilke, for example, writing to a friend while working as Rodin's secretary in Paris, described the effect of viewing the fragments of archaic statuary in the Louvre and in Rodin's collection: 'No one knows what their intention is and (at least for the unscientific) no subject matter is attached to them, no irrelevant voice interrupts the silence of their concentrated reality, and their duration is without retrospect or fear . . . no history casts a shadow over their naked clarity – they are. That is all.'[30] Brancusi's fragments appear to have had a similar impact, since many contemporary accounts of his work were couched in a poetic language that attempted to express the experience rather than the fact of the work. Brancusi himself frequently adopted this form of expression when speaking about his work, as for example in his description of his large marble *Fish* (1930) in 1937. He reportedly told Malvina Hoffman: 'When you see a fish, you do not think of its scales, do you? You think of its speed, its floating, flashing body seen through water . . . Well, I've tried to express just that. If I made fins and eyes and scales, I would arrest the movement and hold you by a pattern, or a shape of reality. I want just the flash of its spirit.'[31] To look at *Fish* and to think of speed and fluidity places our vision in a phenomenological mode. We become less concerned with the detail of naturalistic appearance than with the experience of its movement that we can imagine. For this experience to be communicated effectively, the sculptor resorted to highly polished surfaces for *Fish*, whether marble or bronze (fig.28).

Polish becomes an expressive sculptural feature in Brancusi's work, one that he also included for definition in the *This Quarter* interview: 'High polish is a necessity which certain approximately absolute forms demand of some materials. It is not always appropriate, it is even very harmful for certain other forms.' Thus polish, though always remarked upon as a mark of his technical skill, is a means of underlining what he feels is important in a work, which has attained a form of completion in his thinking. This is particularly appropriate for *Fish*, which more than any other work suggests, without

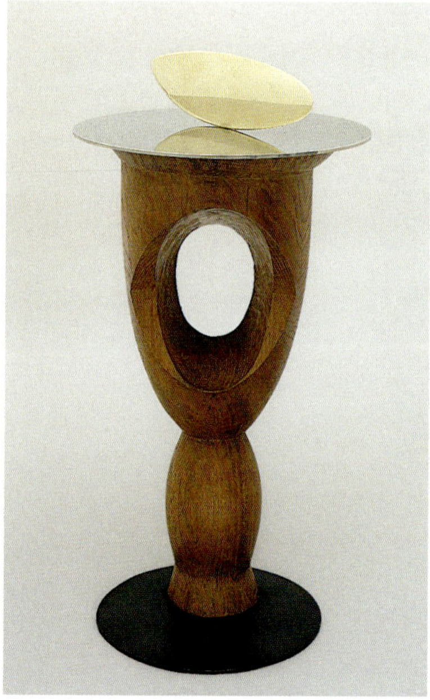

Fig.28 **Fish** 1926
Tate

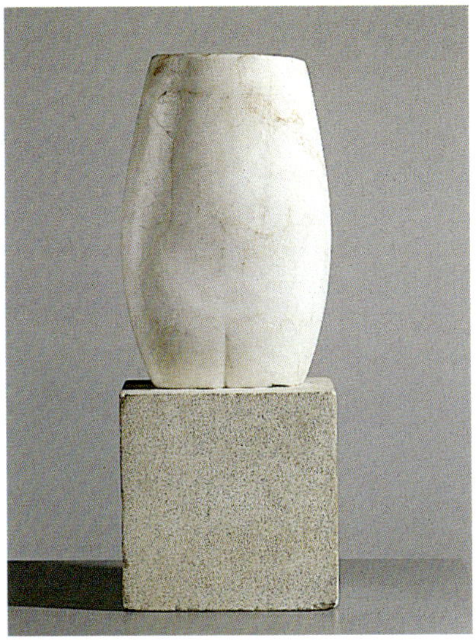

Fig.29 **Torso of a Young Girl** c.1918
Öffentliche Kunstsammlung Basel, Kunstmuseum

resorting to natural appearance, what is most essential in the shape and experience of a fish. Without knowing Brancusi's work, the writer and painter Adrian Stokes described the pleasure he got out of the curves of weathered limestone, by evoking the shape of a fish, which 'affords one the deep sensation of roundness, since it is a flattened or gradual yet rounded shape'.[32]

Thinking about a work like *Fish* brings to mind another important aspect of Brancusi's work: titles. Never considering his sculpture entirely abstract, he used titles to carry residual traces of genres that are meant to bridge form and meaning: portrait, torso, animal. Except for the early *Maiastra* of 1910 or *Prometheus* of 1911 (cat.19), they are not literary, though they function as suggestive clues and, when accompanied by adjectives – 'young', 'in space', 'without end' – describe a state of being without falling into narrative. Works like *Torso of a Young Girl* or *Torso of a Young Man II* (cat.6 & 8) are not amputations or castrations, even if we compare the latter to the more complete *Torso of a Young Man* (1910) by Duchamp-Villon.[33] We are invited to use our imagination in response to the solicitations of the words in the title, as Jeanne Robert Foster did in the presence of *Torso of a Young Girl*, which evoked the lines 'She scarcely knew she was a woman, so gently she grew'.[34] It is not hard to see connotations of growth and life in works made from an organic material like wood or, in the case of *Torso of a Young Man II*, an expressive shape and polished surface. But when Brancusi seeks the same effects in marble, we really experience his skill and sophistication as a sculptor.

Thus in the marble series of *Torso of a Young Girl* (1918 to 1923, fig.29 & cat.6–7), Brancusi has managed to transfer the organic experience of wood to a more obviously static material. One could describe this series as gradually pushing out into a rounded, bulging form, like a bud about to flower. But the 'aesthetic reason for this work', as Slobodkin would say, lies in the tension that Brancusi establishes between the cut-off edge at the top, the polished surface and the roundness of the form. He thus sets up a tension between abstract form, material and image that is characteristic of so many of his works and gives these abstract forms – to quote Brancusi on Arthur Dove's paintings – 'the shock of reality'.[35]

Yet marble is also a sedimentary stone that, even though it is transformed by metamorphic processes, remains, to quote Stokes again, 'a link between the organic and inorganic world'.[36] This becomes palpable in the yellow marble *Hand* that Brancusi sent as a gift to Quinn in 1920 (fig.30). Once again, the title describes what the sculpture is: both a stylised carving in the form of a fragment, suggesting a hand, and a

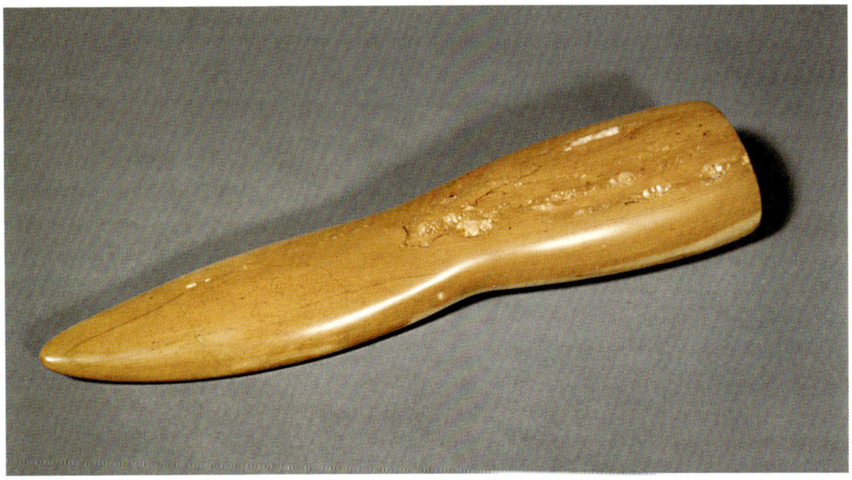

Fig.30 **Hand** 1920
Fogg Art Museum, Harvard University Art Museums, Gift of Mr and Mrs Max Wasserman

metaphorical hand extended as a mark of friendship to his loyal patron. The colour, smooth surface and shape of this work also evoke the propellers of ships or aeroplanes, which, at the time, were made out of wood. Thus he adds a note of 1920s modernity to the age-old paradigm of the sculptor's hand and touch. Paraphrasing Richard Wollheim, we might conclude this section by stating that viewers, instead of responding to the titles in an imaginative way, superimpose emotional states onto the works. These *states* then stand between the spectator and his or her capacity to see that Brancusi's achievement resides in his ability to create objects of art that can be described in non-emotive terms.[37]

Seriality

'Brancusi has set out on the maddeningly more difficult exploration toward getting all the forms into one form,' wrote Ezra Pound, in an essay that profoundly annoyed Brancusi.[38] Despite this, Pound's text has been acknowledged by scholars as constituting the beginning of serious criticism of his art, and has played an important role in formulating a discourse for modern sculpture.[39] With this in mind, it is worth considering whether thinking in terms of 'getting all forms into one form' is a useful description of what is at stake in Brancusi's work.

Pound's formulation may be tested against the series originating in the early 'Rodinesque' work *Sleep* (1907, fig.24), which was developed through the *Sleeping Muses* (cat.20) – a sequence of reclining heads – and ended with what many critics saw as the ultimate egg-shaped forms, *Sculpture for the Blind* and *Beginning of the World* (both *c.*1920, cat.21 & 22). The gradual elimination of naturalistic features (eyes, nose, mouth) in the series seems to follow the progressive refinement of the carving, which will smooth away all traces of the chisel, so visible in the early work. As the mark of the chisel is commonly held to be intimately related to the hand of the artist and to reflect evidence of his work, critics have agreed that works like *Beginning of the World* were 'in some way depersonalised, removed from the tradition of the handmade, individualised *objet d'art*'.[40]

Despite the common denomination of these works as egg-like, it is possible, on closer consideration, to see the slightly flattened oval form of *Sculpture for the Blind* in different terms. Brancusi's authorship of these titles is disputed, but they were clearly given to add a metaphoric value to a work that in the end defies language. In this sense the works are emblematic and poised between signifying and non-signifying. Small wonder that critics, seeking an explanation, have clung to the notion of 'egg', and drawn out all possible cultural connotations and meanings.[41] However, we may perhaps think a little more about what a title like *Sculpture for the Blind* might mean in a symbolist context or, better still, in the context of Duchampian *double-entendres* and correspondences. For here we encounter, taken to its extreme, the poetic trope of seeing with the inner eye, and thus not needing one's eyes to see what really matters. This work, which defies viewers to approach it in an anecdotal manner, also defies that other basic instinct when dealing with sculpture: touching with one's hands. In the same vein, one could read *Beginning of the World* in terms of W.H. Auden's notion of the *Euclidian stone*, 'the transcendent stable reality desired as a haven for the storm tossed mariner', in other words as a form emerging, from the undifferentiated chaos of water, ironically in a state of perfection.[42]

In the 1930s, Brancusi's work came under attack from the Surrealists, who dismissed it as simply too aesthetic to share in their concerns. Yet it was as aesthetic objects that

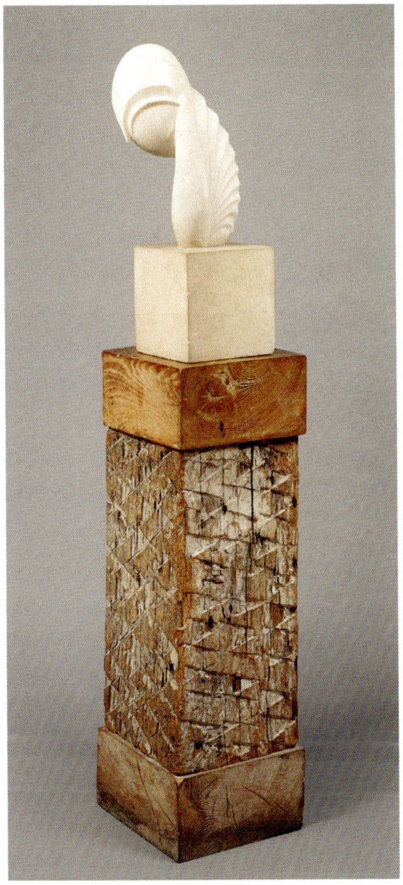

Fig.31 **Mlle Pogany III** 1931
Philadelphia Museum of Art. The Louise and Walter Arensberg Collection, 1950

Brancusi's sculptures were destined to be looked at, because as aesthetic objects they were worthy of attention. For just as so much of Symbolist culture has been relegated to the domain of the arcane, undue emphasis on the object in recent studies has overlooked the fundamental concern of modernism, which was a renewed interest in the nature of attention and process. Only in the last decade has recent scholarship begun to think critically about the historical significance of these important modes.[43]

In order to account for Brancusi's tendency to work on a limited number of subjects and return to the same work again and again, we need to judge his approach to sculpture from the perspective of conventional practices within his field, observing how he turns these conventions to his own advantage. At first adopting traditional market strategies to sell his works, he soon turned the practice of replicating a popular work on demand (something we also see with nineteenth-century sculptors like Rodin) into a creative exercise that he compared to a voyage of self-discovery (like so many painters in the late nineteenth century).[44] He was not alone in this approach. Matisse was also executing works of sculpture in series over a period of time at this date – the *Heads of Jeanette*, or his *Backs* – which might be described as demonstrations in the art of abstracting from the initial naturalistic model. But a different way of looking at these series would be to view them as an ongoing reflection and analysis of the very process of making itself. In the case of the *Mlle Pogany* series in marble (see cat.17) and bronze, Brancusi returned to the same theme again and again, even resorting in the late bronze versions to the assistance of powered tools. This underscores the fact that mere technique was of no consequence, and that something in the image held the artist's attention, which he expressed in the different versions: for example, the permutation of curved forms, eyes taking over the oval of the face, neck subsumed by cascading hair. The third more abstracted version is called *Mlle Pogany III* (fig.31) because it is anchored in *Mlle Pogany I* and carries some of its initial formal concerns and rhythm. But to describe the series as an abstracting process detracts from what is really at stake: namely, the presence of the artist, and the creative process.[45]

Brancusi's work has long been the subject of debates concerned with formalist and extra-formalist criteria for the interpretation of sculpture. His mature works showed an increasing preoccupation with exploring the limits of his forms, though he always tied these to the expression of a figurative image. In order to appreciate what is so distinctive in his work, it is necessary to resurrect the conventions and aesthetic issues that dominated the thinking of his time. His interest lay less in abstraction *per se* than in the process of thinking out an idea in terms of sculptural solutions that ended up as abstracted form. At no point did Brancusi admit the validity of working purely from abstract shapes devoid of connotative associations. What was at stake was removing any sense of narrative in order to privilege the experience. This experience was above all one of looking and attending. By eliminating evidence of the sculptor's touch, Brancusi invited the viewer to experience the finished product, not to imagine its making. The paradox of Brancusi's 'road to Damascus' experience was that it began with stone, a resistant and gravity-laden material, but this opened the way, through the fragment and through a reduction of external virtuosity, to the light and polish of marble and bronze and to a view of the world as meditation.

I wish to thank Alan Marshall, M. Stone-Richards and Marielle Tabart for their comments during the draft stage of this text.

1 Henri-Pierre Roché, 'L'enterrement de Brancusi', in Suzanne de Coninck (ed.), *Hommage de la Sculpture à Brancusi*, Paris 1957, p.29.
2 The following discussion takes up from Sidney Geist (Geist 1978). See also the entries for the Craiova *Kiss* in Brezianu 1976, pp.110–14. For the chronology of the series, see Miller 1995, pp.69–74. For the abbreviations used in the notes, see Selected Reading.
3 See Geist 1978 and the essay by Marielle Tabart, appropriately termed 'Plein/Creux', in *Sculpture, de Derain à Séchas*, exh. cat., Centre Georges Pompidou, Paris and Carré d'Art–Musée d'art contemporain, Nîmes 2003, p.34.
4 As one critic, reviewing Brancusi's 1914 exhibition at Alfred Stieglitz's Photo-Secession Gallery in New York, put it: 'We have passed beyond the stage of art where sculpture must be imitation of nature. Rodin contents us with the suggestion only.' See Edgar Chamberlain writing in the *New York Evening Mail*, quoted in *Camera Work*, no. XLV, June 1914, p.38. See also Auguste Rodin, *L'Art, Entretiens réunis par Paul Gsell*, Paris 1911. For an excellent analysis of the context of Auguste Rodin's ideas, see Debora L. Silverman, *Art Nouveau in Fin de Siècle France: Politics, Psychology, and Style*, Berkeley 1989.
5 For an account of Rodin's *Kiss*, see David Rosenfeld, 'Rodin's Carved Sculpture', in *Rodin Rediscovered*, exh. cat., National Gallery of Art, Washington 1981, pp.85–7.
6 These assistants were known as *praticiens*. Just such a position was open to Brancusi when he turned down the offer of working for Rodin with the famous statement, 'Nothing grows under a great tree.' For a discussion of studio practices see Geist 1978 and Anne Pingeot, Antoinette Le Normand-Romain and Isabelle Lemaistre, *La Sculpture au française au XIXè siècle*, exh. cat., Galeries nationales du Grand Palais, Paris 1986.
7 Brancusi was one of the few, if not the only, sculptors at the beginning of the twentieth century to have benefited from a comprehensive art education as a sculptor in the Beaux Arts tradition, and as a trained artisan in a technical school, the Craiova School of Arts and Crafts. See Brezianu 1976, pp.273–284 and Miller 1985, pp.24–48. Although we do not know the precise details of his training, his early carved stone works were given titles that indicate an awareness of carved architectural motifs – *Fragment of a Capital, Caryatids*. Architectural carving was taught at institutions like the Craiova School of Arts and Crafts. But see Matthew Gale's essay in this catalogue.
8 See Alexandra Parigoris, 'Writing on Brancusi in a Postmodern World', in the symposium papers, *Brancusi at his Zenith. And What Next?*, Bucharest 2001, pp.98–106.
9 Roger Fry reviewing the Allied Artists' Exhibition in London in *The Nation*, 2 Aug. 1913, pp.676–7.
10 See, for example, the plaster version of the Craiova *Kiss* that Brancusi gave to his friend and supporter Cecilia Cutsescu-Storck, in Brezianu 1976, p.114, or the plaster of *Tête de femme* c.1908, given to Guillaume Apollinaire reproduced in Tabart and Lemny 1997, p.145, no.37.
11 See Milton W. Brown, *The Story of the Armory Show*, New York 1988, pp.249–50, and, for a general context, Pingeot, Le Normand-Romain and Lemaistre 1986.
12 As Patrick Elliott has shown, this concern only emerged in France after Rodin's death with the ensuing scandal of his works in marble continuing to be produced by his assistants. See Patrick Elliott, *La Sculpture en taille directe en France de 1900 à 1950*, Saint-Rémy-les-Chevreuse 1988.
13 Brancusi's words first appeared in French as 'Réponses de Brancusi sur la Taille Directe, le Poli et la Simplicité dans l'Art', in the Paris-based American periodical *This Quarter* (no.1, 1925, p.236). They appeared in this English version the following year, in the catalogue of Brancusi's first exhibition at the Brummer Gallery in New York. See 'Selected aphorisms' in this catalogue.
14 See Geist 1978, p.23.
15 See Geist 1978, p.52 and Brezianu 1976, p.112.
16 See Albert Elsen, *The Partial Figure in Modern Sculpture: From Rodin to 1969*, Baltimore Museum of Art 1969.
17 Robert Morris, 'Form-Classes in the Work of Constantin Brancusi', unpublished M.A. thesis, Hunter College, New York 1966, pp.84–5.
18 Louis Slobodkin, *Sculpture, Principles and Practice*, New York, originally published in 1949, reprinted New York 1973, p.241.
19 Letter to Walter Pach, dated 4 Oct. 1916 (Quinn Collection, New York Public Library). See the catalogue entry for this work by Ann Temkin in Bach, Rowell and Temkin 1995, p.142.
20 Chave 1993, in particular chapter 1, entitled: 'Figuration and Disfiguration: the Vanishing Muse', pp.23–65.
21 Roger Vitrac, 'Constantin Brancusi', *Cahiers d'Art*, no. VIII–X, 1929, pp.383–4.
22 Ibid. My translation from the French.
23 Ibid.
24 For this incident, in which the work was forcibly removed having been judged obscene, see Chave 1993, pp.93–123, and Alexandra Parigoris, '*La Princesse X*: Cherchez la femme' in Marielle Tabart (ed.), *Princesse X, Les Carnets de l'Atelier Brancusi*, Centre Georges Pompidou, Paris 1999, pp.16–31.
25 The best critical account of this well known incident, in which US Customs charged import duty on the work because it looked like a manufactured object, is found in Thierry De Duve, 'Réponse à la question "qu'est-ce que la sculpture moderne?"' in *Qu'est-ce que la sculpture moderne?*, exh. cat., Centre Georges Pompidou, Paris 1986.
26 See Marielle Tabart's important discussion of Matisse's reaction to the work in 'Les Avatars de la Princesse X', in Tabart 1999, pp.9–12.
27 See Parigoris 1999, p.22, which discusses and illustrates Roger Fry's letter to Vanessa Bell, dated 12 April 1922, in which Fry describes a visit to Brancusi and sketches both versions – the early one from the photograph and the finished one from the bronze bust, which Brancusi defended in earnest.
28 Roger Vitrac, *Brancusi*, exh. cat., Brummer Gallery, New York 1933, pp.383–5.

29 This despite Bach 1987, and his 'Brancusi: the Reality of Sculpture' in Bach, Rowell and Temkin 1995, pp.22–37. See also Marielle Tabart, 'L'atelier comme lieu de mémoire' in Tabart and Lemny 1997, pp. 68–137. Chave 1993 also studies this question at some length.

30 Letter to Lou Andreas-Salomé, 15 Aug. 1903, cited by Stephen Mitchell, discussing Rilke's 1908 poem, 'Archaic Torso of Apollo', in Stephen Mitchell (ed.), *Selected Poetry of Rainer Maria Rilke*, New York 1982 , p.303. I am grateful to Alan Marshall for having pointed out this poem to me.

31 Malvina Hoffman, *Sculpture Inside Out*, New York 1939, p.52.

32 Adrian Stokes, *Stones of Rimini* (1935), in *The Critical Writings of Adrian Stokes*, vol.1, London 1978, p. 209.

33 Which retains, if only in vestigial form, evidence of its masculinity. See Chave's discussion of gender in these works, Chave 1993, pp.98–102. See also the important new information brought to light in the Brancusi archives, *La Dation Brancusi, dessins et archives*, Marielle Tabart and Doina Lemny (eds.), Centre Georges Pompidou, Paris 2003, pp.158–9.

34 Jeanne Robert Foster, 'New Sculptures by Constantin Brancusi: A Note on the Man and the Formal Perfection of his Carvings', *Vanity Fair*, May 1922, pp.68 and 124.

35 See letter from Arthur Dove to Stieglitz dated 20 or 21 June 1928, in Ann Lee Morgan, *Dear Stieglitz, Dear Dove*, Delaware 1988, p.150.

36 Stokes devotes many pages to the physical and poetical quality of materials in 'Stones of Rimini', (1935), in *The Critical Writings of Adrian Stokes*, vol.1, London 1978, p.196.

37 Richard Wollheim, *Art and its Objects*, second ed., Cambridge 1980 (first published 1968), section 19, p.33.

38 Ezra Pound, 'Brancusi', in *The Little Review*, Autumn 1921, p.5. Pound apologised profusely, see letter dated 14 October 1921, reproduced in Hulten, Dumitresco and Istrati 1988, p.141.

39 Chave discusses the essay at length in the introduction of her book on Brancusi (Chave 1993), and Alex Potts concurs with many of Pound's views while discussing the performativity of Brancusi's works in *The Sculptural Imagination*, New Haven and London 2000, pp.132–44. See also Alexandra Parigoris, 'La Bête Noire de Brancusi', in *Ligea*, Brancusi issue, Nov. 2003.

40 Chave 1993, p.160.

41 Most of these views are summarised in Chave 1993, pp.124–63. It should be noted, however, that Brancusi himself never spoke of his works as 'eggs'.

42 See W.H. Auden, *The Enchafèd Flood or the Romantic Iconography of the Sea*, London 1951, p.77. I wish to thank M. Stone-Richards for this point.

43 See Bach in Bach, Rowell and Temkin 1995; and Michel Frizot, 'Les Photographies de Brancusi, une Sculpture de la Surface' and Lucien Stéphan, 'Formes et Matières dans la sculpture de Brancusi', *Cahiers du Musée National d'Art Moderne*, no. 54, Winter 1995. See also Jon Wood, 'Brancusi's White Studio', in *Sculpture Journal*, vol.VII, 2002, pp.108–120.

44 See Richard Shiff's discussion of 'series' in his review of John House, 'Monet: Nature into Art', in *The Art Bulletin*, March 1991, pp.149–156.

45 See Richard Wollheim, 'Minimal Art', *Arts Magazine*, Jan. 1965, reprinted in Gregory Battcock, *Minimal Art: A Critical Anthology*, New York 1968, pp.387–99.

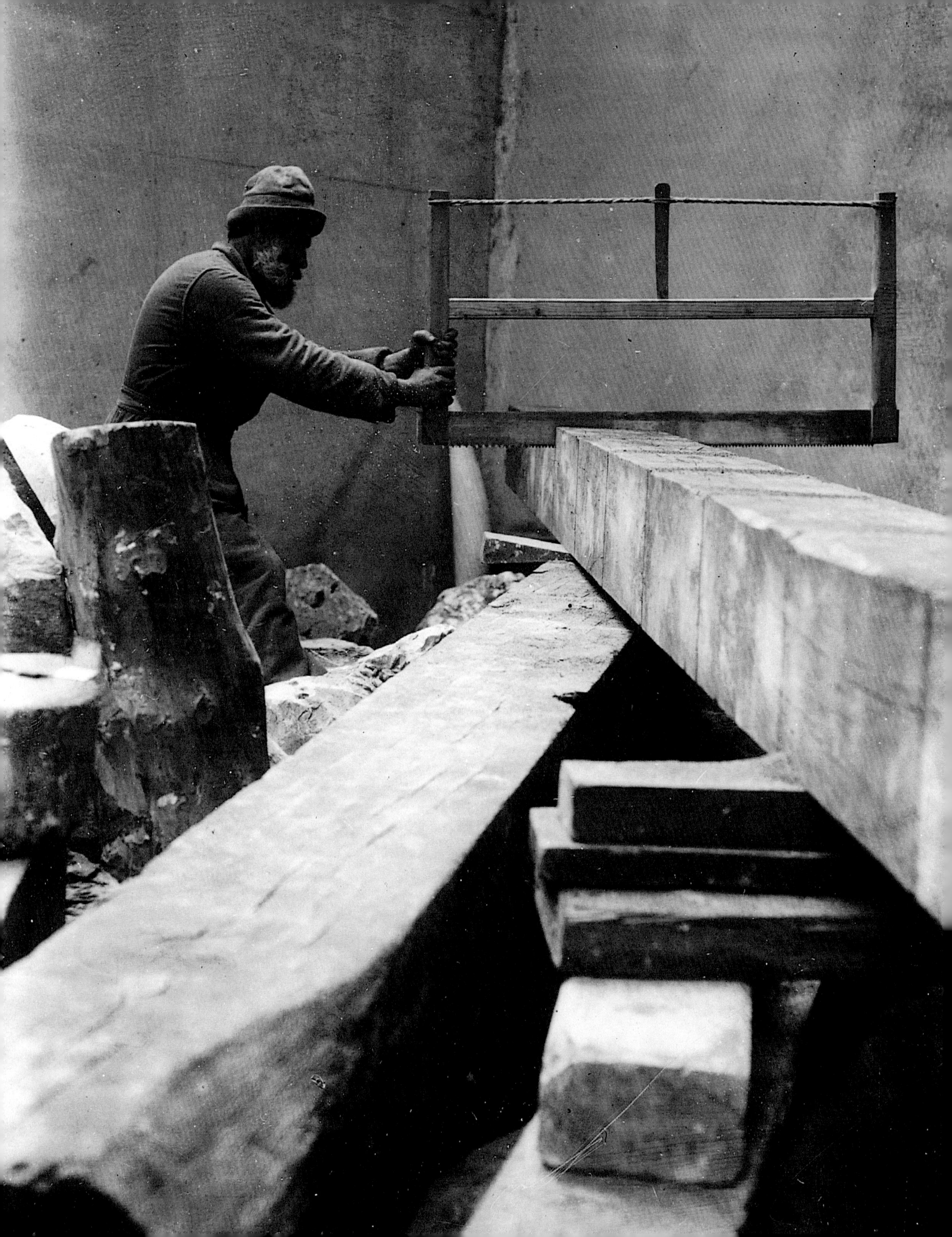

When we are no longer children: Brancusi's wooden sculpture c.1913–25

JON WOOD

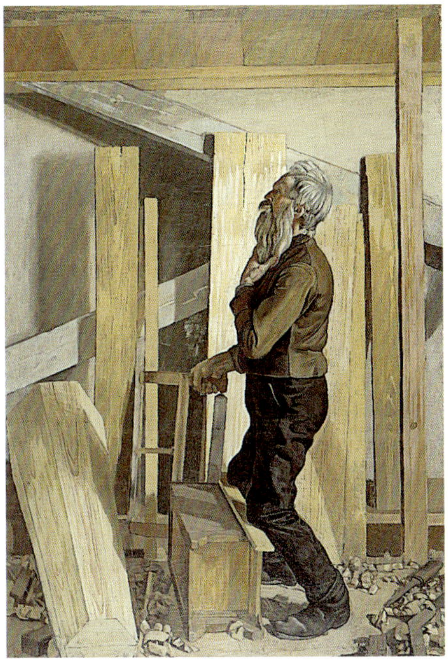

Fig.33 Ferdinand Hodler **Glimpse into Eternity** 1884
Kunstmuseum, Bern

Saw in hand, the old carpenter suddenly stops work on the child's coffin that he is making. He stares into the distance, beyond the physical confines of his workshop, deep in thought and stroking his beard (fig.33). Ferdinand Hodler's painting *Glimpse into Eternity* (1884) is the portrayal of an epiphany: the realisation of the relationship between birth and death, between childhood and old age. It is also a portrayal of the 'philosophical worker': the artisan who has acquired philosophical knowledge about 'eternity' and human existence through the direct, solitary and one-to-one experience of his materials and craft.

The themes of the artisanal worker, the child and the philosopher were also important to Constantin Brancusi and, in particular, to his work in wood. He was, of course, a trained carpenter as well as a trained sculptor. Looking, however, at the series of photographs that Brancusi took of himself in 1924, working on a version of *Endless Column*, it is no longer easy to see the vestigial presence of this symbolist figure (fig.32). Instead, we might see his deliberate self portrayal as the Romanian peasant woodcutter, the outdoor sculptor of Voulangis and then Târgu Jiu, the proto-minimalist maker of abstract sculpture, or the serial carver, carrying simplification further. It can be difficult, in photographs such as this, to see the wood from the trees.

Indeed, by the mid-1930s Brancusi himself had deliberately blurred the metaphorical distinctions between 'wood' and 'tree'. Wood, in all its forms (be it block, beam, trunk, log or stump), was not only 'alive' and connotative of organic growth, but also, in turn, 'rooted' in the ground like a tree.[1] Wood was, for Brancusi, a living material, full of transformatory and metamorphic potential. It was also an aspirational material with an inherent verticality that Brancusi (at less than five feet tall) must surely have admired. In his aphoristic statements, his fables and his 'real life' stories, he purposefully identified himself as an artist with trees and wood.[2] Others such as Jeanne Robert Foster already had done so, for example in her 1923 poem, in which Brancusi wishfully transforms himself into a tree.[3] 'Nothing grows under a great tree,' Brancusi said of his relationship to Rodin, and in his anecdotes about the *Crocodile Log* (1925, visible in fig.1) and the *Chestnut Tree Trunk* (1933–4) he cast himself as the special beneficiary of their magical and curative properties. Friedrich Teja Bach has shown how cleverly Brancusi complemented such tales with photographic illustration, for instance mapping his own seated body onto a sprouting trunk.[4] Similar anxieties of uprootedness and detachment can be observed even in Brancusi's little-known nature studies, such as the *Cicatrices d'arbres* photograph of *c.*1924.[5] Here, Brancusi has captured the 'scars' and traces left by a climbing plant, once it has been removed.

This essay returns to Brancusi's wooden sculptures made during the decade before these 1924 photographs – when he was first turning to wood as a sculptural material and before these metaphorical resonances had become established. Not only does this period mark his first carved work in wood, but it also stands as a crucial time in his career and oeuvre as a whole (Brancusi, it should be remembered, turned fifty in 1926). It witnessed his first international achievements as an avant-garde artist, his close

Fig.32 **Brancusi working on Endless Column**, *c.*1924
Centre Pompidou, Paris (AM4002-729, PH719, modern print)

friendships with Eric Satie (who died in 1925) and Marcel Duchamp, his relationships with American collectors and supporters such as John Quinn (who died in 1924) and Walter Pach, and, after 1916, his first attempts (through drawing, photography and the staging of his studio-home environment at 8 impasse Ronsin) to craft an identity for himself as an avant-garde sculptor in Paris.

Such circumstances are highly important to the understanding of the making and meanings of his early wooden works, and in particular pieces such as *The First Step* and *The First Cry* (1913), *Plato*, which became reduced to *(Child's) Head* (1919–20), *Little French Girl* (1914–18) and *Socrates* (1921–2). In these works, Brancusi's ideas of the child and the philosopher are closely interrelated, if not inextricably linked, as themes.[6] Many of these wooden works were made over an extended period during and immediately after the First World War; they were carved and re-carved, destroyed and decapitated; they did not generate a series *per se* and were all made out of oak. They were diminutive sculptures and, carefully finished, all were made for indoor display. They are some of the most extraordinary, and oddest, works that Brancusi ever made, and have proved very difficult to date and document, as well as to interpret. *Little French Girl*, for example, is not only a child figure, but also another early version of *Plato*: it acquired its title, according to Sidney Geist, through James Johnson Sweeney (Brancusi's titles are notoriously difficult to rely upon).[7]

There has been much debate over his influences, but it is now widely acknowledged that Brancusi was highly responsive to the example of African sculpture and African wood-carving and that this interest was facilitated by his Romanian cultural background.[8] *The First Step* (1913), as Geist has suggested, was perhaps made through an awareness of African sculpture,[9] whilst also based on a real person, the infant George Farquhar. This was Brancusi's first wood-carving, and both the child subject and the title reflected this, characteristically using the metaphor of the 'journey' to evoke this beginning. Growth and development are thus implicitly cast as both vertical and horizontal: growing up and travelling forwards. His later wooden sculpture *The Prodigal Son* (1915) continues this poetry of the journey of wood-carving. What is also crucial here is that *The First Step* was carved from a single block of oak. This was also the case with works such as *Little French Girl* (cat.26)[10] and *Plato* (now destroyed except for the head, cat.25), which were, and are, extraordinary given their assembled and articulated look. Brancusi could certainly carve wood with skill and delicacy, as his early student pieces from Craiova demonstrate. But there were now new tricks at stake. These were manifestly virtuoso performances designed to show that he could not only compete technically with African wood-carving, but could also respond with skill and conceptual sophistication to its contemporary avant-garde appropriation.

Other avant-garde artists were also working in wood during the 1910s. There are examples to be found in the work of Cubists and Dadaists in particular, but rarely were they carving complicated pieces out of single blocks of wood as Brancusi was. After Picasso's Gauguin-inspired pre-1910 experiments, Henri Laurens, Jacques Lipchitz and Alexander Archipenko worked in wood, but their sculptures were most often painted and multi-component in structure – indeed in 1915 Lipchitz made some 'detachable' works that invited the manual participation of the viewer. Their playfulness was also reflected in their subjects – frequently dancers, musicians and clowns. It was, however, the Dadaist wooden works of Sophie Taeuber-Arp and Jean Arp that had most in common with Brancusi's wooden sculptures. Though made in Zurich rather than Paris, and given a painted surface, they brought together portraiture, caricature and puppetry in ways that were comparable to Brancusi's wooden sculptures.

The photographs of Brancusi's first studio at 8 impasse Ronsin (where he lived from

1916 to 1927) reveal it to be largely populated with wooden sculpture, wooden bases and wooden furniture.[11] Something of Brancusi's relationship to these wooden works can be gauged by looking at a 'work-in-progress' photograph of *Figure* (which may have been an earlier incarnation of *Little French Girl*), placed under his wooden *Arch* (1915–16) (fig.34). *Figure* was also carved out of a single block, as can be seen by its composition, its chalk markings and its dimensions in relation to those of the oak uprights of the *Arch* that frames it. Wood thus frames wood, with a material echo that provided the smaller sculpted figure with a shrine-like enclosure and a private spatial environment of its own. The wood of *Arch* was a salvaged material, which was deemed full of character and age by Brancusi, rather than merely antique looking, as he stated in a letter to John Quinn, its first owner.[12] As the commentary of Walter Pach (Quinn's intermediary) suggests, it may also have had an aura of grandeur for Brancusi, since it was oak salvaged 'from some noble house that was being torn down'.[13] This wooden frame, to the sculptor's mind, could obviously do much to enhance the presence of things. He even photographed himself, pausing mid-work, between its posts.[14] It served as a sculptural stage for a curious kind of puppetry. If Rodin, and *The Thinker*, were respectively aloof

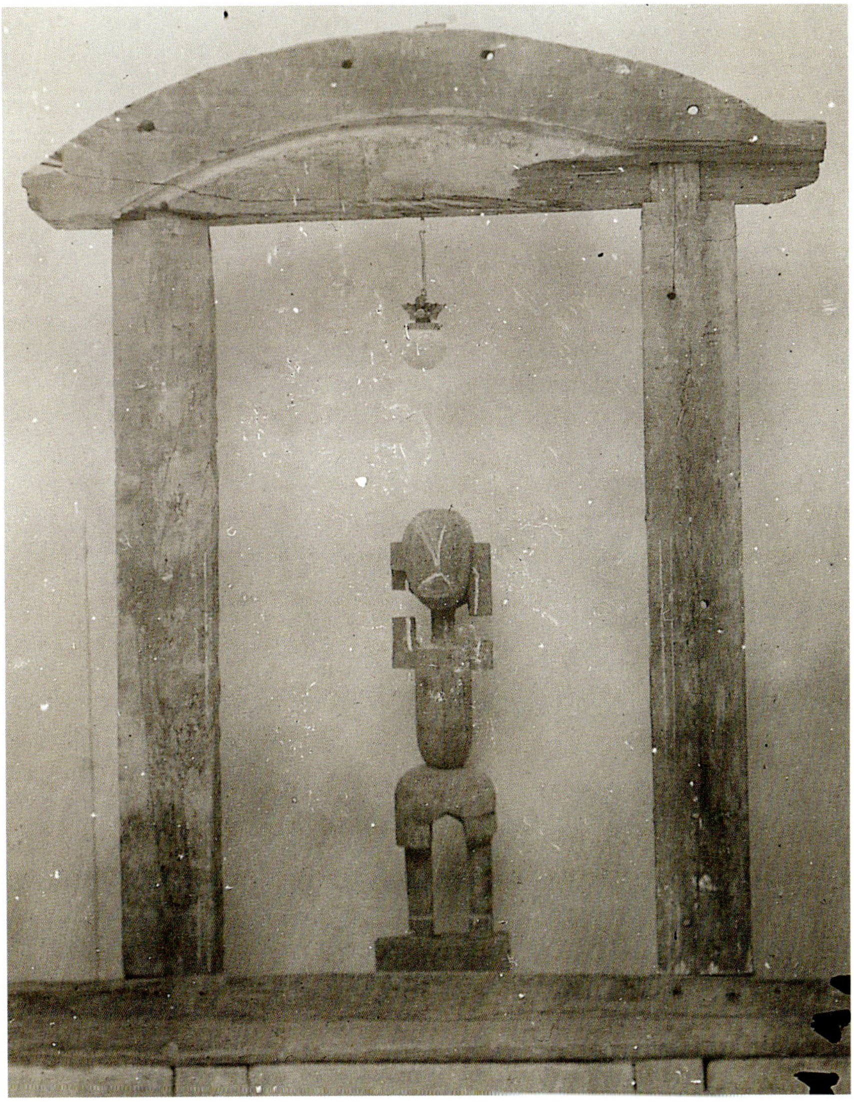

Fig.34 **Figure and Arch**, 1915–16
Centre Pompidou, Paris (PH592B)

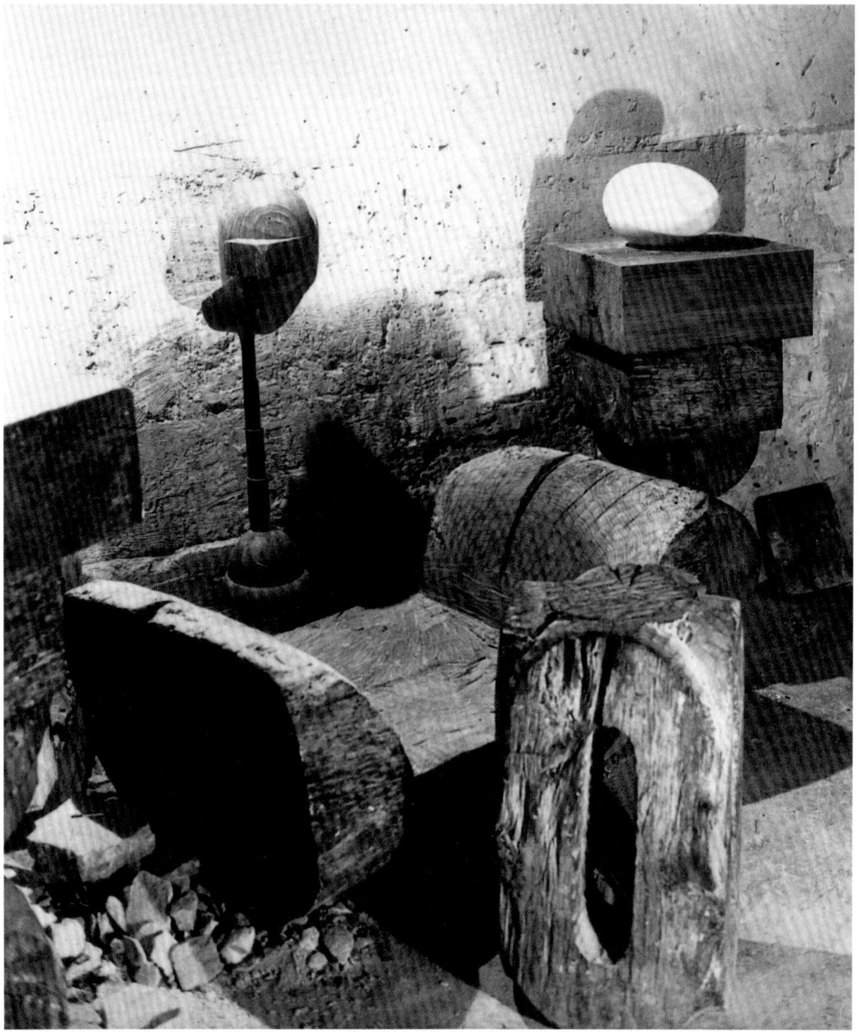

Fig.35 **Plato, bench and Newborn**, *c.*1923
Centre Pompidou, Paris (PH45)

from physical labour and seated pedestal-like on top of his *Gates of Hell*, Brancusi has here positioned himself, as he did with his wooden sculpture *Figure*, as the artisan at the very centre of his own work.

Between 1919 and 1924, his two-legged wooden sculpture *Plato*, which he never sold, featured to such a large extent in his studio photographs that it clearly seems to have been allocated not only the role of guardian of his first studio, but also of personal mascot, and was possibly a form of three-dimensional self-portrait (fig.35, see also figs.9, 12 & 40). Once again the example of Rodin – and the close identification in the public imagination of him with the image of *The Thinker* (after his death in 1917 when the sculpture functioned as a funerary monument to the sculptor) – is, I would suggest, an important one for Brancusi's *Plato* self-portraiture. Indeed, given the kind of sculpture *Plato* was, perhaps there is also a playful sending up not only of Rodin, but also of himself in this – a caricature of the idea of the sculptor as an intellectual man of letters. Before Brancusi's own exposition of his 'philosophy of Plato' working practice (as quoted by Adlow in 1927) the awkward wooden figure of *Plato* certainly seems an ill-fitting counterpart.[15] That *Plato* was carved out of wood, and not made of stone or bronze, highlighted the artisanal character of his work and the title cast the sculptor as a Platonic craftsman, his studio as Plato's cave.

Plato was later destroyed, and only the head survives (cat.25). Provided with a visor-like eye, which continues around the head to serve as an ear as well, this helmet-like head is clearly a highly 'sensitised' wooden object: all eyes, ears and mouth. Although *Plato*, like *Little French Girl*, was carved from a single block, in the photographs it looks like a seven-part sculpture, comprising head, neck, torso/pelvis and two wooden legs and feet (figs.9 & 38). Its resemblance to an articulated puppet or toy (that looks as if it might move) is noteworthy in the light of the formal components of the puppets of Arp and Taeuber of 1918. *Plato*, however, is not a marionette but a freestanding figure, to be moved about by hand, not from above with strings.[16] The fact that it does stand upright, without strings, is an important part of its sculptural achievement, wit and charm: there are no gaps between, or string within the parts. It is a highly self-contained sculpture, an aspect emphasised by the pelvic body of the earlier *Little French Girl* (cat.26), which resembles a tortoise's shell. This is a curious characteristic: more than simply a utilisation of the tortoise-shell quality of oak grain, it indicates a reading of wood as connotative of a protective carapace (and as containing 'inner life'). There may be an Aesopian twist here, in which the tortoise's shell reads as 'house',[17] an image that was dear to Symbolists such as Huysmans and d'Aurevilly. However, rather than crafting a neck and head peeping out from a hole at the side of the shell as one might expect, Brancusi has provided both *Plato* and *Little French Girl* with 'collapsible', telescopic necks that rise vertically, and impossibly, out of the top of these shell-like bodies.

The serrations of this telescopic neck in the case of *Little French Girl* might give it an African look, as has been stated, but in and amongst the deliberately jumbled iconographies of these works might we not also find the telescopic neck of Lewis Carroll's Alice? In *Alice's Adventures in Wonderland* (1865), having drunk a potion labelled 'DRINK ME' and shrunk to ten inches in size, Alice exclaims: 'What a curious feeling! . . . I must be shutting up like a telescope.' And after eating a cake marked 'EAT ME', she finds herself 'opening out like the largest telescope that ever was! Good-bye, feet!'[18] It is impossible to imagine Carroll's imaginative articulation of shifts in scale and distance, his ground-breaking representation of the child's point of view and repertoire of fantastical, speaking animals not appealing to Brancusi, who (even if he hadn't read the book or seen John Tenniel's extraordinary illustration) is likely to have known about the story from friends, perhaps indeed from Duchamp and Katherine Dreier, who bought *Little French Girl* directly from the sculptor in 1920.[19] The notion of the 'child-like' to be found in Brancusi's wooden work has this Carrollesque quality to it: which, like Satie's, is at once Symbolist and also Dadaist.

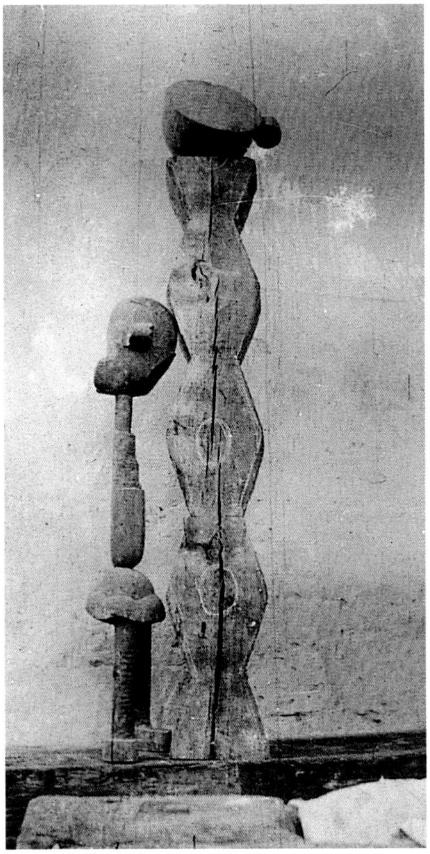

Fig.36 **The Child in the World: Mobile Group**, 1917
Centre Pompidou, Paris (AM4002-662, PH629, modern print)

When *Little French Girl* was first photographed in 1917, it was presented within an ensemble (also comprising *Cup* and *Column*), which Brancusi gave the name *The Child in the World* (*L'Enfant au monde*) (fig.36). This ensemble was offered to Quinn in 1917, who turned it down, saying that he preferred the sculptor's work in stone to wood.[20] The fact that these works stayed put in 8 impasse Ronsin led to them being reworked and acquiring more private, reified associations. Brancusi was tremendously attached to his sculptures and invested them with personal meaning, often legible only to 'initiates'. Henri-Pierre Roché once described him as being 'like a child weeping over his toys'.[21] *The Child in the World* ensemble, in particular, took on a 'philosophical' meaning for the sculptor, later read by him as a portrayal of the death of Socrates, through the presence of Plato and the cup of hemlock. Brancusi was here, by this point, referring as much to the philosophers Plato and Socrates, as he was to himself and the composer Eric Satie, whose own opera *Socrate* was performed in 1920.[22] Brancusi and Satie nicknamed each other 'Plato' (and 'son of Socrates') and 'Socrates' respectively (Satie was the elder by exactly ten years). As Conrad Satie's notebooks of the period demonstrate, they had a very lively friendship – full of leg pulling and in-jokes.[23]

Brancusi's later description of *The Child in the World* clearly reveals his sense of Plato's child-like relationship to Socrates: 'The whole universe flows through . . . Nothing escapes the great thinker. He knows all, he sees all, he hears all. His eyes are in his ears, his ears in his eyes. Not far from him, like a simple and docile child, Plato seems to be soaking up his master's wisdom.'[24] Both Brancusi and Satie shared a preoccupation with the figure of the child. Brancusi's conflation of this figure with that of Plato demonstrates a Symbolist and, in particular, a Baudelairean appreciation of the 'man-child' (*l'homme-enfant*). Indeed, and in keeping with their mutual valetudinarianism, the heightened imaginative life of the poet's 'man-child' was held to be equivalent to that of the convalescent.[25] His aphorism, 'When we are no longer children we are already dead', was a statement that unequivocally confirmed the sculptor's commitment to such concerns.[26]

The two-legged wooden sculptures were toys *of* adults *for* children and *vice versa*. *Plato* and the 1921–2 sculpture *Socrates* (fig.37), with their variously balanced heads and narrow, articulated necks, resemble the two main types of wooden *bilboquet*, a popular French toy. A simple game, but extremely difficult to play, it was aimed both at children and adults, and popular among artists in Paris at the time. Indeed, Duchamp not only owned one, but also signed it and gave it to the painter Max Bergmann in 1910 – making it a candidate for his first 'readymade'.[27] *Plato*'s head is 'spiked' on a stick and *Socrates*'s is 'held' in a cup; once again Brancusi has articulated two wooden parts in the same block. He 'played' with his sculptures (rather like toys), trying out and photographing different balancing acts, as can be seen in his combination of *Socrates* and *Cup*, in which Satie's trademark bowler hat has been turned upside down through the sculptor's addition of his wooden cup (fig.37). Such play emphasises the association between this group of wooden works and the symbolist motif of the severed head, so central to Brancusi's oeuvre.

It was the dialectic of simplicity/difficulty as much as that of innocence/experience in relation to the 'childlike' that interested both Brancusi and Satie as a dynamic within their work. For Brancusi, simplicity was a state of being only to be achieved, or arrived at, through the childlike absence of sophistication or self-consciousness: 'Simplicity isn't a goal in art, but one arrives at it despite oneself in approaching the real meaning of things.'[28] Satie's piano pieces, which were given strange, childlike titles, were deceptively difficult pieces which could nevertheless be played by adult and child alike. He provided his sheet music with bizarre directions and annotations, part helpfully poetic, part parodic of their own didactic function. In his 1913 composition, 'Sketches and Provocations of a Portly Wooden Mannequin', for example, he glossed the music with phrases such as: 'down in the throat', 'With the tip of the eyes and held back in advance', 'Fairly slow, if you don't mind', and 'Without your finger blushing'.[29]

With its complicated and ambiguous iconography, Brancusi's *Plato* stands as a nice companion piece for such concerns and would be at home in front of Satie's piano. (Curiously, the eye in Brancusi's sculpture echoes that of Matisse's child in his painting *The Piano Lesson* of 1916.)[30] Music again comes to mind in the presence of Brancusi's large-scale wooden sculpture *Adam and Eve* (cat.27), which was made over an extended period in these years, simultaneously with works such as *Plato*. The contrasting forms, contours and surfaces of this work are highly evocative of sound, from the smooth and slick to the rough, unpolished and throaty: the whole work seems to stand as a sculptural equivalent to the syncopated rhythms and voices of jazz.[31]

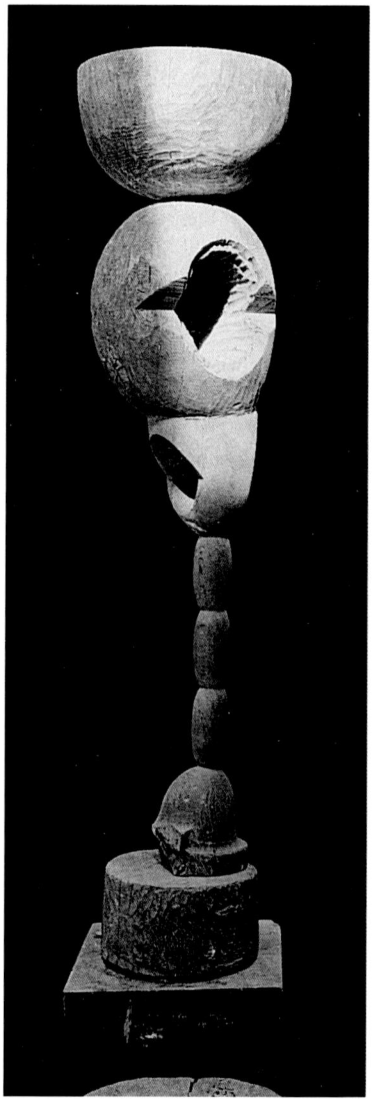

Fig.37. **Socrates and Cup**, 1922
Centre Pompidou, Paris (AM4002-696, PH670)
modern print

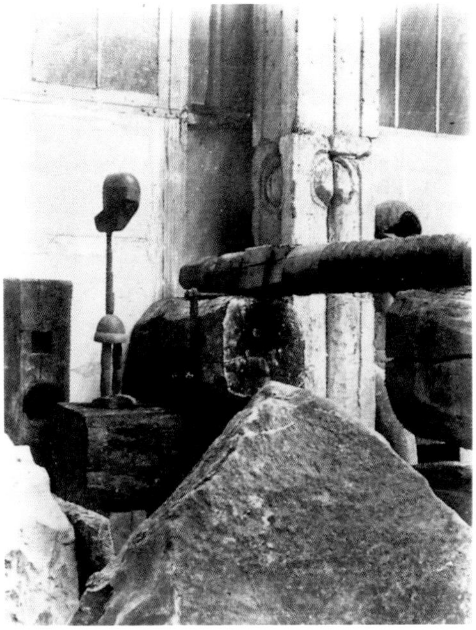

Fig.38 **Studio view with Plato, Socrates and oil press**, *c.*1921–2
Centre Pompidou, Paris (AM4002-260, PH15)

Similarly, Brancusi's black and white photographs were never silent documents, and the sculptor (whose French was not fluent) relied heavily on them to communicate his work and his ideas about it. Both *Plato* and *Socrates* feature in one of the most intriguing studio photographs that Brancusi took during these years, and in which sound (and, in turn, the perceptual apprehension of sound) plays a decisive role (fig.38). A staged environment is comprised of stone boulders, blocks of wood and the sculptor's oil press. These props, whilst situated of course inside the studio, can be understood as evoking an outdoor setting: a landscape of mountains and a bridge (provided by the horizontal oil press). Within this a narrative can be detected, the operation of which is dependent upon the reading of sound in the photograph in the highly charged spaces in between the works and objects. In this way, the wooden block can be read as a head with two eye-holes, square nose and circular mouth agape, which appears to be uttering a howl. This sends *Plato* (himself screaming with his *Newborn*-like mouth) running in flight up towards the bridge, which leads out of the frame of the photograph and into the studio interior. To activate this drama in sound, Brancusi has provided an actor-audience, *Socrates* (to the right), who, since 'his ears are his eyes' (according to the shared mythology of Brancusi and Satie), can comprehend the scene even though positioned out of sight behind the *Column of the Kiss*.

This particular photograph reminds us how evocative was Brancusi's actual wooden sculpture of sound and speech. Paul Morand touches upon this in his 1926 introduction to the Brummer Gallery exhibition in New York: 'His woods speak of the happiness of their new life. His *Socrates* strikes us as a wireless post which is broadcasting.'[32] The fact that wood had 'resonance' was not lost on Brancusi, who was not only a musician but had also made his own violin. That this was an emotional matter can be gauged from a letter to his friend Blaise Cendrars in late 1921: 'If you had heard my violin just now, you would understand my soul's distress.'[33] Brancusi would never make a wooden sculpture of a musical instrument or of a musician (as did Lipchitz or Zadkine) rather, he turned to what he saw as the expressive quality of wood itself. Each piece of wood had its own grain, its own character, its own voice: the texture, surfaces, weight and density of wood carried sonic correspondences and different ways of being heard. Brancusi furnished his studio with objects carved and crafted from the same resonating material to create an ostensibly non-hierarchical studio environment, which levelled sculptures and functional objects into a self-consciously, almost operatic, harmonised whole. Like the sculptor's *Cup*, which featured at first in his *The Child in the World* ensemble, these wooden objects constituted Brancusi's equivalent to Satie's *Musique d'ammeublement*, that atmospheric, household music that surrounds the hearer and evaporates if he or she stops to try to listen to it.

Other wooden works are to be 'heard' as much as seen. Compared to the sealed inner mouths of *The Kiss* and elegant, tight lips of *Mlle Pogany* and *Sleeping Muse* (in stone and bronze, cat.1–3, 17, 20), his wooden sculptures are very noisy, talkative, exclamatory and outspoken. After 1914 when the head of *The First Step* becomes *The First Cry* (see cat.23), we find a range of mouths and 'see' a repertoire of voices: the singing of *Eve* (cat.27), the woof and bark of *Watchdog* (cat.29), the crow of the *Cock* (cat.30), the guffaw of *The Chief*, the declaration of *King of Kings* (cat.31), the beaming smile of his *Child's Head*,[34] the chatter of the *Telephone Chair* (especially when the sculptor sat on it, whilst on the phone). Indeed, given the later self-identification with wood noted at the beginning of this essay, we might hear a linguistic twist to such correspondences, since *branchu* ('branchy' and 'connected' in French) is homophonically close to the Romanian pronunciation of 'Brancusi'.

Revisited through these metaphors, we get a different sense of the noisy combination of wooden sculptures that constituted Brancusi's *The Child in the World* (fig.36). Looking at the way in which he has placed the mouth of the figure into the wedge-shaped cut of the column brings something else more mournful to this yelling. The wooden head of the child, which leans onto the column, could almost fit into this hollow. Indeed the cut itself seems connotative of a wailing mouth, as if this carved wooden, abstract column were evocative of grief – a sculpture in mourning (articulated through the vertical repetition of the cuts) – and as if it functioned in a funerary manner within this ensemble. There is seriousness here, not play. The wooden 'endless column' was, of course, the prototype for his later Târgu Jiu memorial. And we are, once again, reminded that if wood is connotative of animation and life, it is by the same token connotative of mortality and death.

1 This view is developed in the doctoral thesis of Alexandra Parigoris, where the idea of 'rootedness' is set in the cultural context of Romanian nation building. See Alexandra Parigoris, 'Constantin Brancusi, a Peasant in Paris: A Study of the Persona and Work of Constantin Brancusi from a Post-Symbolist Perspective', Ph.D., University of London, 1997.

2 Also titled 'The Girls of the Bois de Clamart', the tale is quoted in Hulten, Dumitresco and Istrati 1988, p.210. For the abbreviations used in the notes, see Selected Reading.

3 Jeanne Robert Foster, 'Constantin Brancusi', *Rock-Flower*, New York 1923. The poem was also printed in *Brancusi*, exh. cat., Arts Club of Chicago 1927.

4 Friedrich Teja Bach, *Brancusi: Photo Réflexion*, Paris 1991, p.141, n.49.

5 *Cicatrices d'arbres* (*c*.1924), Centre Pompidou, Paris (AM4002-1003).

6 This has also been observed by Eric Shanes in 'Brancusi in the Tate Gallery: A working philosophy', *Apollo*, May 1989, p.311.

7 For a useful summary of the links between these works, see Ann Temkin's catalogue entry for the *Little French Girl* in Bach, Rowell and Temkin 1995, p.154. For other readings see Edith Balas, 'Brancusi, Duchamp and Dada', *Gazette des Beaux-Arts*, vol.XCV, Apr. 1980, p.170; Gregory Salzman, 'Brancusi's Woods', unpublished MA thesis, Courtauld Institute of Art, University of London, 1972, p.8. Salzman notes the figure of the 'Little American Girl' from *Parade* (1917), with music by Eric Satie. On this, see also Miller 1995, p.184. On the two re-workings of *Plato*'s head (the earlier with 'ears'), see Geist 1975, cat. nos. 122–3, p.183 and Bach 1997, cat. nos. 158–9, p.458.

8 See K.J. Michaelsen, 'Brancusi and African Art', *Artforum*, Nov. 1971, pp.72–7; Sidney Geist, 'Brancusi', in William Rubin (ed.), *'Primitivism' in the Twentieth Century: Affinity of the Tribal and the Modern*, exh. cat., Museum of Modern Art, New York 1984, pp.344–67; Edith Balas, *Brancusi and Romanian Folk Traditions*, Eastern European Monographs, CCXXIV, 1987; and Parigoris 1997.

9 According to Geist, Senufo and Bidjogo figures in particular. Geist 1975, pp.348–50.

10 Confirmed by Eleanor Nagy, Conservator, Solomon R. Guggenheim Museum, New York, in a message to Tate, 8 Oct. 2003.

11 For a recent reading of the ways Brancusi (and his supporters) used his studio to stage his 'artistic identity' see Jon Wood, 'Brancusi's "white studio"', *Sculpture Journal*, Vol. VII, 2002, pp.108–20.

12 Letter from Brancusi to Quinn, 4 Oct. 1916 (Pach's translation), Quinn archive, New York Public Library.

13 Walter Pach, *Queer Thing, Painting: Forty Years in the World of Art*, New York and London 1938, p.173.

14 'Brancusi in his studio' (1914–15), Centre Pompidou, Paris (PH708).

15 Dorothy Adlow, 'Brancusi', *Drawing and Design*, London, Feb. 1927, p.37.

16 One of Sophie Taeuber's puppets was reproduced in *Variétés* on 15 January 1930, in the company of Brancusi's *The First Step* (1913).

17 The association between the tortoise and the house is made by Aesop in 'How the Tortoise Got its Shell', *Fables of Aesop*, Harmondsworth 1954, p.68.

18 Lewis Carroll, *The Annotated Alice: Alice's Adventures in Wonderland and Through the Looking Glass*, Harmondsworth 1965, pp.31 and 35.

19 Indeed, as Geist has stated, *Little French Girl* was once known as *Mlle Brancusi*. Geist 1968/1983, p.66.

20 Letter from Quinn to Brancusi, 26 Oct. 1918, Quinn archive, New York Public Library.

21 Roché to Quinn, 15 May 1922, Quinn archive, New York Public Library.

22 On the Brancusi/Satie relationship see Balas

1980, pp.165–74; Miller 1995, pp.183–4. It is noteworthy that in Satie's own self-portrait drawings he portrayed himself as a portrait bust.

23 'Satie and Brancusi used to tease one another unmercifully, untiringly for hours on end, without getting annoyed, throwing jokes like paving stones into one another's face. The spectators would become exhausted. Not they. They were carried along by the purity of their character and work.' Conrad Satie's entry of July 1925 in his 1914–25 notebook, quoted in Ornella Volta, *Satie Seen Through His Letters* (trans. Michael Bullock), London and New York 1989, p.211.

24 Hulten, Dumitresco and Istrati 1988, p.148.

25 See Charles Baudelaire, *Le Peintre de la vie moderne*, Paris 1965, p.447.

26 *The Little Review*, New York, Autumn 1921, p.236. See also 'Selected aphorisms' in this catalogue.

27 For information about this work, see Francis Naumann, *Marcel Duchamp: The Art of Making Art in the Age of Mechanical Reproduction*, New York 1999, pp.40–1, 57, n.1 and 2; Francis Naumann and Achim Moeller, *Marcel Duchamp: The Art of Making Art in the Age of Mechanical Reproduction*, exh. cat., Achim Moeller Fine Art, New York 1999, p.16.

28 Roger Vitrac, 'Brancusi', *Cahiers d'art*, 1929, p.382. See also 'Selected aphorisms' in this catalogue.

29 Eric Satie, 'Croquis & Agaceries d'un Gros Bonhomme en Bois', *Gymnopédies, Gnossiennes and Other Works for Piano*, New York 1989, pp.144–53.

30 Geist 1968/1983, p.149.

31 I am grateful to Matthew Gale for this observation.

32 Paul Morand, *Brancusi*, exh. cat., Brummer Gallery, New York 1926.

33 Tabart and Lemny 2003, p.176.

34 See Geist 1975, cat. no. 203, p.190 for this little-known, more abstract *Child's Head*.

OVERLEAF

Fig.39 **Studio view with Cocks and King of Kings**, c.1945–6
Centre Pompidou, Paris
(PH140, modern print)

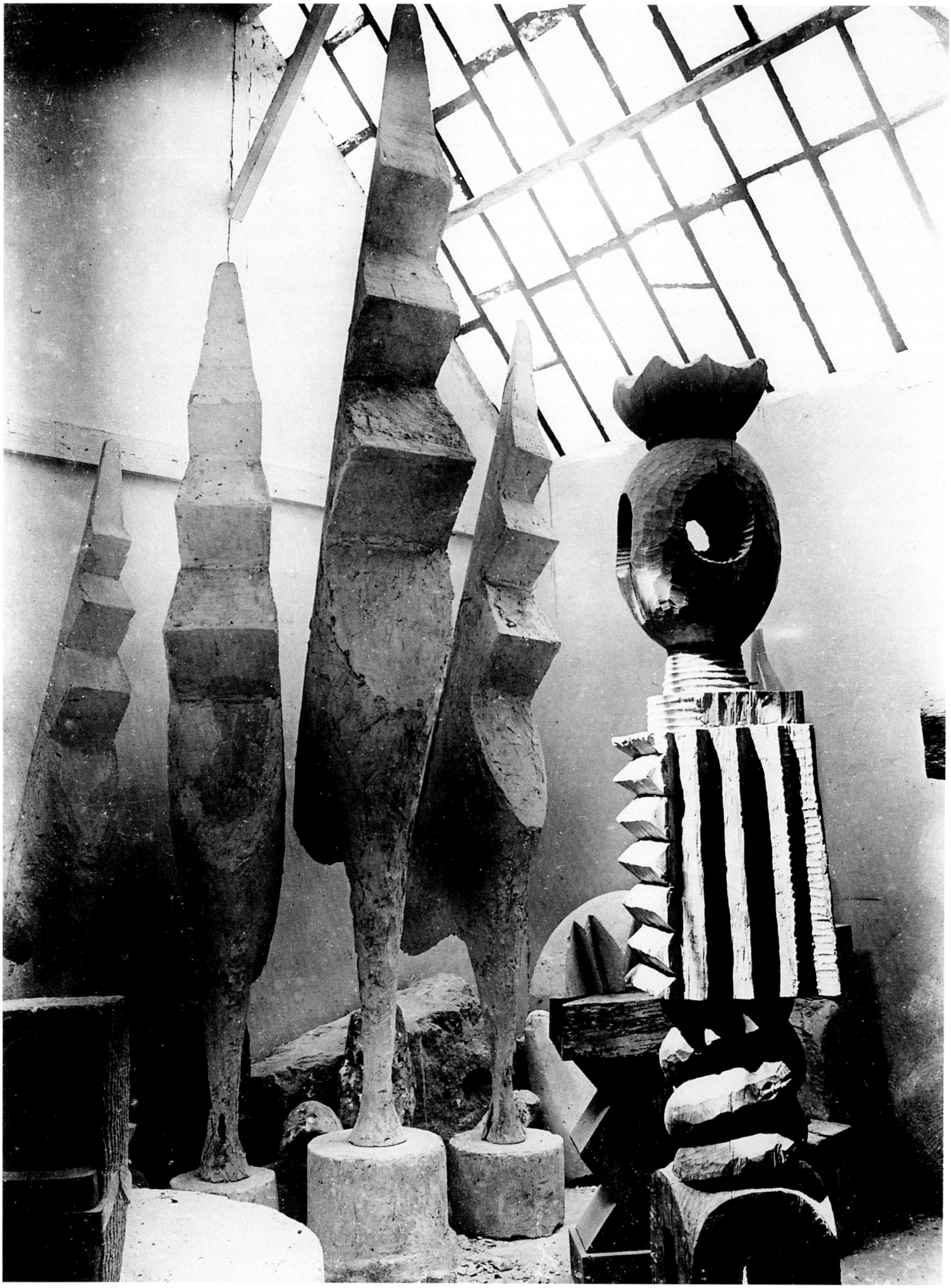

Catalogue

Dimensions are given in height, width and depth, centimetres preceding inches

An asterisk (*) indicates that the base supporting the sculpture is not original.

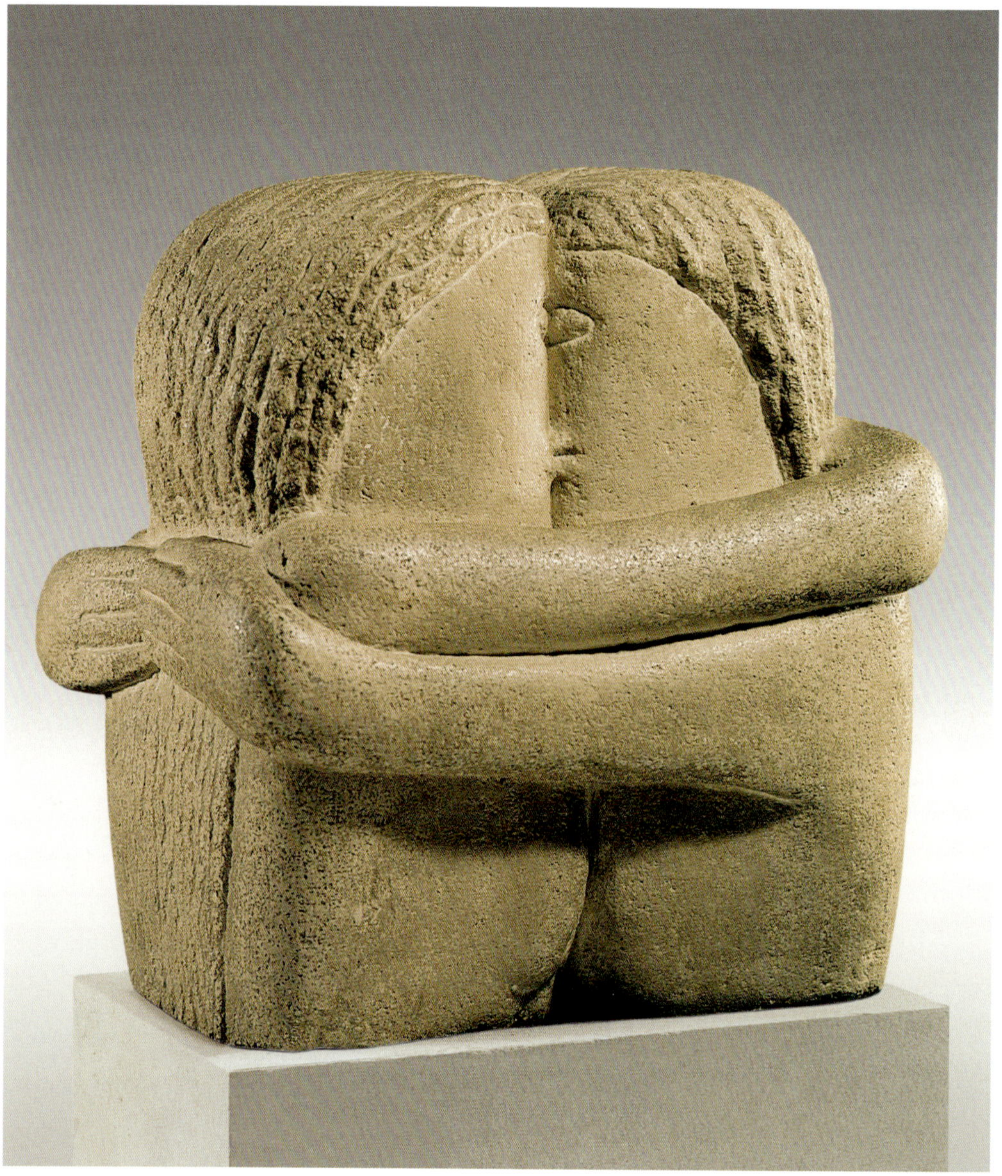

1 **The Kiss**
1907–8
Stone
28 × 26 × 21.5 (11 × 10$\frac{1}{4}$ × 8$\frac{1}{2}$)
Muzeul de Artă, Craiova

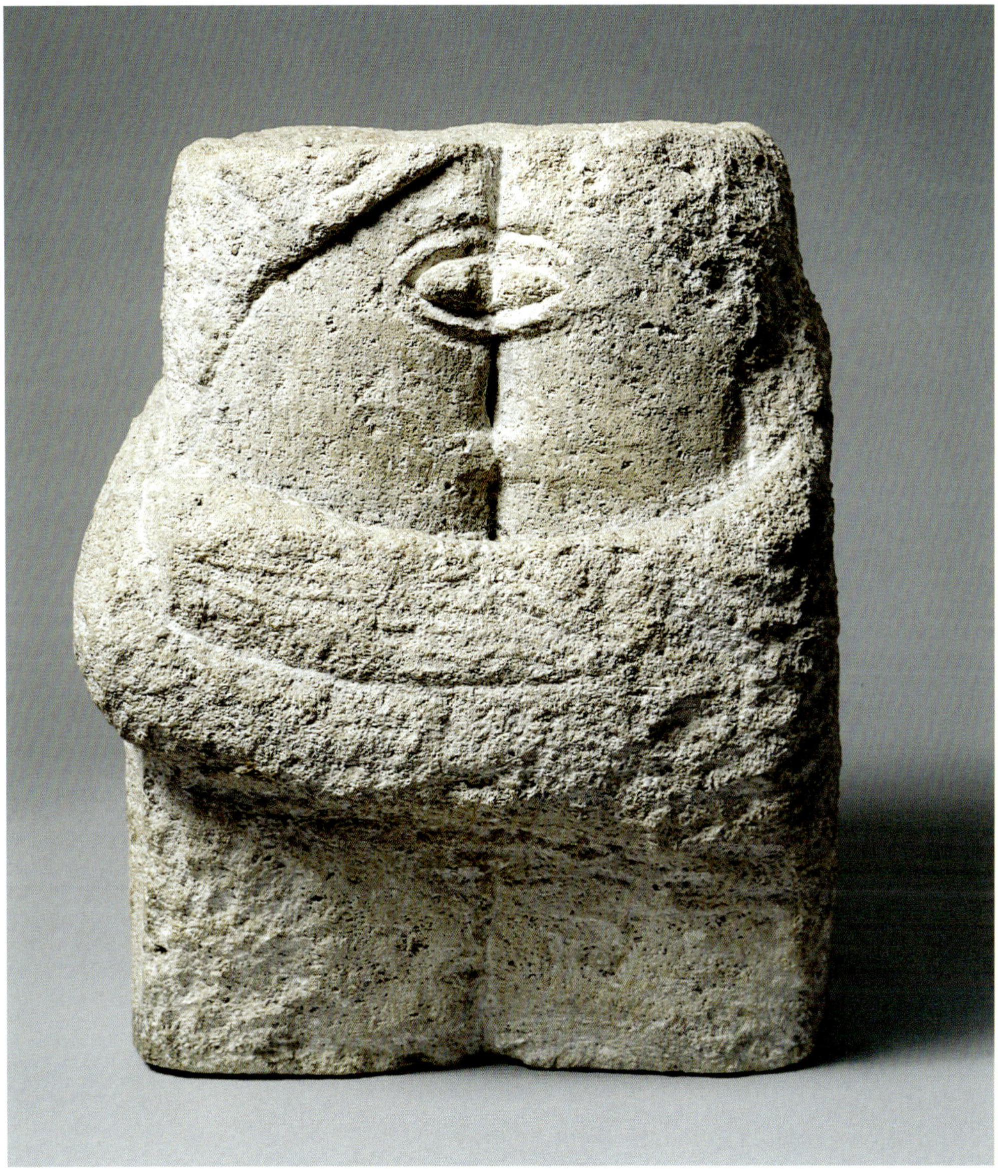

2 **The Kiss**
1908
Stone
32 × 25 × 21 ($13^3/_4 \times 9^7/_8 \times 8^1/_4$)
Private Collection
[Exhibited London only]

3 **The Kiss**
1916
Limestone
58.4 × 33.7 × 25.4 (23 × 13¼ × 10)
Philadelphia Museum of Art:
The Louise and Walter Arensberg
Collection, 1950

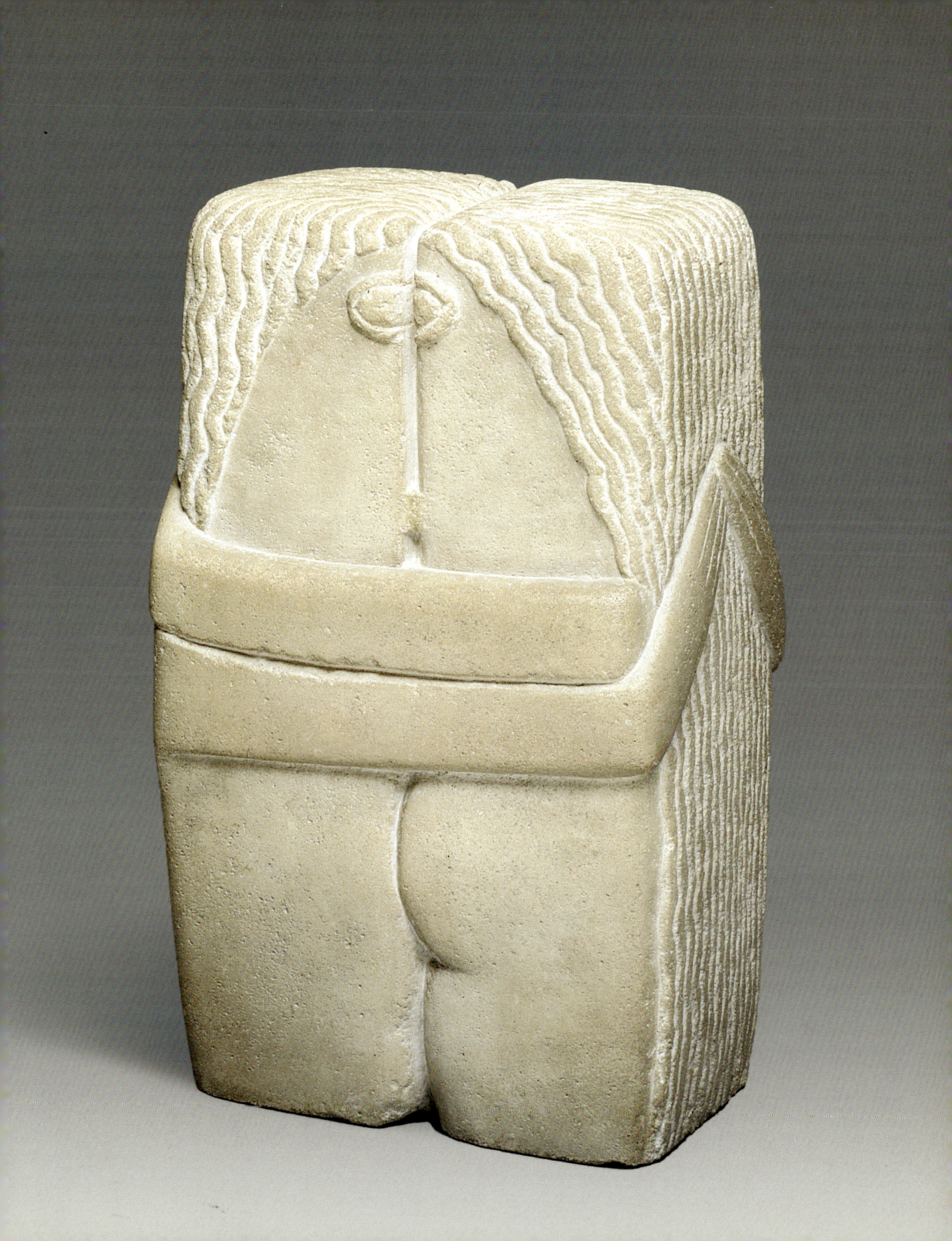

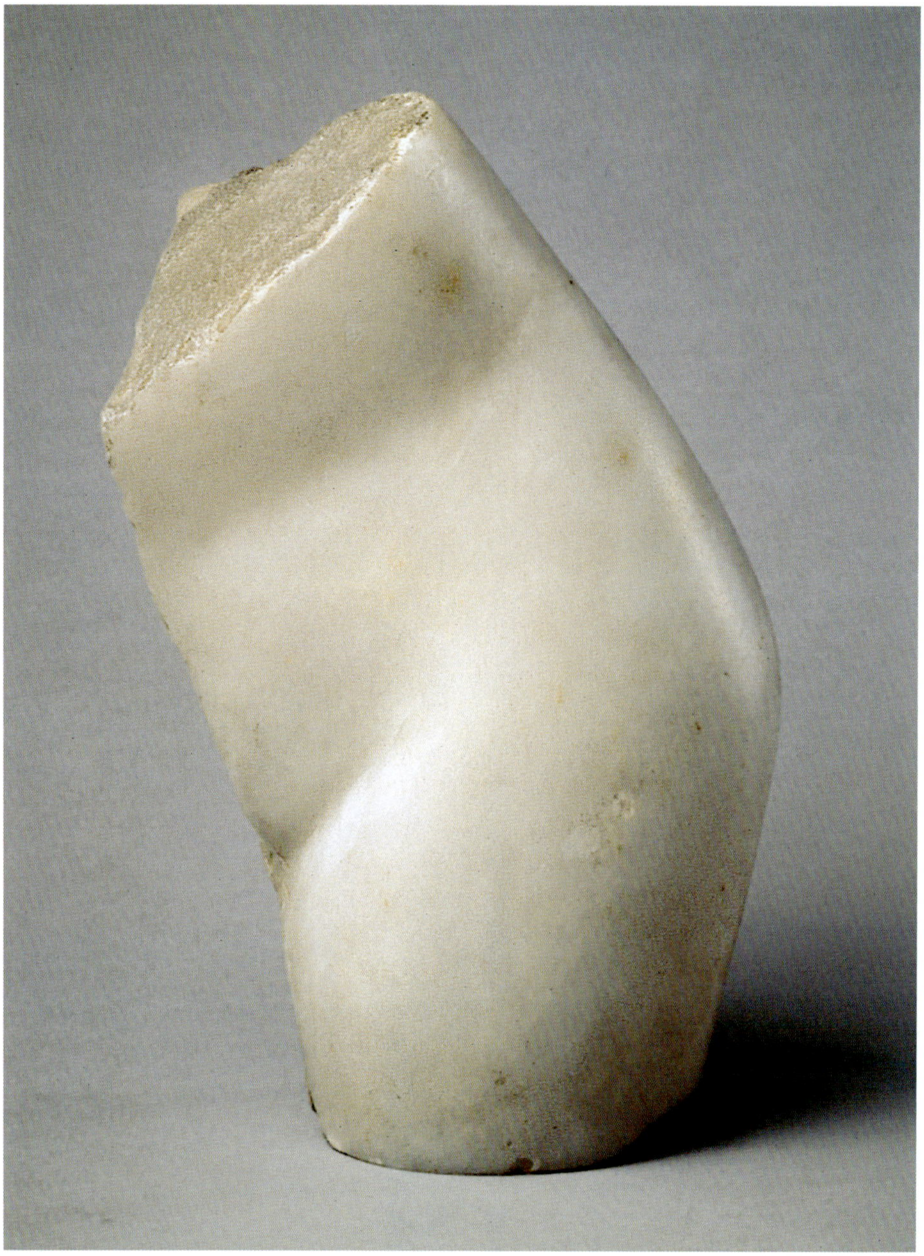

4 **Torso (Fragment of a Torso)**
1909–10
White Marble
24.4 × 16 × 15 (9 5/8 × 6 1/4 × 5 7/8)
Muzeul de Artă, Craiova

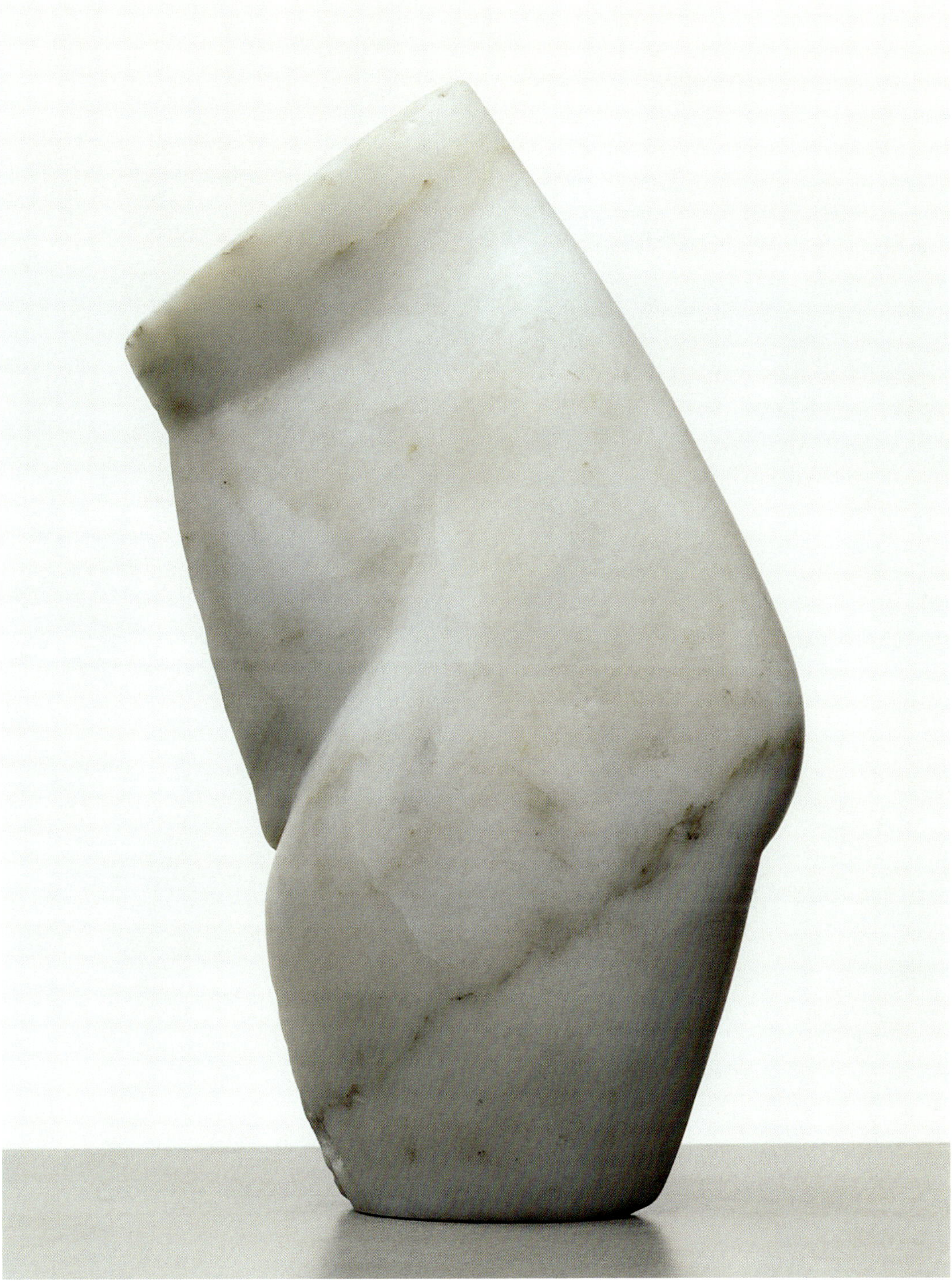

5 **Torso**
1912
White Marble
31.5 × 18 × 14 ($12^3/_8 \times 7^1/_8 \times 5^1/_2$)
Staatsgalerie Stuttgart
[Exhibited London only]

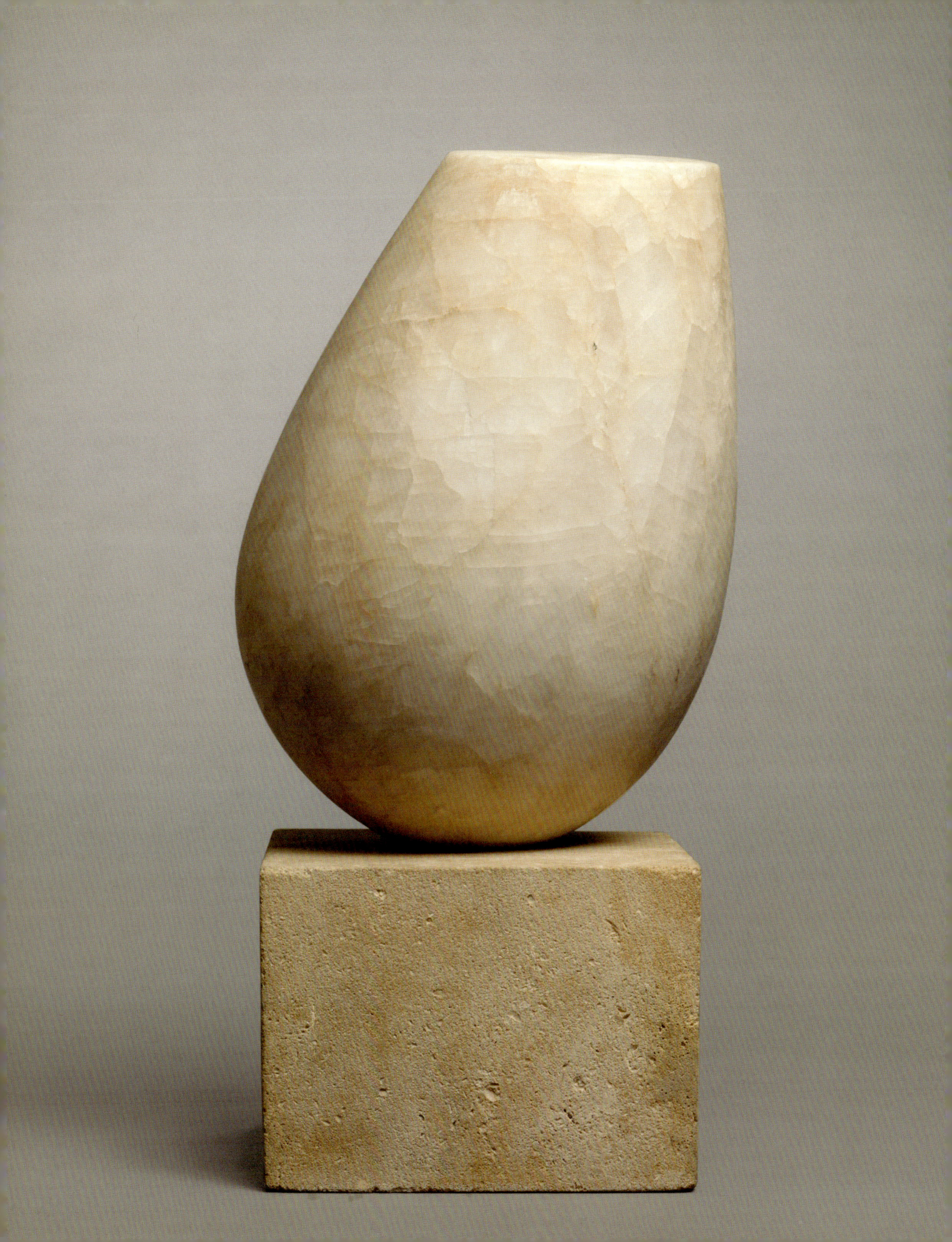

OPPOSITE

6 **Torso of a Young Girl**
1922
Onyx
45.4 × 22.9 × 21 (17⅞ × 9 × 8¼)

Limestone base
14.3 × 19.4 × 18.1 (5⅝ × 7⅝ × 7⅛)
Courtesy of the Fogg Art Museum,
Harvard University Art Museums,
The Lois Orswell Collection

7 **Torso of a Young Girl II**
1923
White Marble
34.9 × 24.8 × 15.2 (13¾ × 9¾ × 6)

Limestone base
15.6 × 22.9 × 22.5 (6⅛ × 9 × 8⅞)
Philadelphia Museum of Art:
A.E. Gallatin Collection, 1952

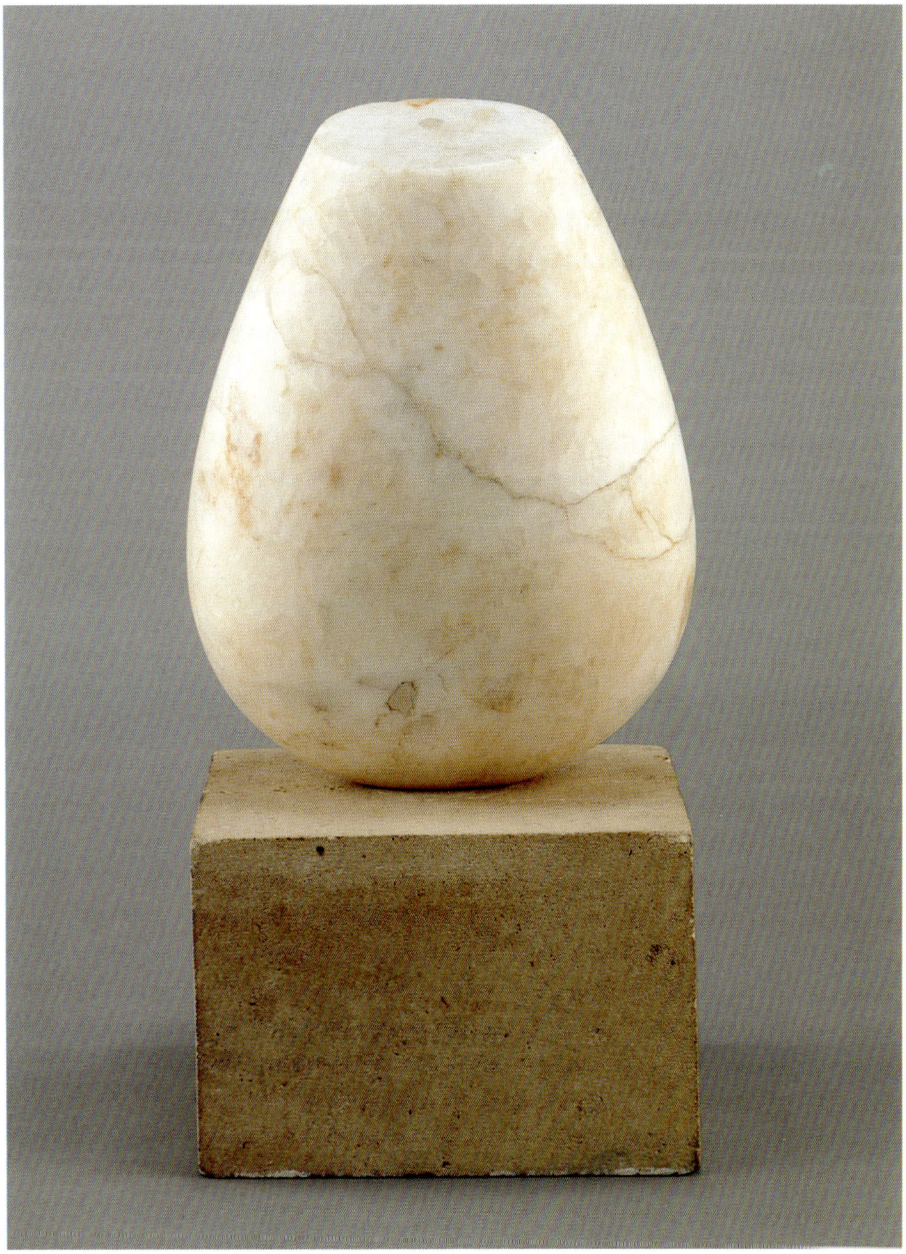

8 **Torso of a Young Man II**
1923
Walnut
42.7 × 28.4 × 14.6 (16 3/4 × 11 1/4 × 5 3/4)

Limestone base
13.4 × 22.5 × 18.4 (5 3/8 × 8 7/8 × 7 1/4)
Musée National d'Art Moderne,
Centre Georges Pompidou, Paris.
Brancusi Bequest, 1957

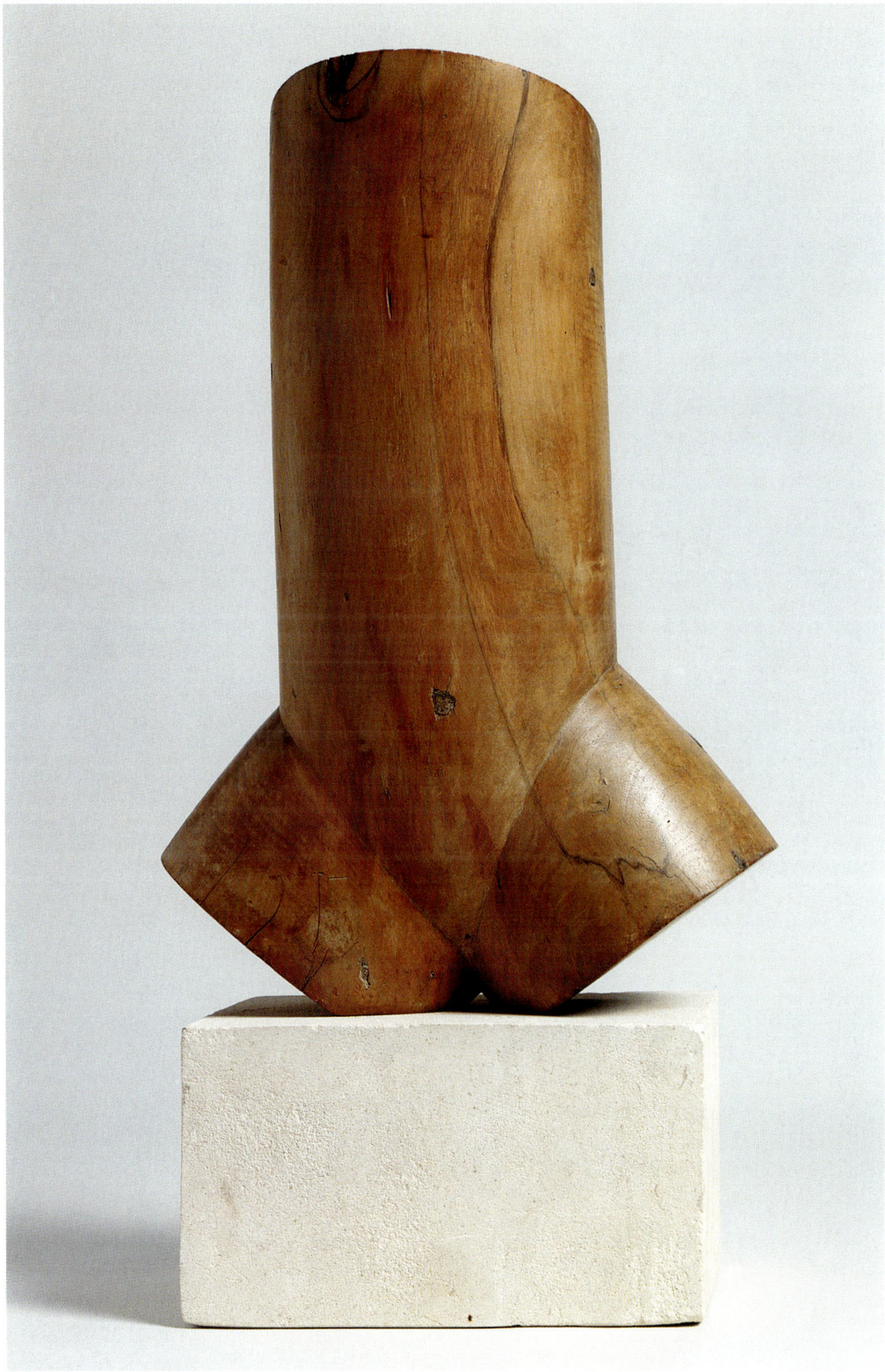

9 **Young Bird II**
1925
Veined Marble
41 × 21.5 × 30 (16 × 8 × 11)

Two-part base of limestone and oak
Limestone base
24.5 × 29.2 × 28.9 (9 5/8 × 11 1/2 × 11 3/8)
Wood base
60.3 × 26.4 × 27.6 (23 3/4 × 10 3/8 × 10 7/8)
Private Collection

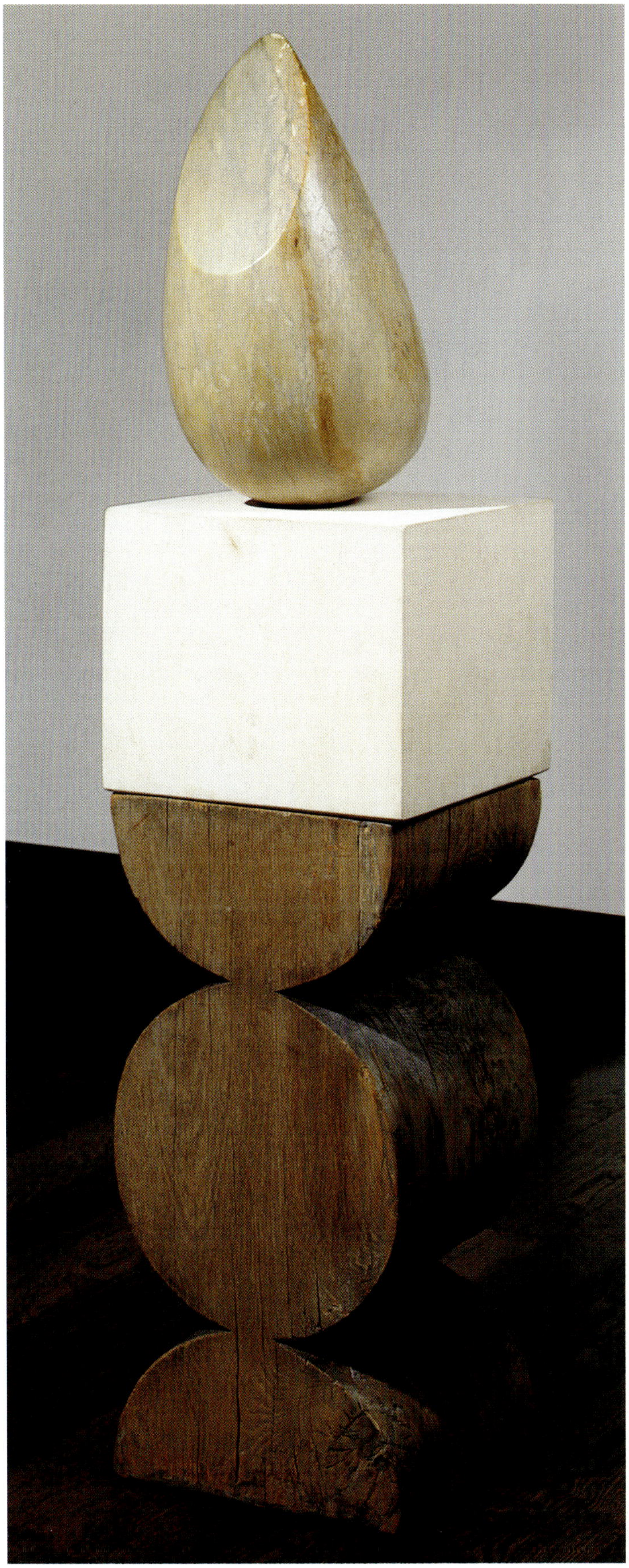

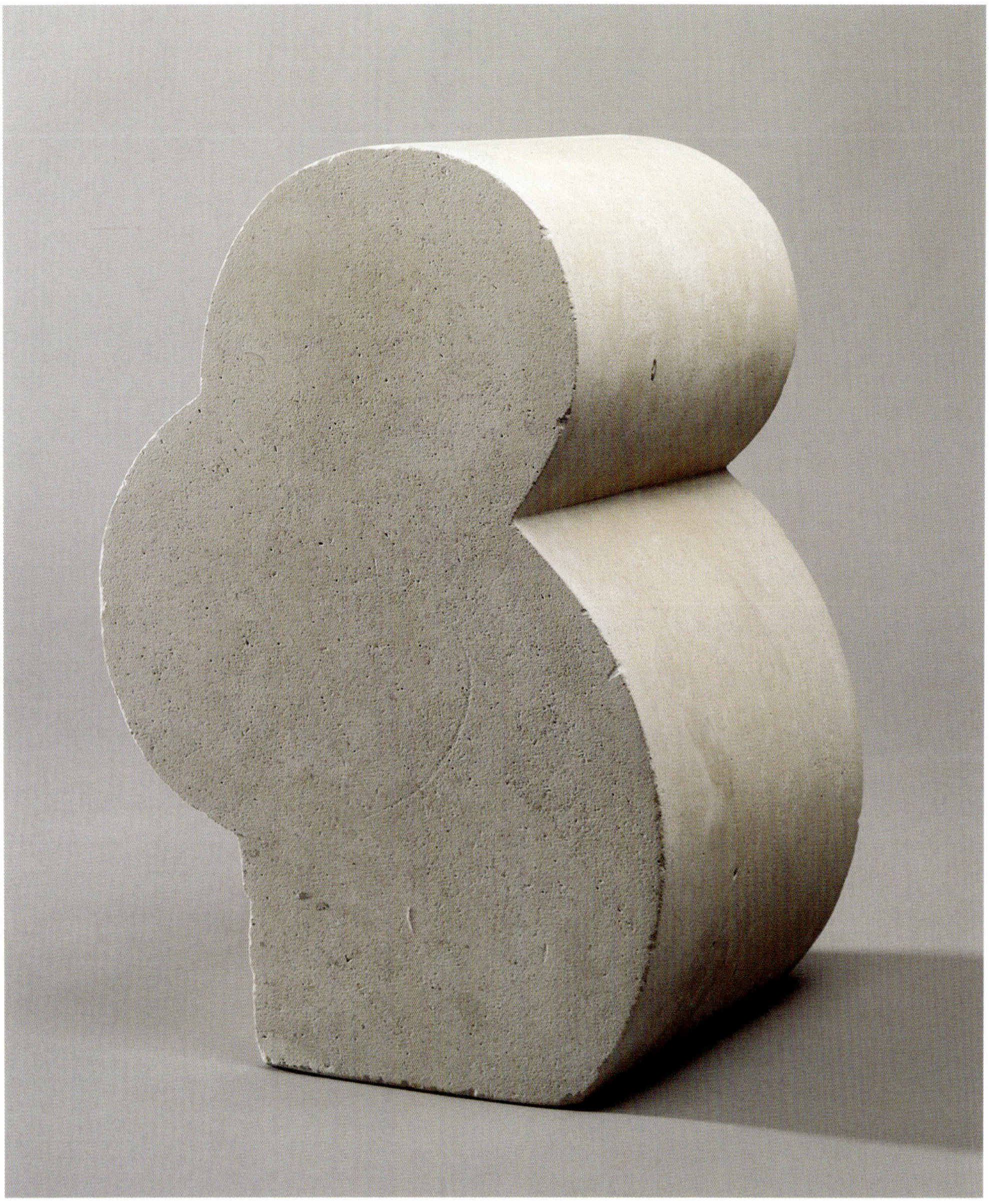

10 **Timidity**
1917
Limestone
36.5 × 24.2 × 22 (14 3/8 × 9 1/2 × 8 5/8)
Musée National d'Art Moderne,
Centre Georges Pompidou, Paris.
Brancusi Bequest, 1957

OPPOSITE
11 **Eileen Lane**
1923
White onyx
28.1 × 21.5 × 15.2 (11 × 8 1/2 × 6)

Limestone base
15 × 26 × 25 (5 7/8 × 10 1/4 × 9 7/8)
Musée National d'Art Moderne,
Centre Georges Pompidou, Paris.
Brancusi Bequest, 1957

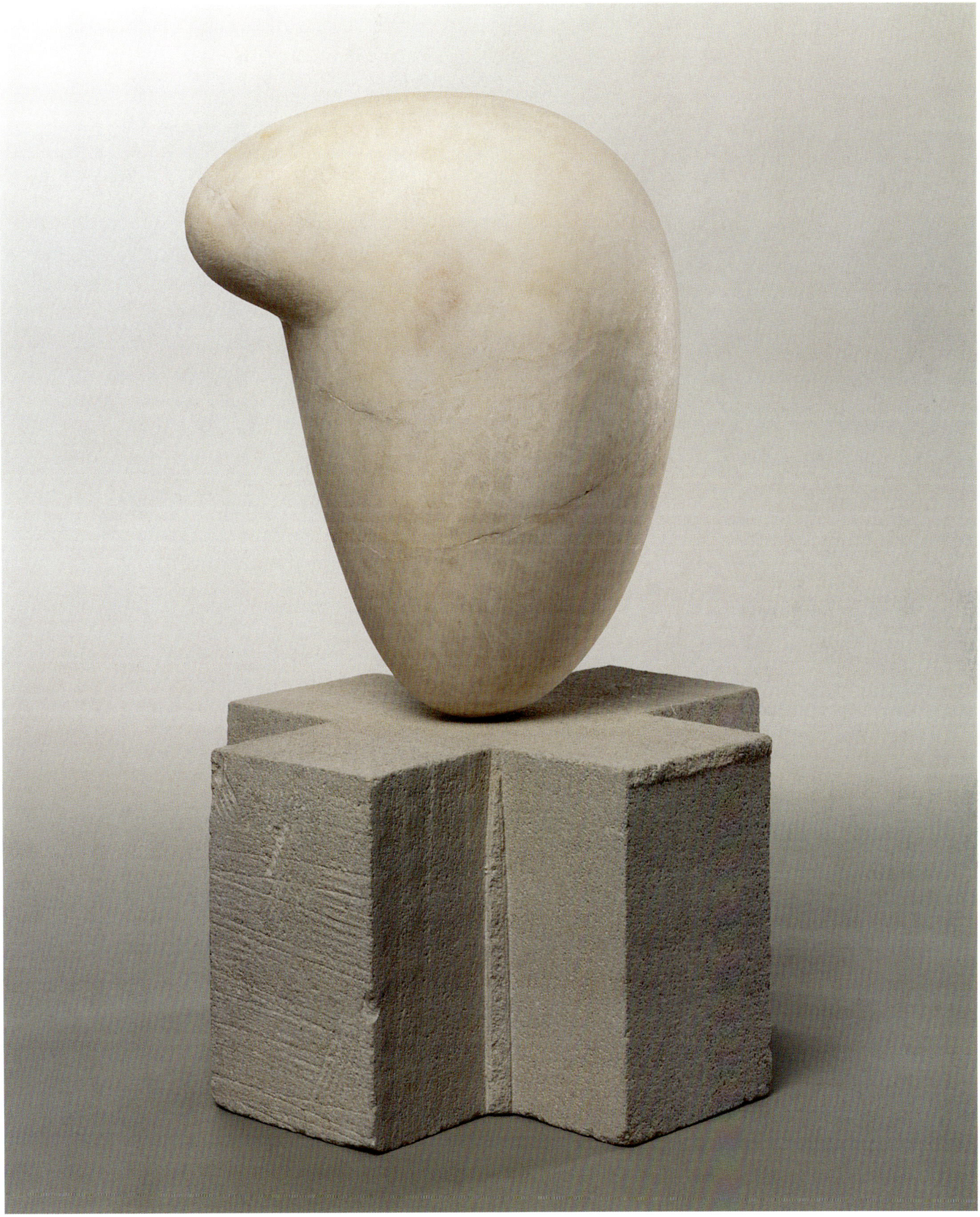

12 **Danaïde**
*c.*1907–9
Sandstone*
33 × 26 × 24 (13 × 10¼ × 9½)
Muzeul Național de Artă al României,
Bucharest
[Exhibited London only]

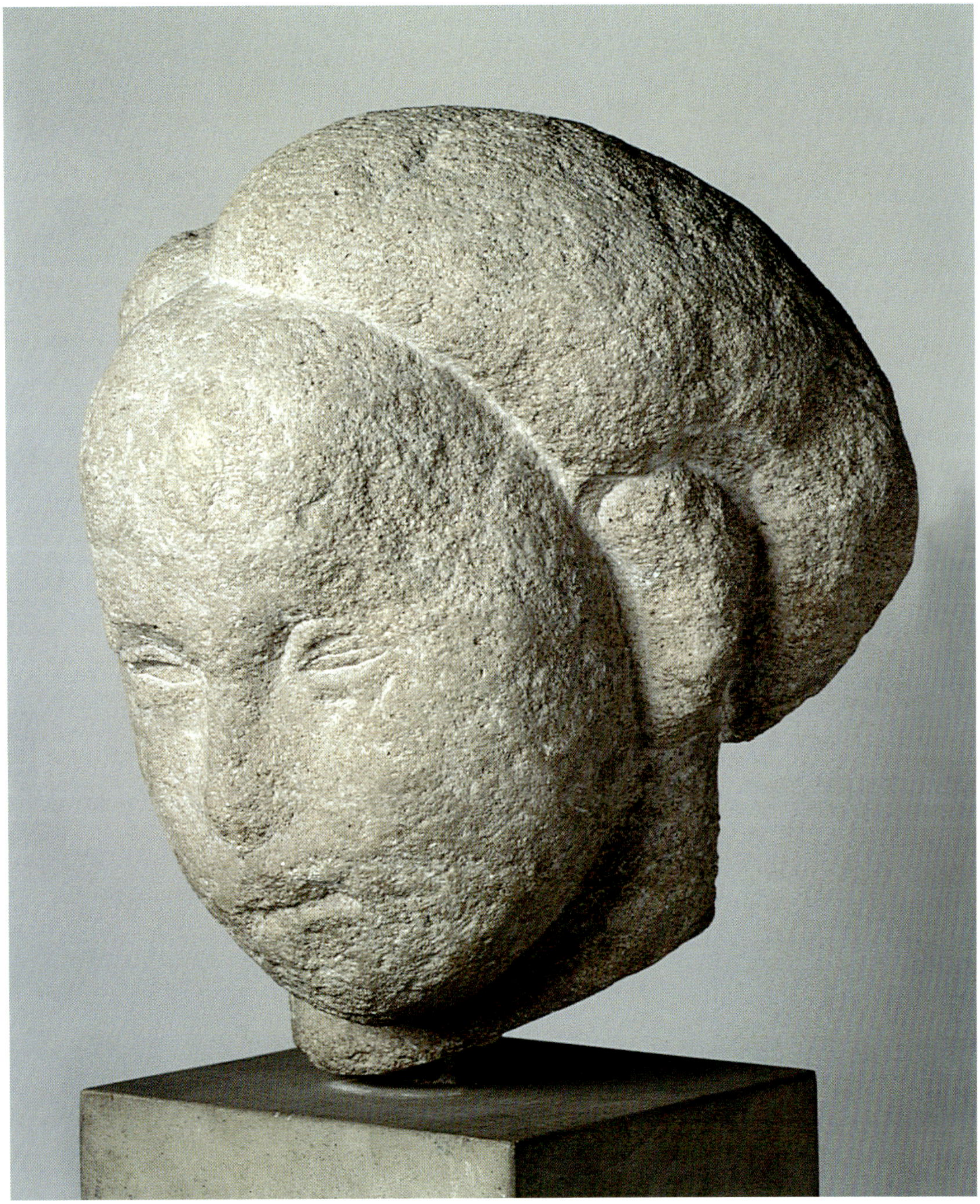

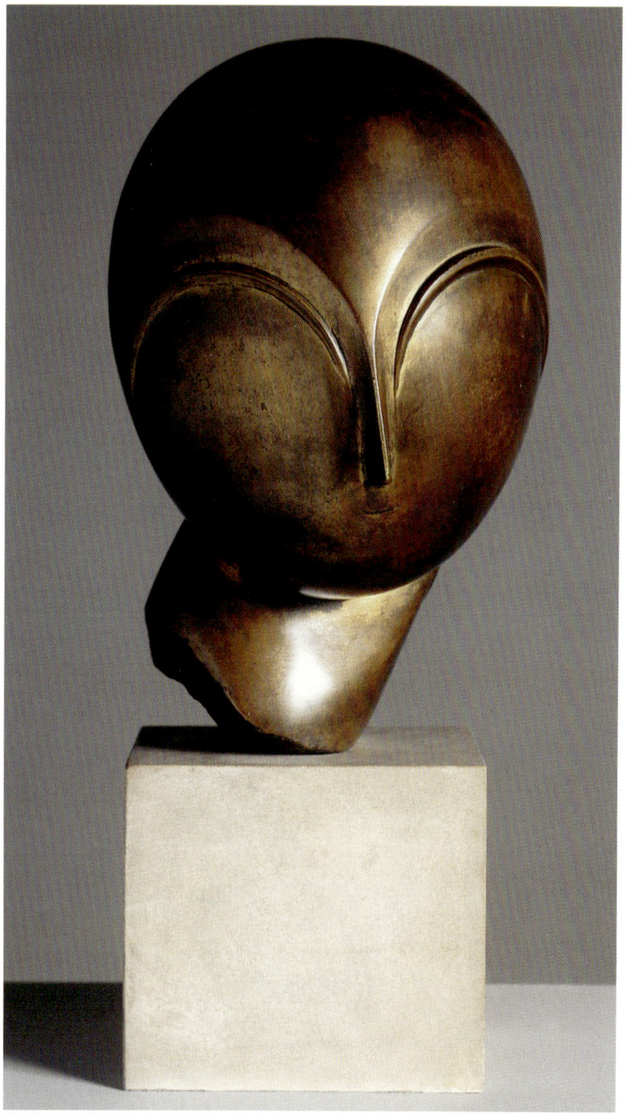

13 **Danaïde**
1913
Bronze
27.9 × 17.1 × 21 (11 × 6 3/4 × 8 1/4)

Limestone base*
11.5 × 14 × 13.5 (4 1/2 × 5 1/2 × 5 1/4)
Tate. Presented by Sir Charles Clore 1959

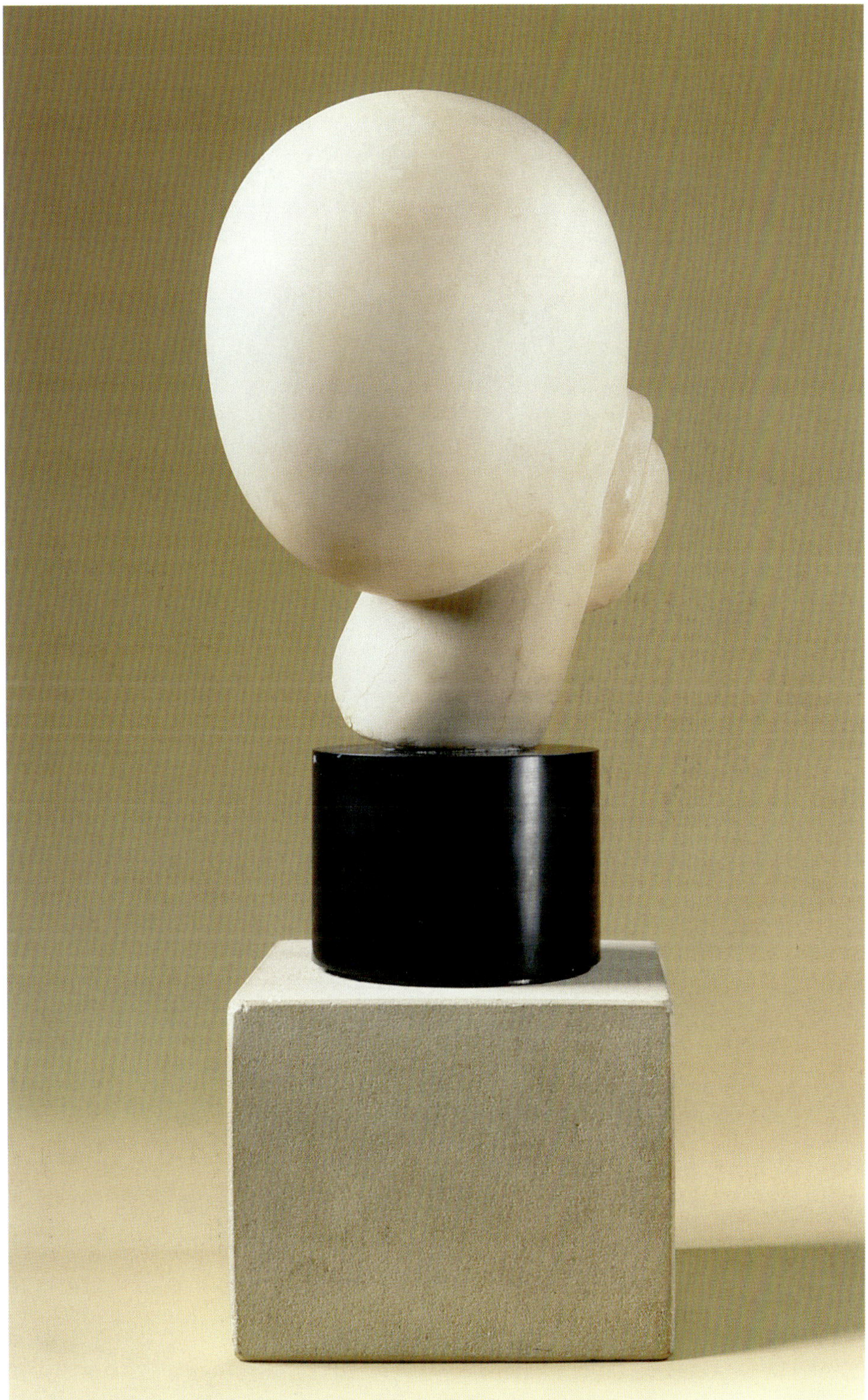

14 **Head of a Woman (Abstract Head)**
1910–25
Marble on two-part black marble and stone base
28.6 × 20 × 18 (11¼ × 7⅞ × 7⅛)
Private Collection
[Exhibited London only]

15 **Muse**
1912
White Marble
45 × 23 × 17 (17 3/4 × 9 × 6 3/4)

Mounted on
Oak base
1920
Oak, three sections
97.5 × 47.3 × 47 (38 3/8 × 18 5/8 × 18 1/2)
The Solomon R. Guggenheim Museum, New York

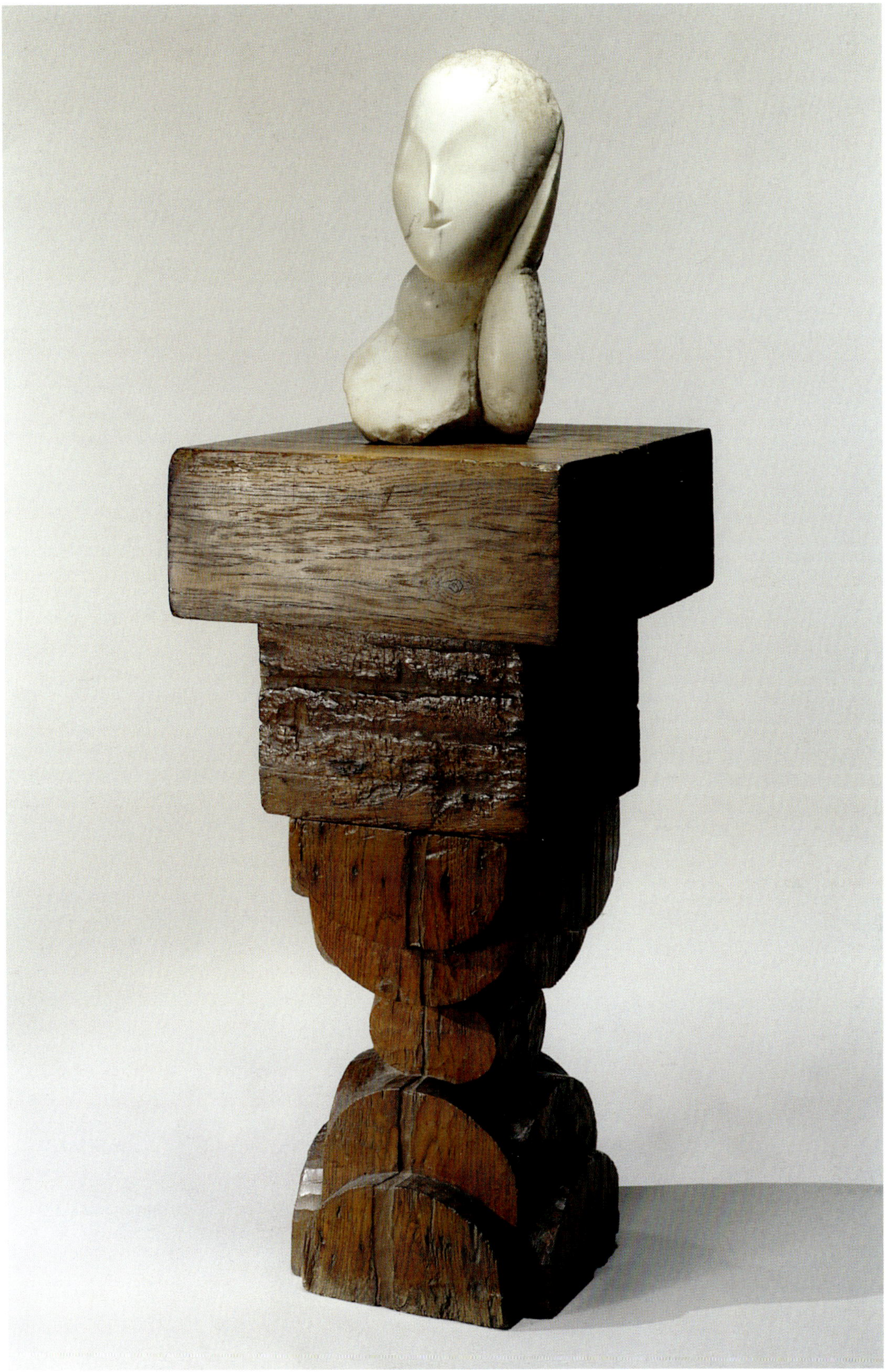

16 **Princess X**
1915
White Marble
55.9 × 27.9 × 22.9 (22 × 11 × 9)

Caen limestone base
16.2 × 16.2 × 14 (6 3/8 × 6 3/8 × 5 1/2)
Sheldon Memorial Art Gallery and Sculpture Garden, University of Nebraska, Lincoln.
Gift of Mrs Olga N. Sheldon in memory of Adams Bromley Sheldon

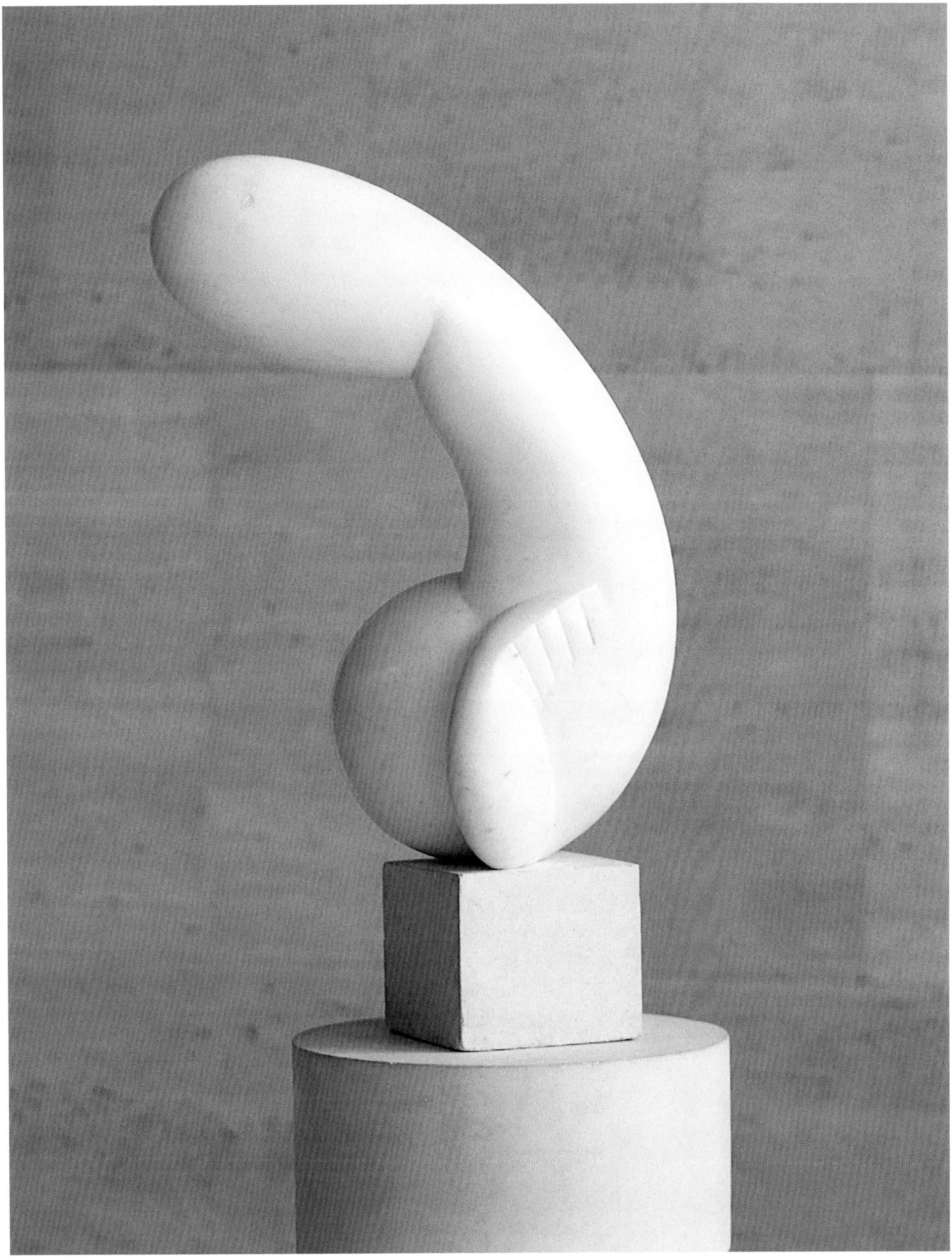

17 **Mlle Pogany II**
1919
Veined Marble
44.2 × 20 × 27 ($17\frac{3}{8} \times 7\frac{7}{8} \times 10\frac{5}{8}$)

Five-part base of limestone and wood
Limestone base
26.4 × 24.1 × 22.5 ($10\frac{3}{8} \times 9\frac{1}{2} \times 8\frac{15}{16}$)
Wood base
97.8 × 41.3 × 40.3 ($38\frac{1}{2} \times 16\frac{1}{4} \times 15\frac{7}{8}$)
Private Collection

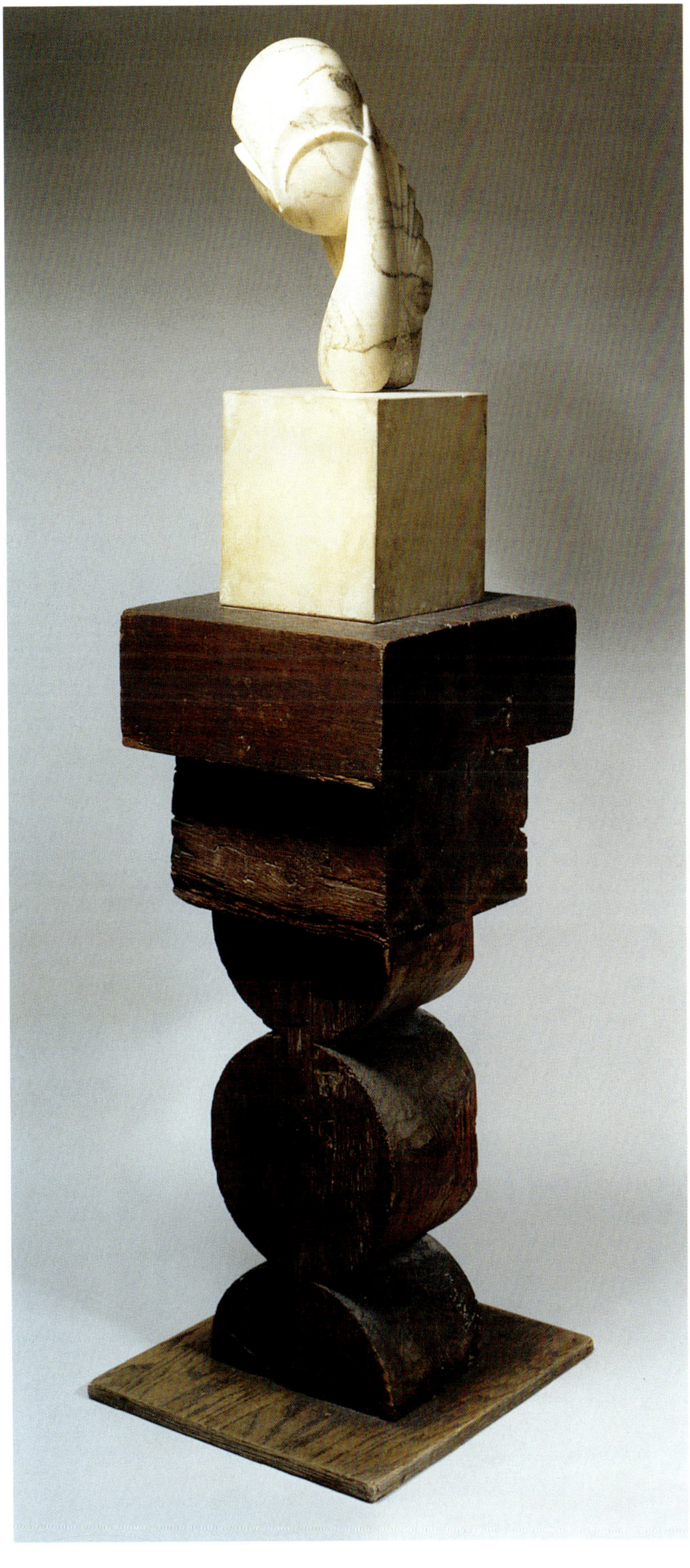

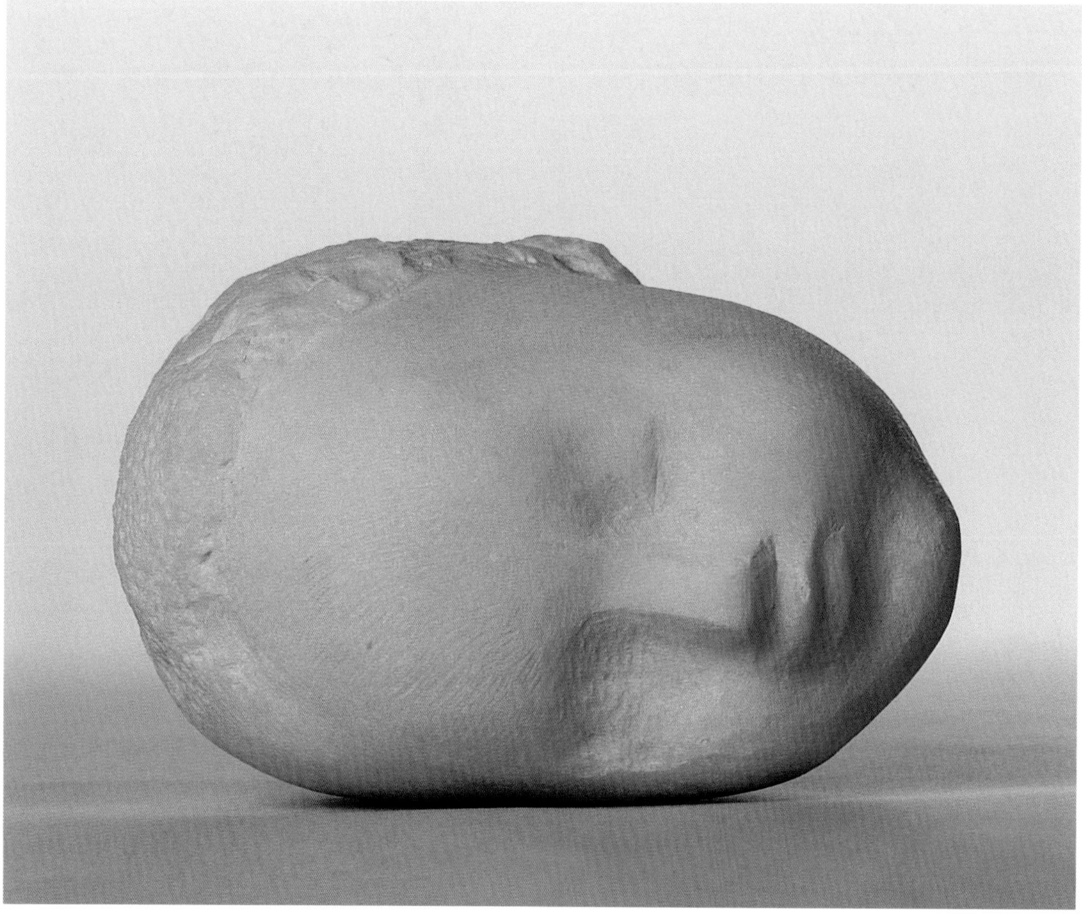

18 **Head of a Sleeping Child**
*c.*1908
White Marble
10.5 × 16.5 × 15 ($4\frac{1}{8} \times 6\frac{1}{2} \times 5\frac{7}{8}$)
Musée National d'Art Moderne,
Centre Georges Pompidou, Paris.
Brancusi Bequest, 1957

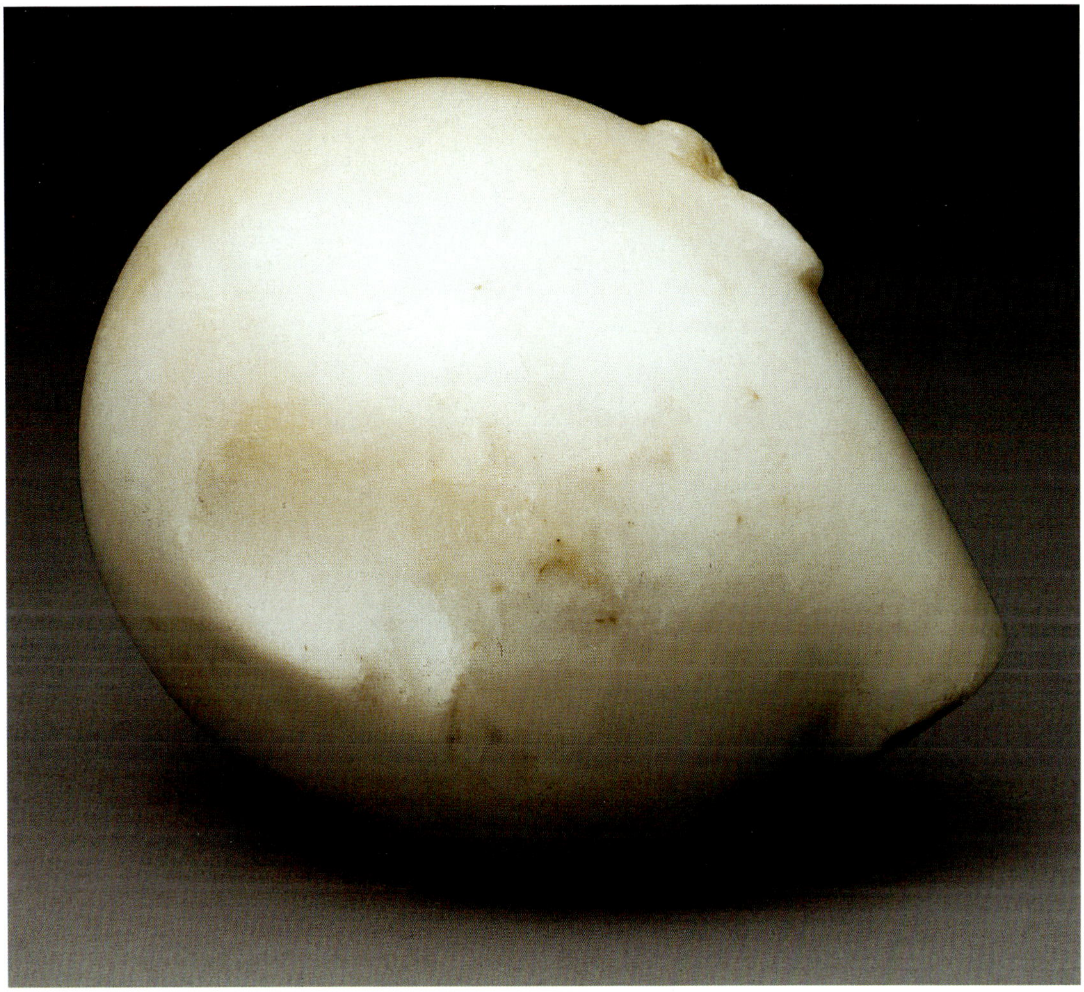

19 **Prometheus**
1911
White Marble
13.8 × 17.8 × 13.7 (5 3/8 × 7 × 5 3/8)
Philadelphia Museum of Art.
The Louise and Walter Arensberg
Collection, 1950

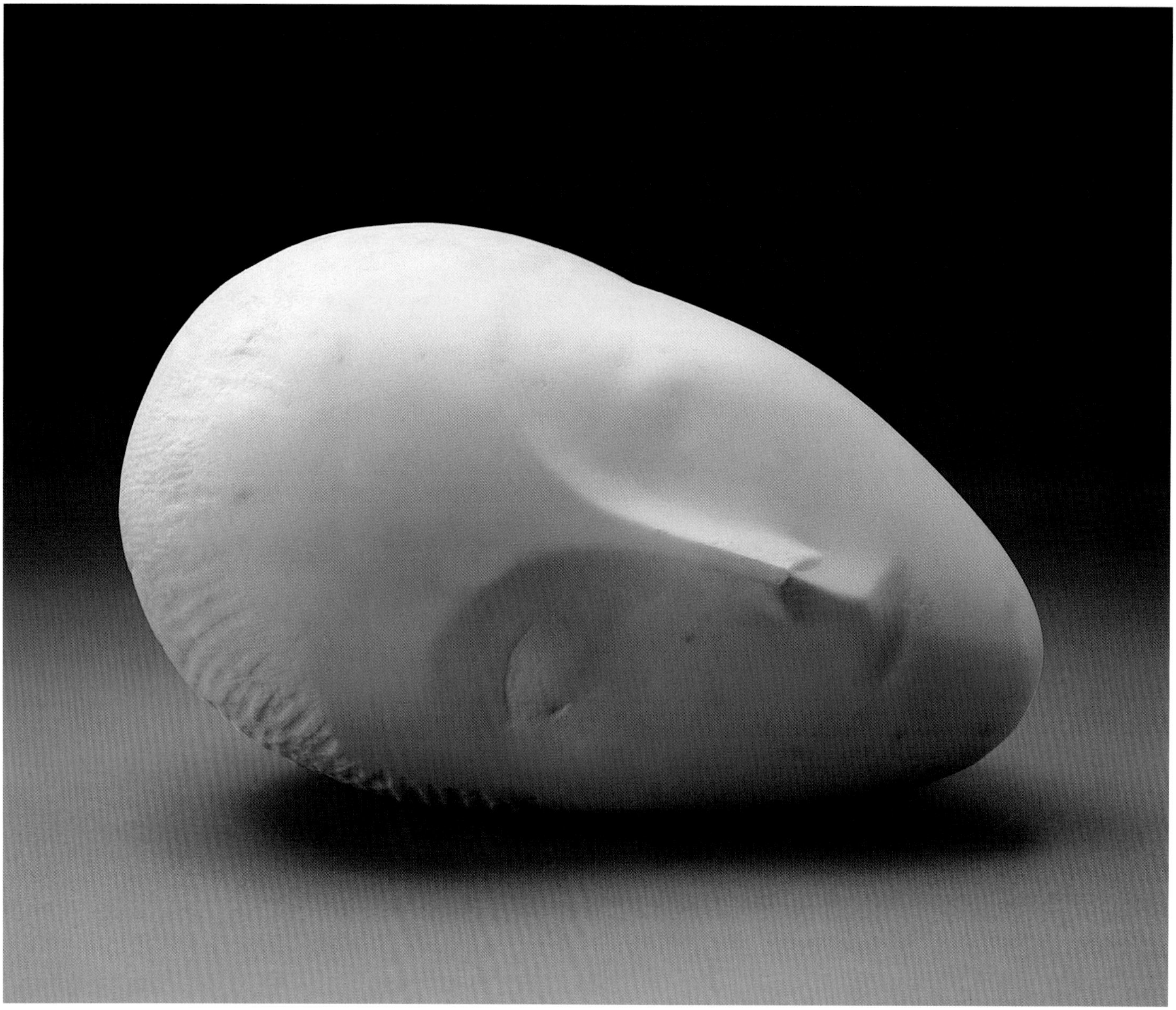

20 **Sleeping Muse I**
1909–10
Marble
17.2 × 27.6 × 21.2 ($6\frac{3}{4} \times 10\frac{7}{8} \times 8\frac{3}{8}$)
Hirshhorn Museum and Sculpture Garden.
Smithsonian Institution,
Gift of Joseph H. Hirshhorn, 1966

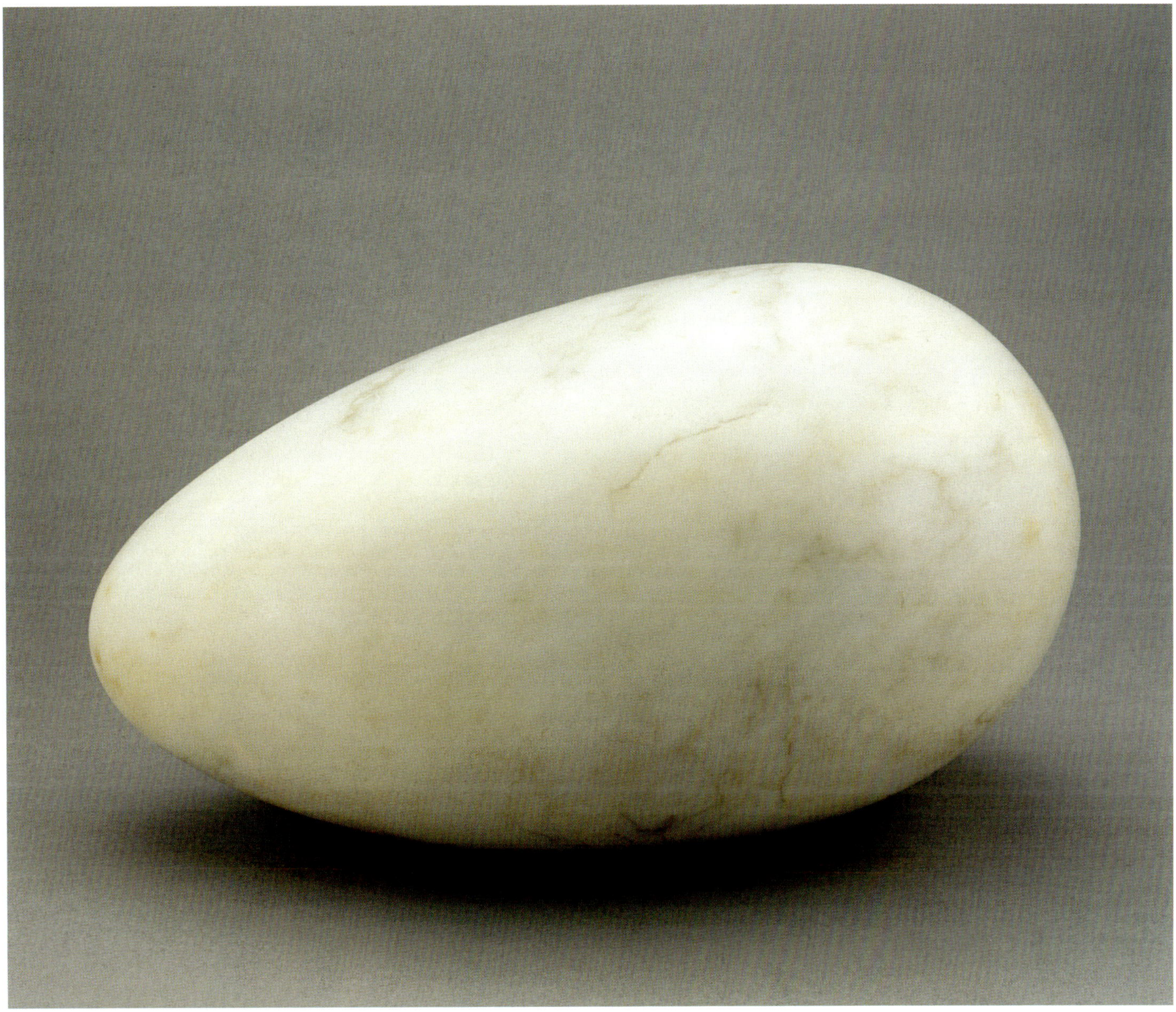

21 **Sculpture for the Blind**
*c.*1920
Veined Marble
17 × 29 × 18.1 (6 3/4 × 11 3/8 × 7 1/8)
Philadelphia Museum of Art.
The Louise and Walter Arensberg
Collection, 1950

22 **Beginning of the World**
*c.*1920
Marble
18.4 × 27.9 × 18.4 (7¼ × 11 × 7¼)

Base of polished steel and limestone, overall height: 57.2 (22½)
Dallas Museum of Art: Foundation for the Arts Collection; gift of Mr and Mrs James H. Clark

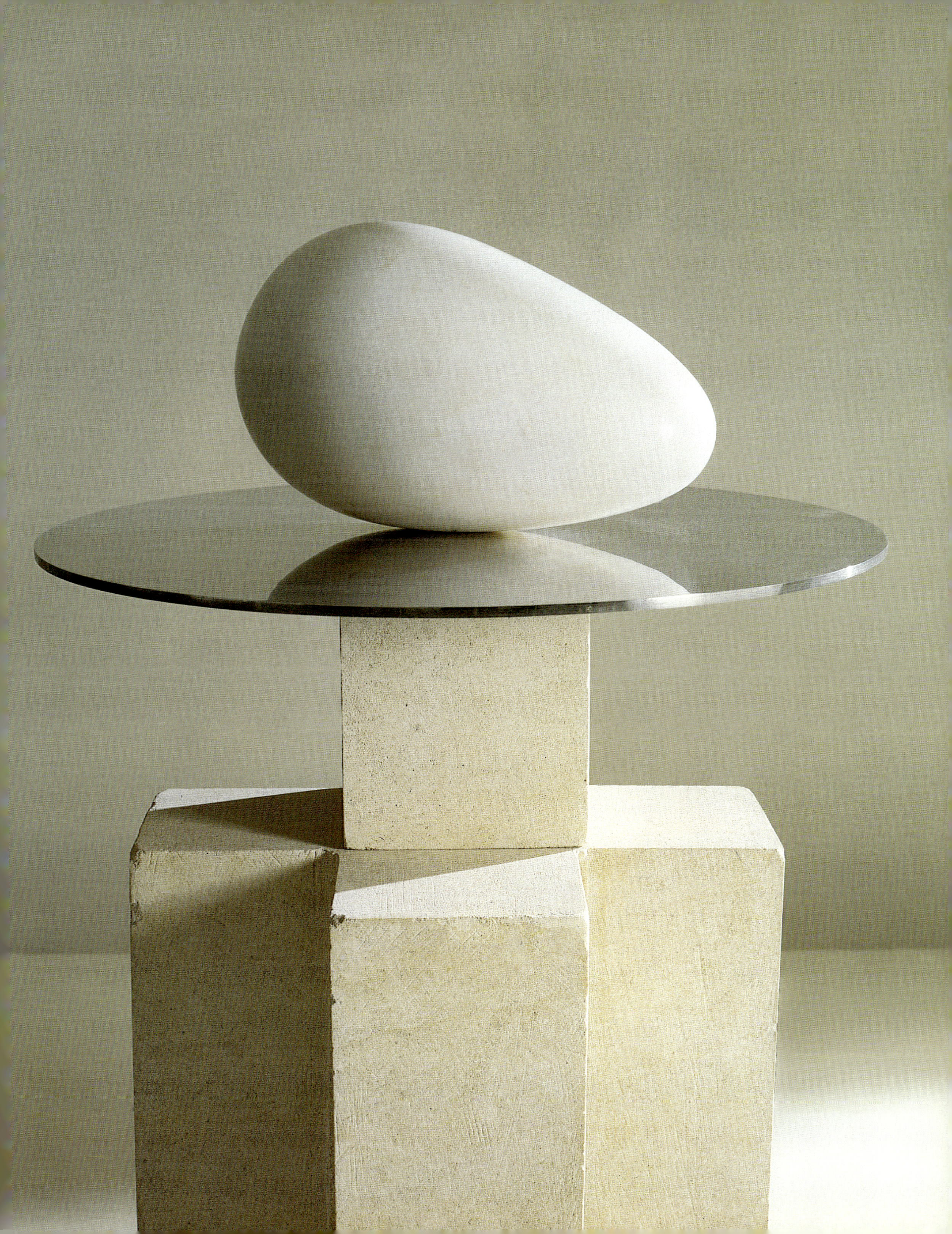

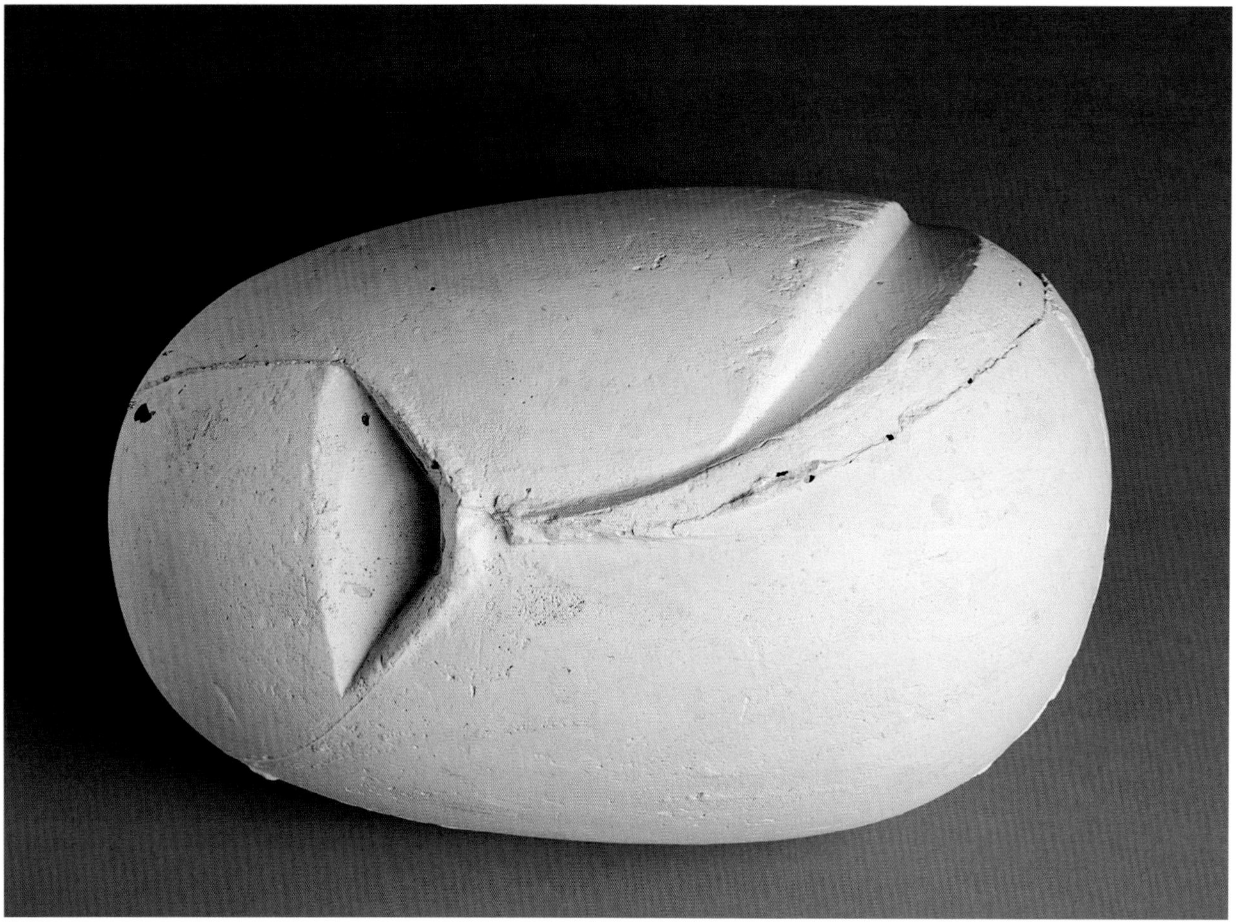

23 **Head of a Child (The First Step)**
1917
Plaster
16.9 × 26 × 19 (6 3/8 × 10 1/4 × 7 1/2)
Musée National d'Art Moderne,
Centre Georges Pompidou, Paris.
Brancusi Bequest, 1957

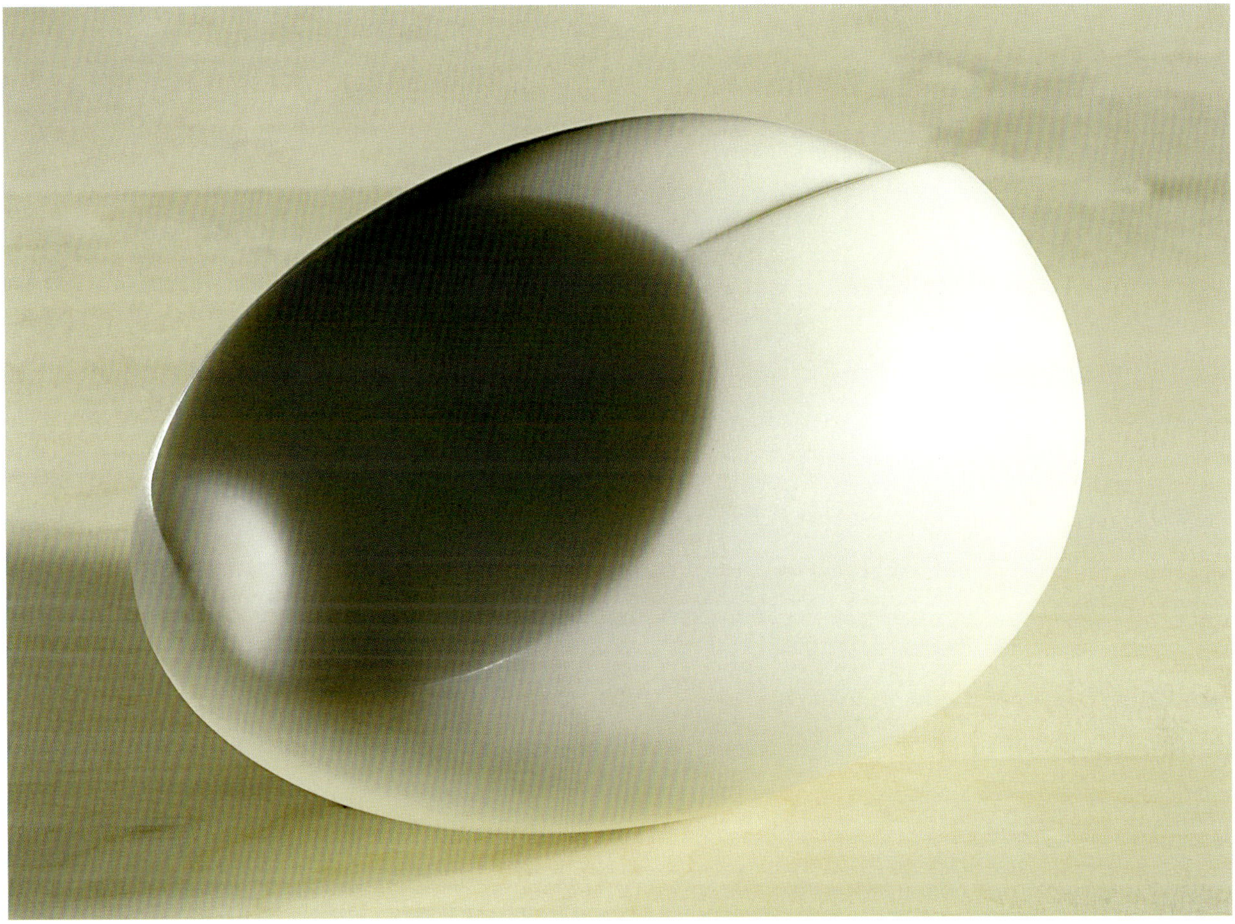

24 **Newborn II**
1919–21
White Marble
16.5 × 25 × 17.5 ($6\frac{1}{2} \times 9\frac{7}{8} \times 6\frac{7}{8}$)
Moderna Museet, Stockholm.
Acquisition 1961 with contributions
from MMV, Gerard Bonnier, Sten Heller,
Charles Nilsson, Hildur Nordin, Ivar Philipson

25 **Head**
1923
Oak
29.2 × 19.4 × 21 (11½ × 7⅝ × 8¼)
Tate. Purchased 1980

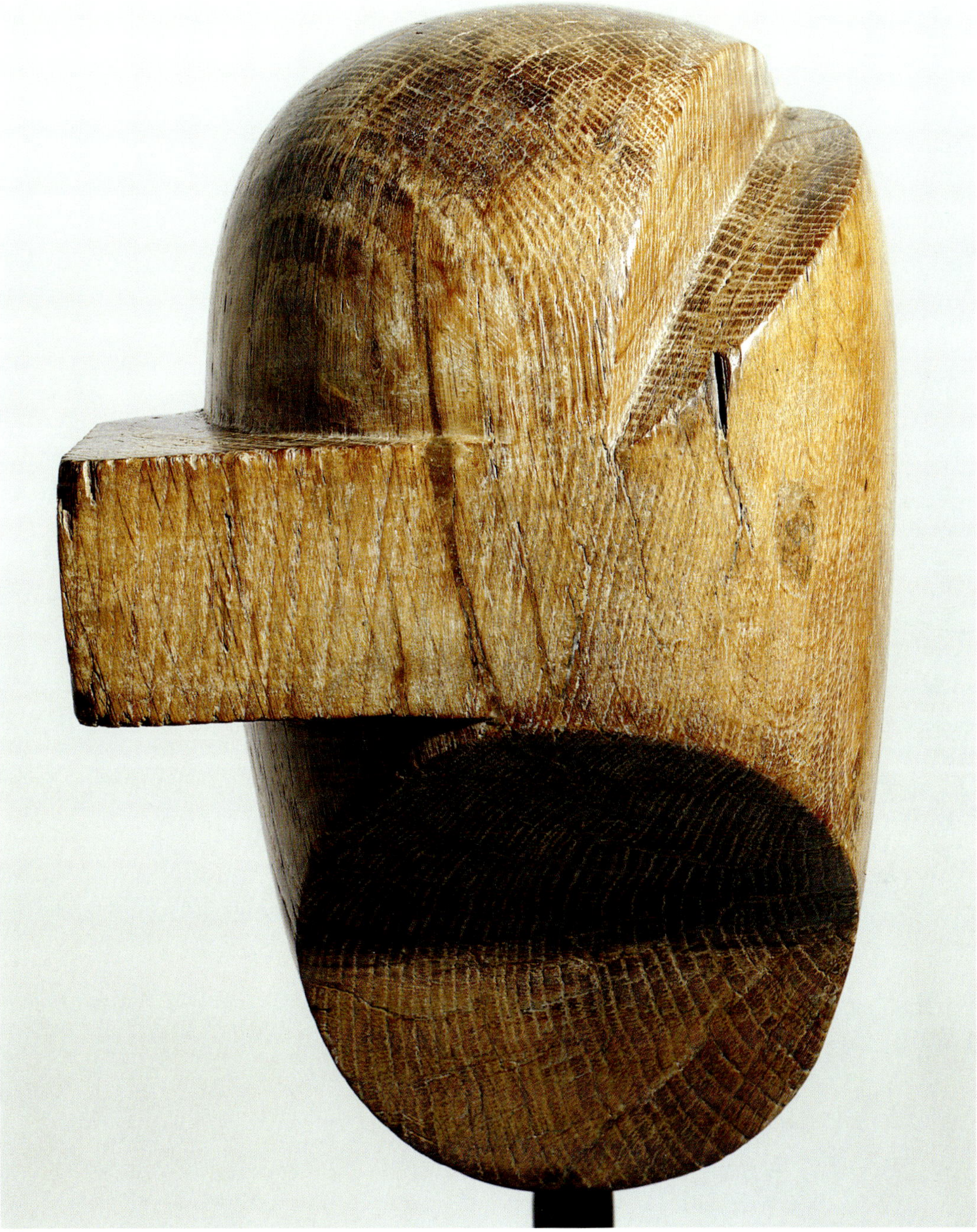

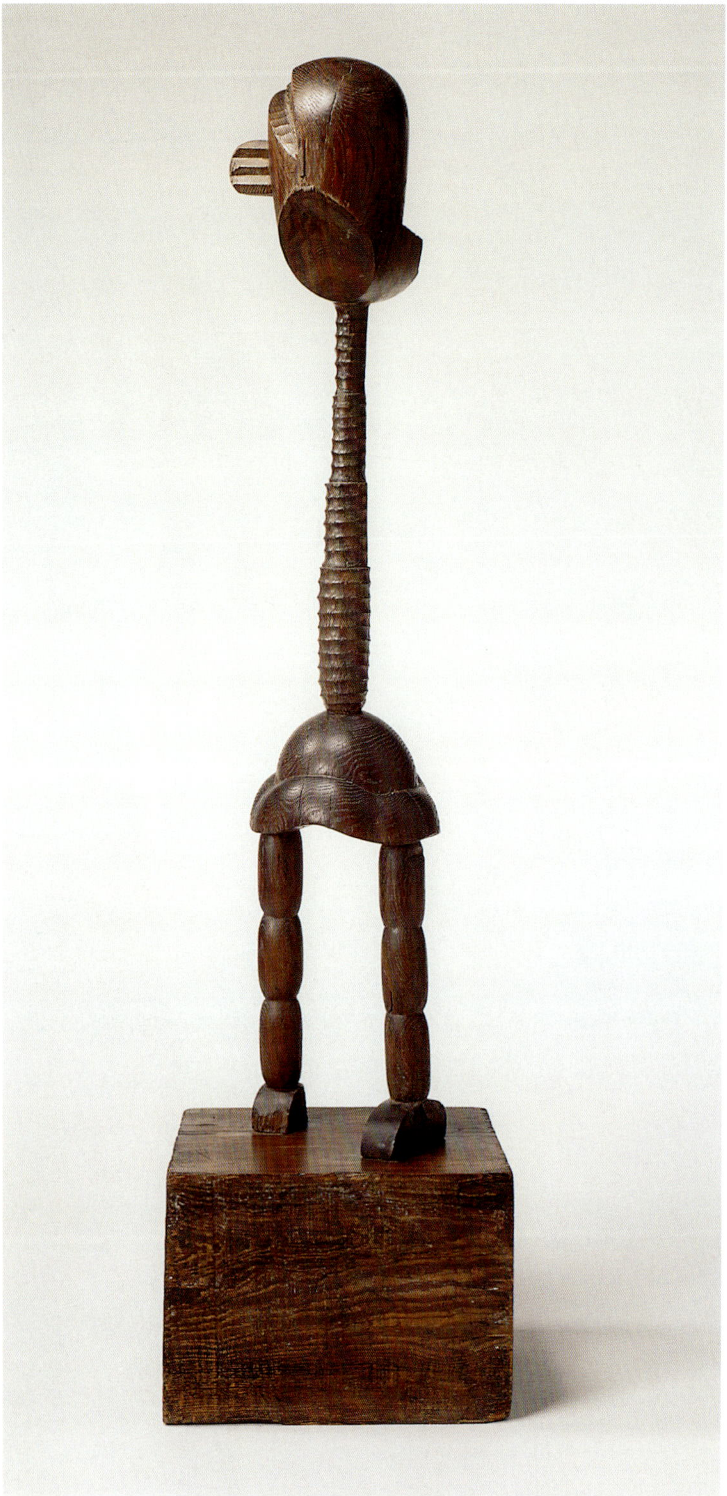

26 **Little French Girl (The First Step III)**
*c.*1914–18
Oak
123.5 × 23.8 × 23.5 ($48\frac{5}{8} \times 9\frac{3}{8} \times 9\frac{1}{4}$)
The Solomon R. Guggenheim Museum, New York.
Gift, Estate of Katherine S. Dreier, 1953

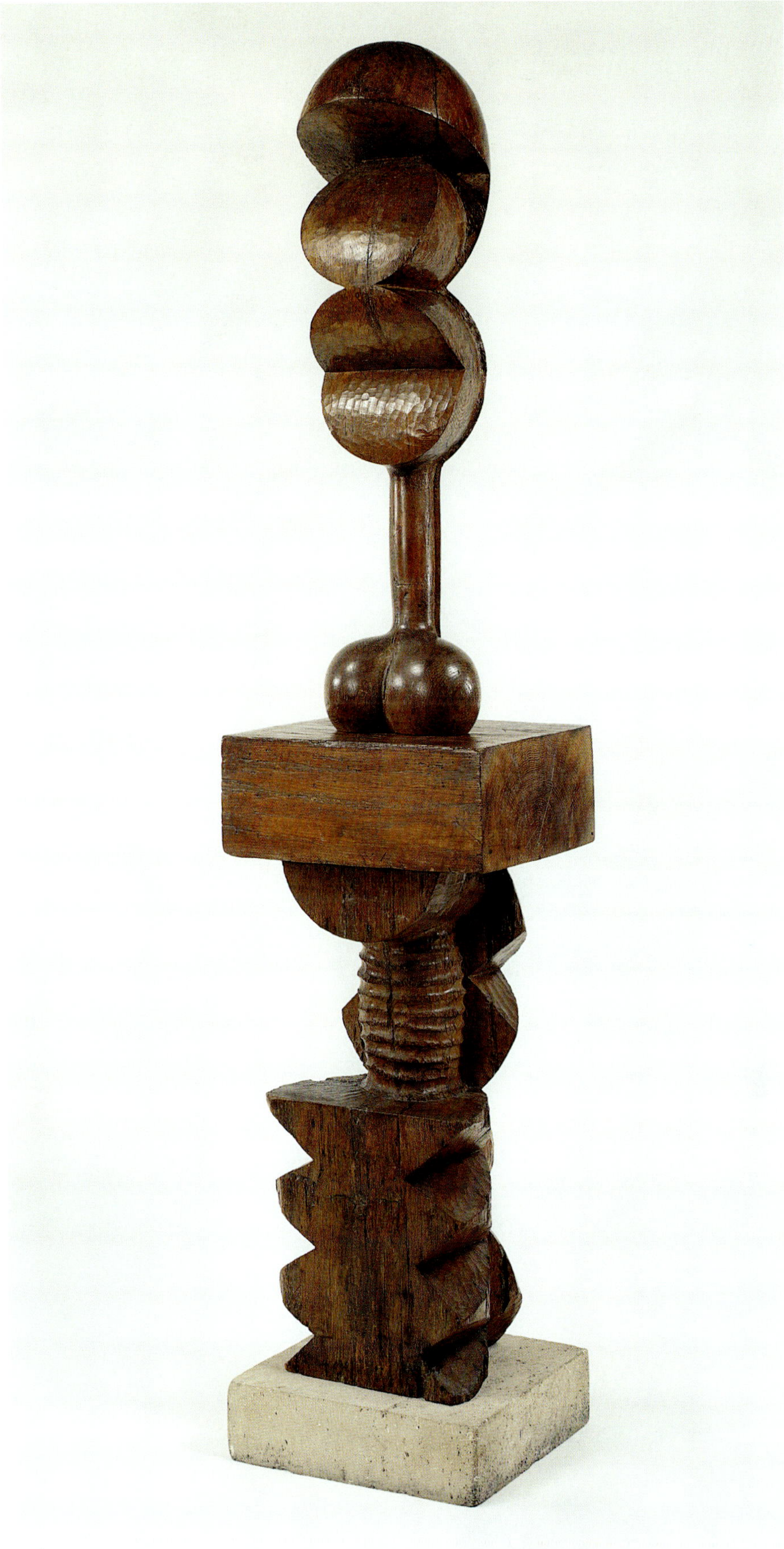

27 **Adam and Eve**
1921
Eve (above): oak
116.5 × 30.8 × 30.2 (45 7/8 × 12 1/8 × 11 7/8)
Adam (below): chestnut
108.9 × 47.5 × 43.5 (42 7/8 × 18 3/4 × 17 1/8)

Limestone base*
13.3 × 46.4 × 46.4 (5 1/4 × 18 1/4 × 18 1/4)
The Solomon R. Guggenheim Museum,
New York

28 **Caryatid II**
1914 and 1926
Red Oak
165.4 × 42.6 × 46 ($65\frac{1}{8}$ × $16\frac{3}{4}$ × $18\frac{1}{8}$)
Fogg Art Museum, Harvard University
Art Museums, Cambridge.
Gift in part of William A. Coolidge,
Joseph H. Hazen Foundation Inc., and Mrs Max Wasserman;
purchase in part from the Francis H. Burr Memorial and
Alpheus Hyatt Funds

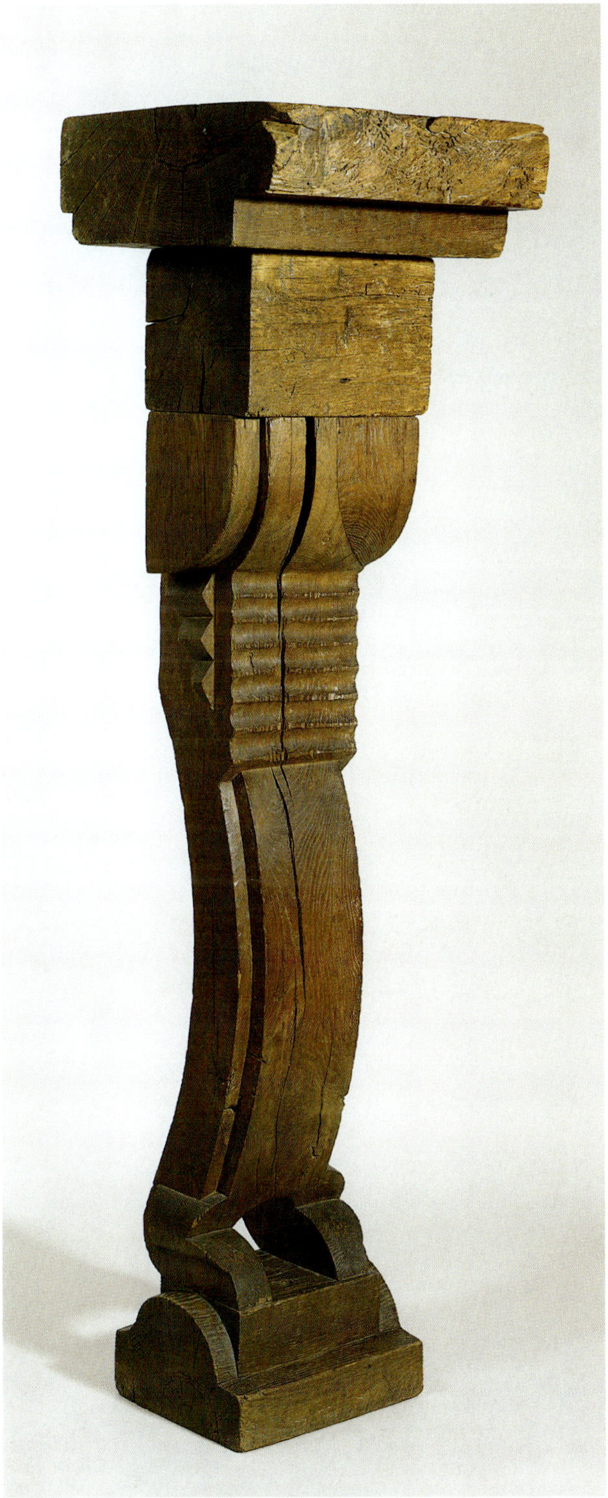

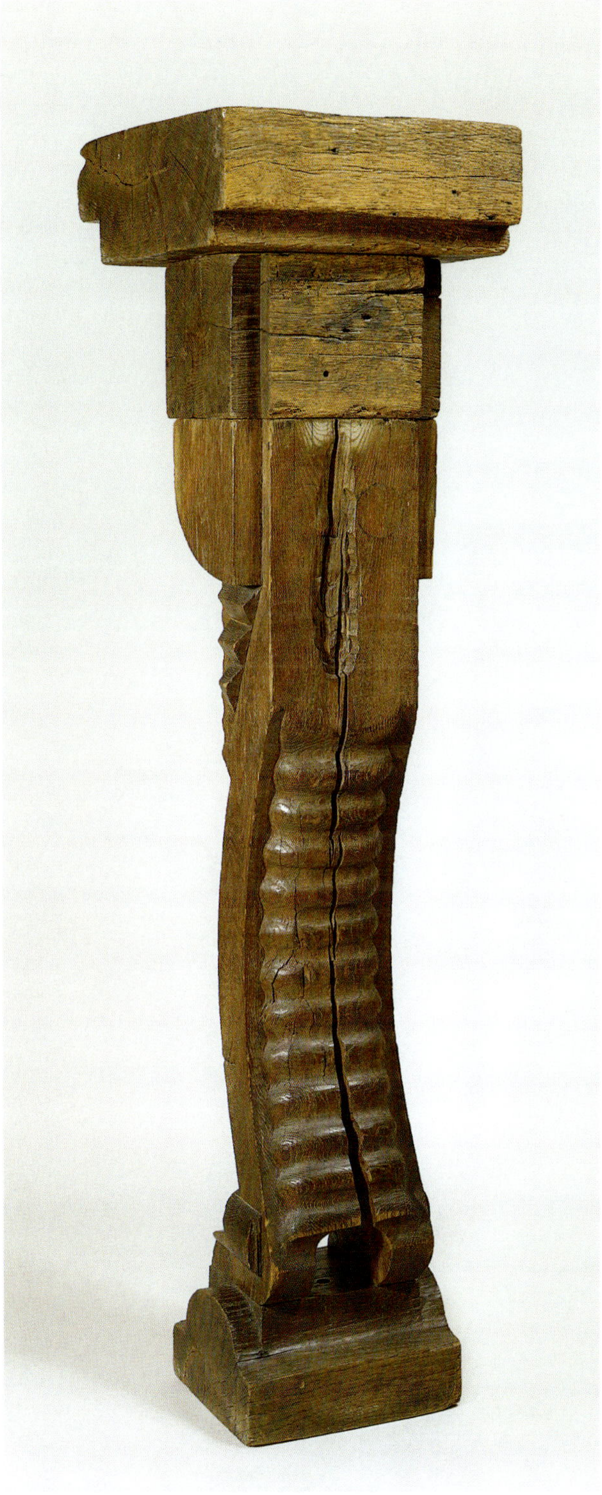

29 **The Sorceress**
1916–24
Walnut
99.1 × 48 × 64.1 (39 × 19 × 25 1/4)

Limestone base
14.9 × 28.6 (5 7/8 × 11 1/4)

Mounted on
Watchdog
1916
Oak
74 × 38.5 × 36 (29 1/8 × 15 1/4 × 14 1/4)
The Solomon R. Guggenheim Museum, New York

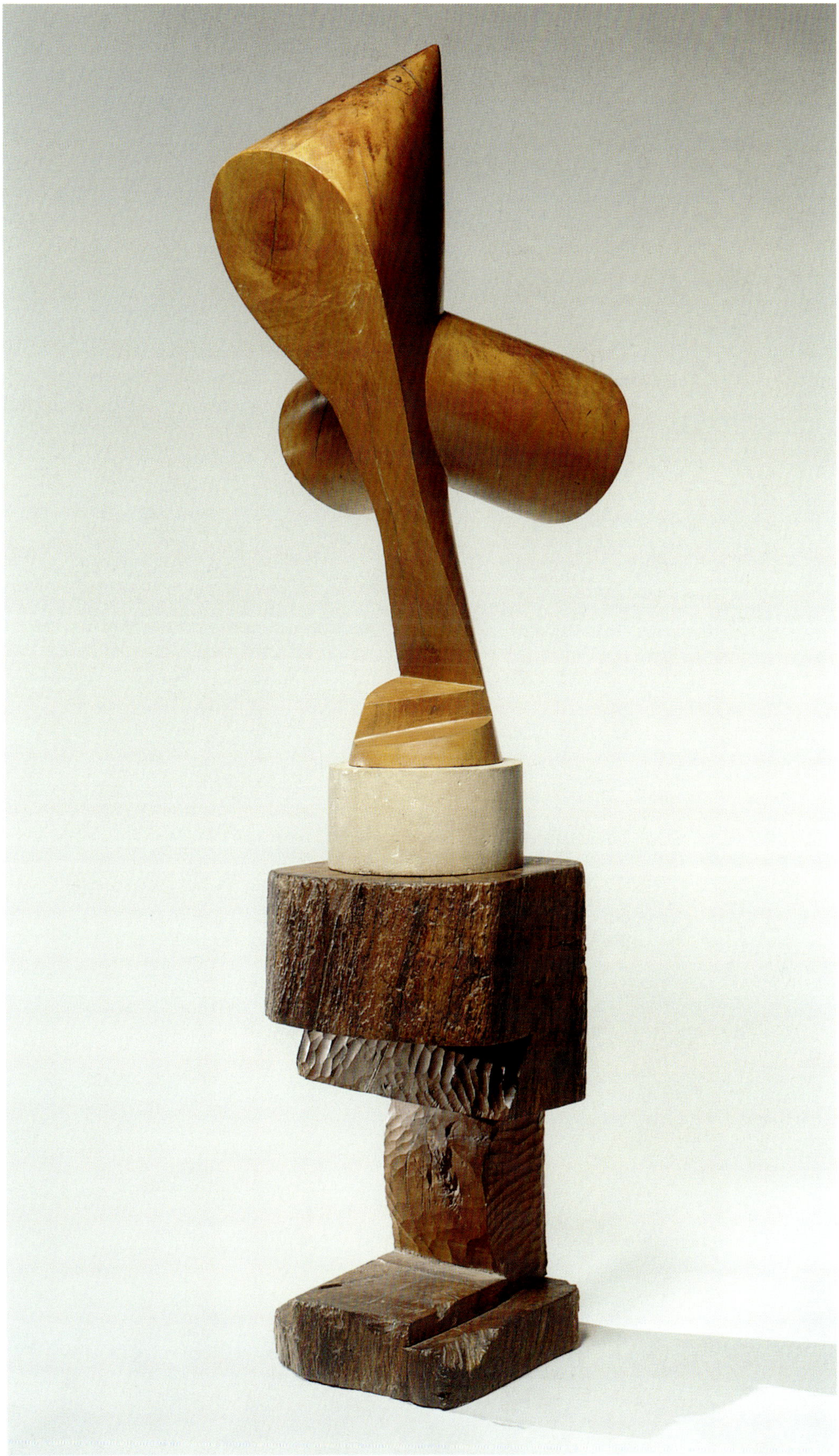

30 **The Cock**
1924
Wild Cherry
121 × 46.3 × 14.6 (47 5/8 × 18 1/4 × 5 3/4)
(including cylindrical base)
The Museum of Modern Art, New York.
Gift of LeRay W. Berdeau, 1959

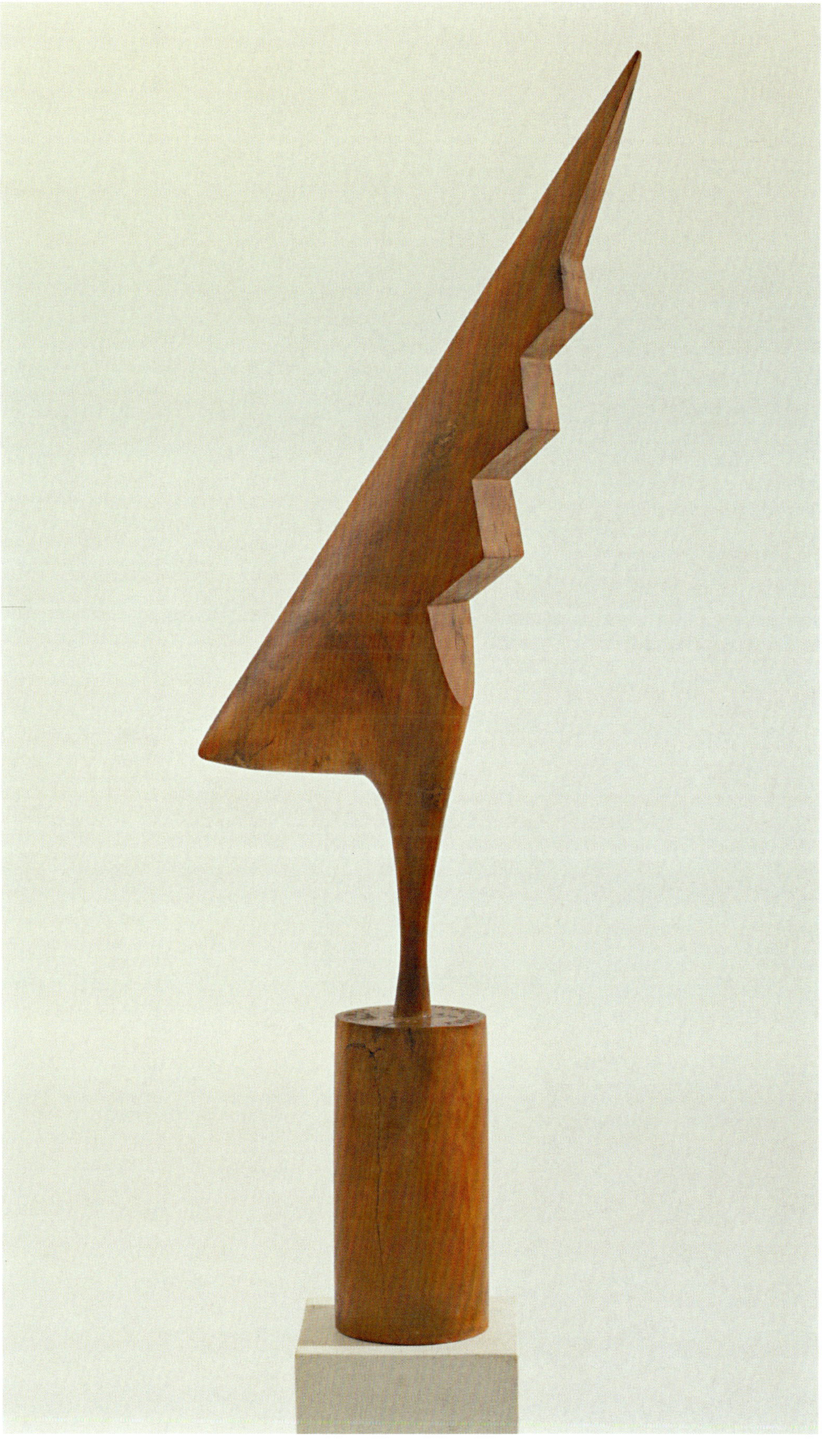

31 **King of Kings**
*c.*1938
Oak
300 × 48.3 × 46 (118 3/8 × 19 × 18 1/8)
The Solomon R. Guggenheim Museum,
New York

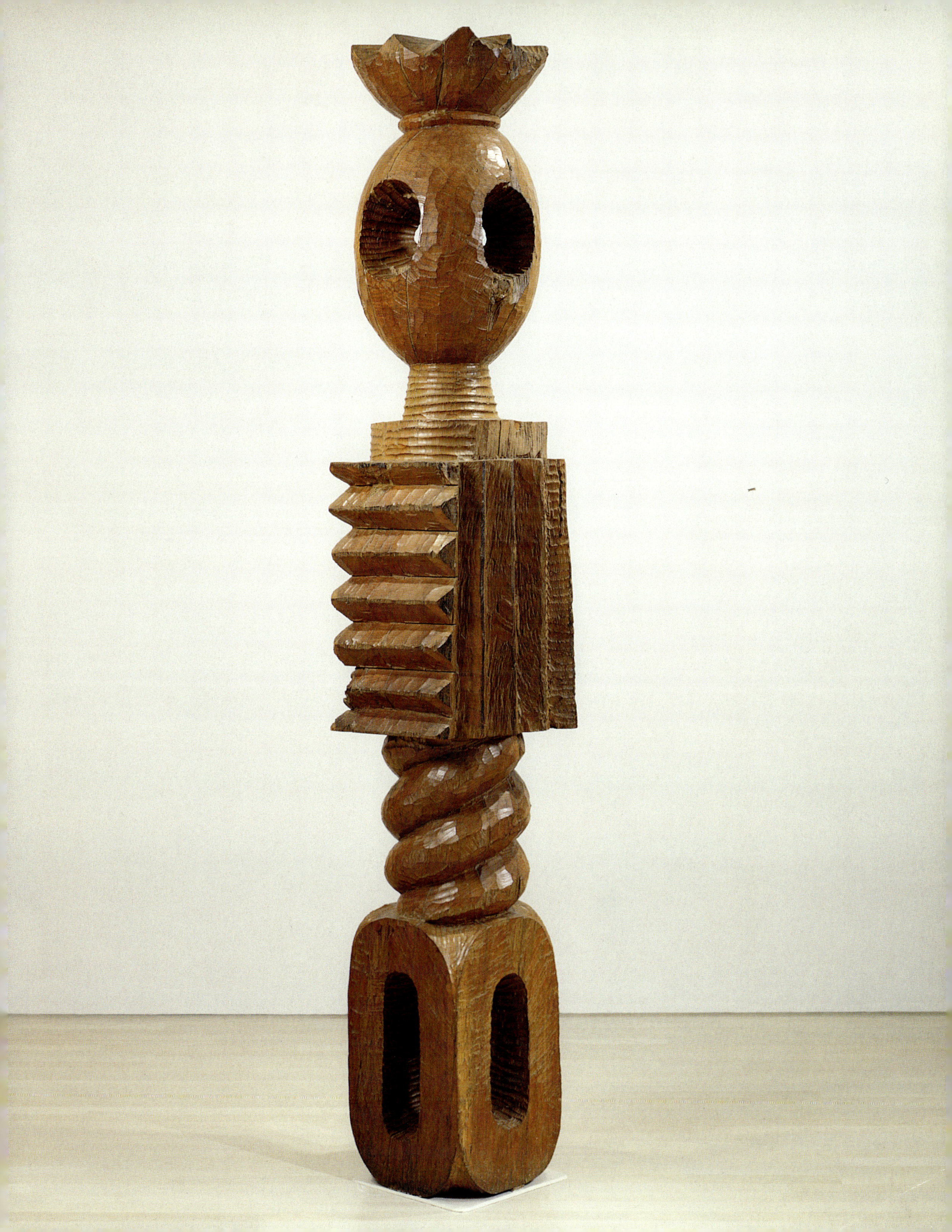

32 **The Seal (Miracle)**
1924–36
White Marble
108.6 × 114 × 33 (42 3/4 × 44 7/8 × 13)

Three-part base of white marble and limestone
44.5 × 149.5 (21 1/2 × 58 3/4)
The Solomon R. Guggenheim Museum, New York
[Exhibited New York only]

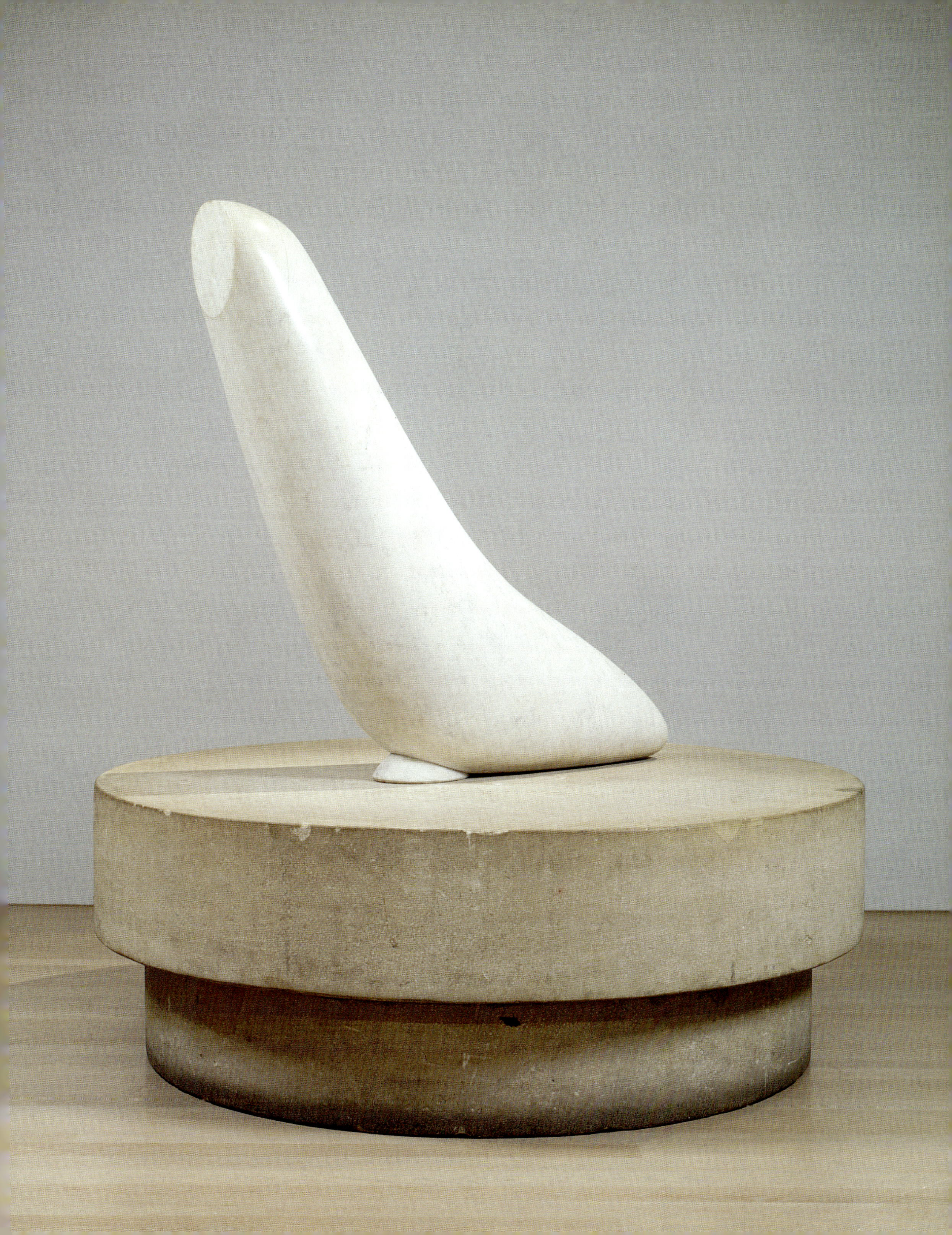

33 **Flying Turtle (Turtle)**
1940–45
White marble on limestone base
31.8 × 93 × 69 (12½ × 36⅝ × 27⅛)
The Solomon R. Guggenheim Museum, New York

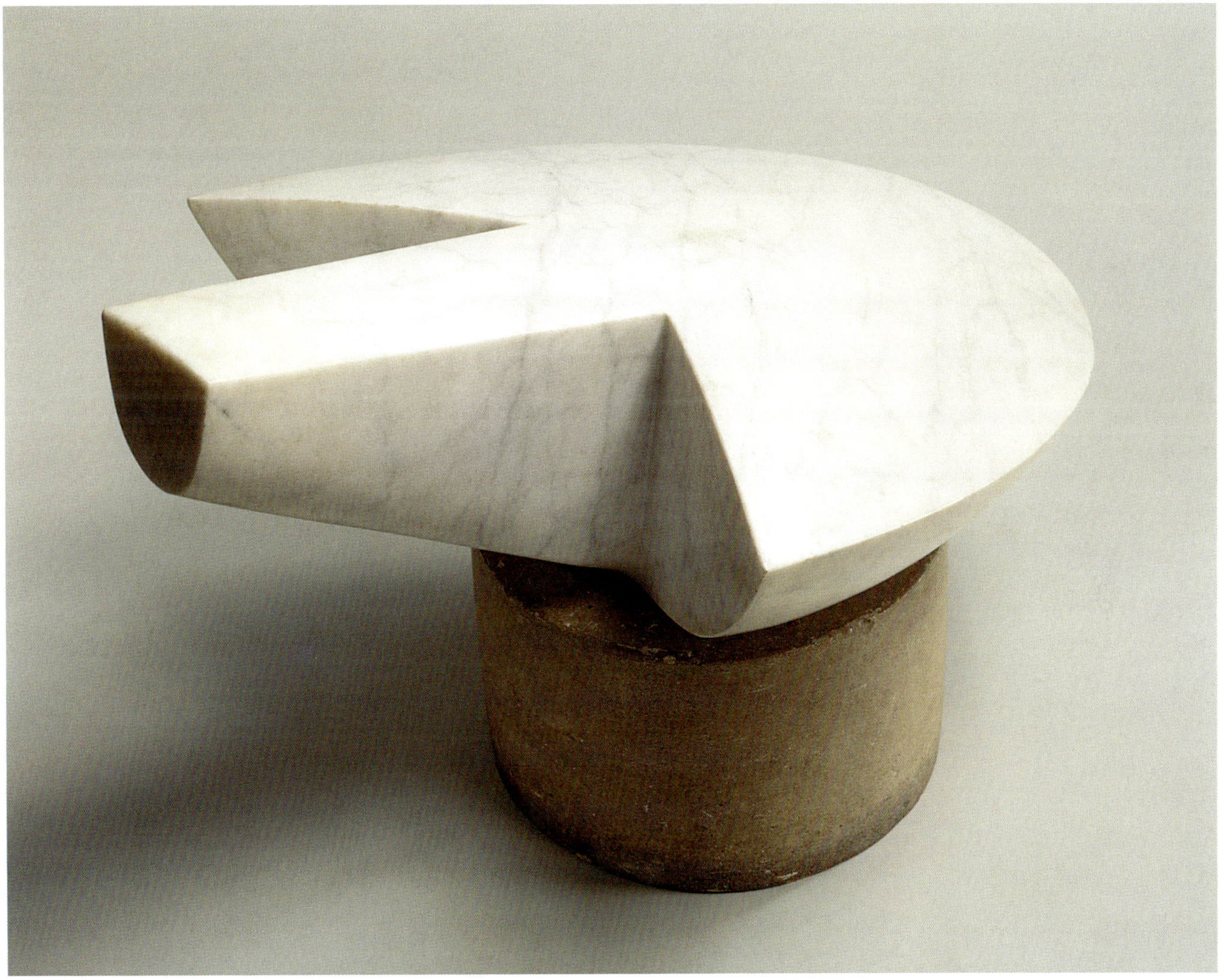

34 **Maiastra**
1912
Bronze
55.5 × 17 × 17.8 (21 7/8 × 6 3/4 × 7)
Circumference: 59.7 (23 1/2)

Two-part limestone base
33.5 × 22 × 19 (13 1/8 × 8 5/8 × 7 1/2)
Tate. Purchased 1973

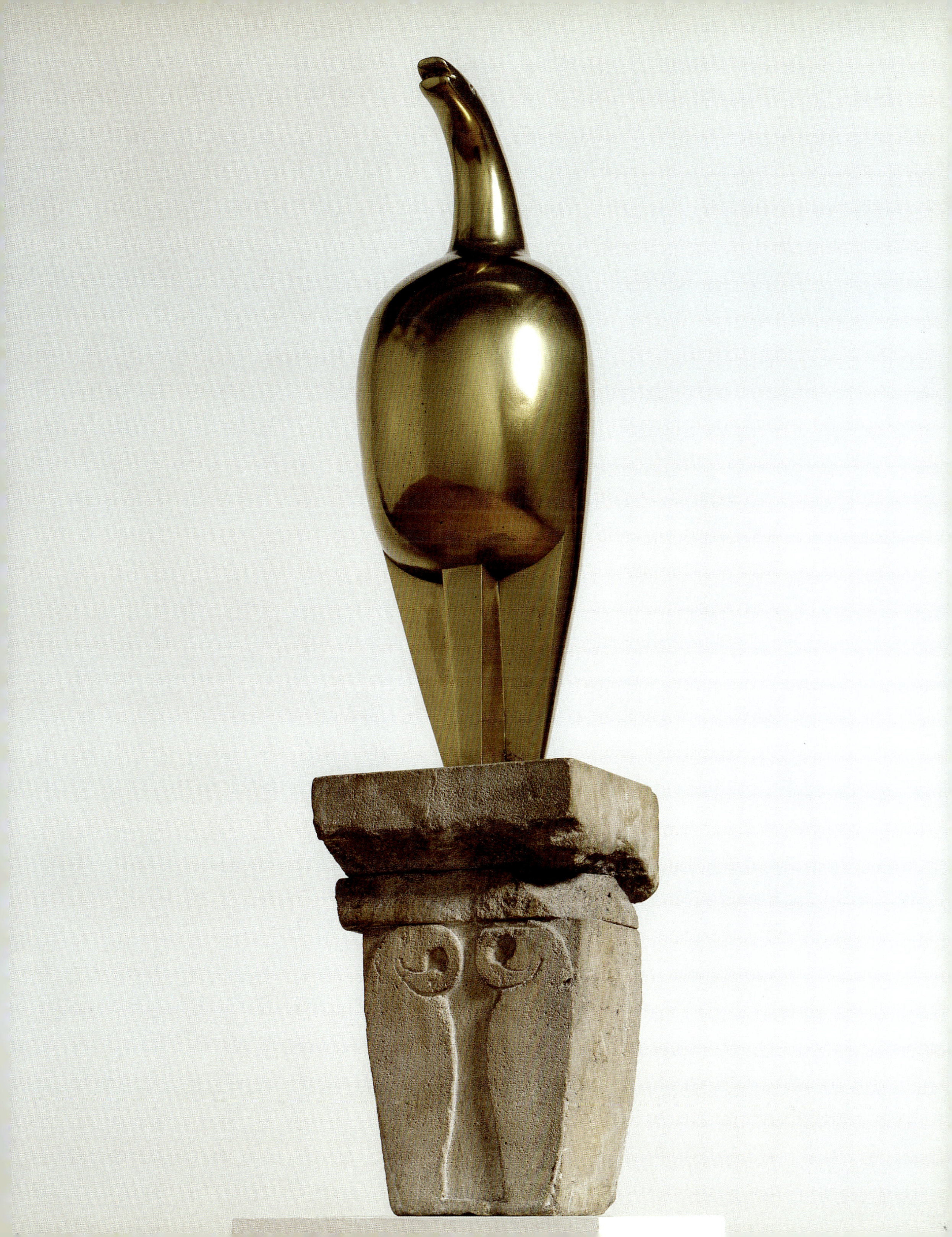

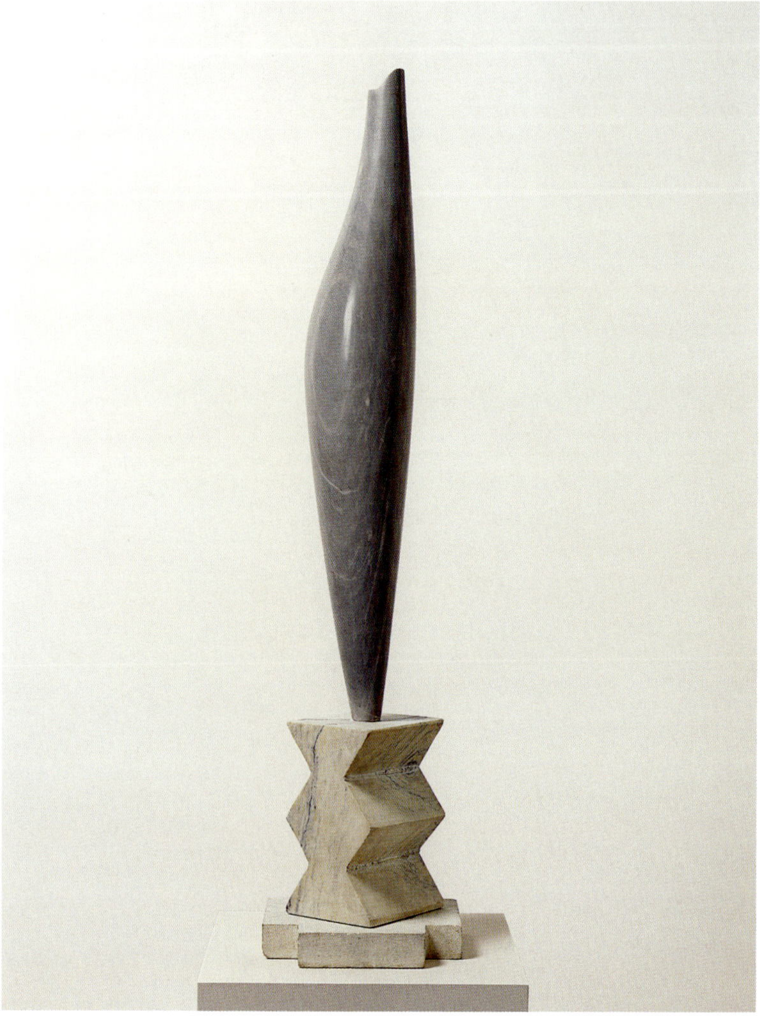

35 **Bird**
1923–47
Blue-grey marble
Height: 89.2 (35 1/8)
Circumference 48.1 (19)

Two-part base of veined marble and limestone
Overall height: 31.2 (12 1/2)
Fondation Beyeler, Riehen/Basel

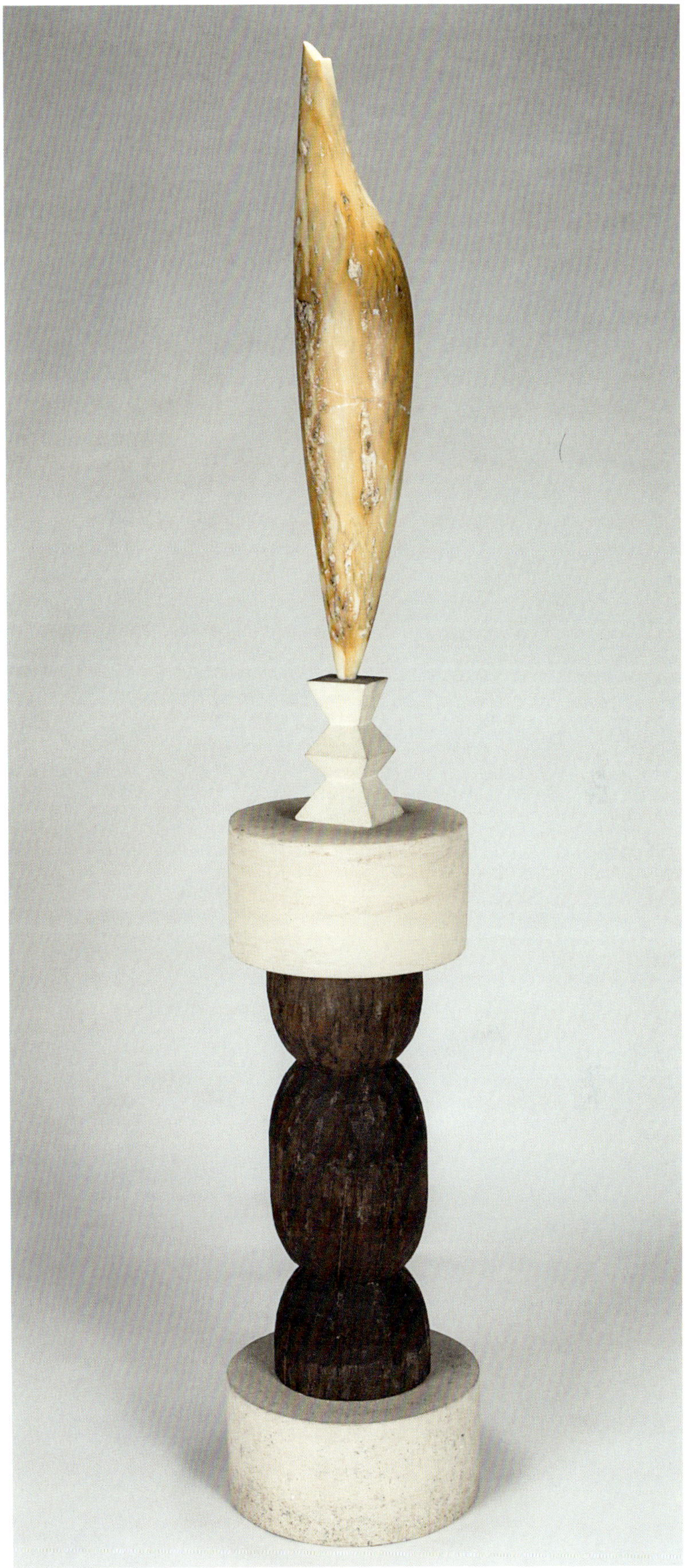

36 **Yellow Bird**
1919
Yellow marble
Height: 92 (36¼)
Circumference: 52.1 (20½)

Four-part base of limestone and oak
Overall height: 221.6 (87¼)
Yale University Art Gallery, New Haven.
Collection of the Société Anonyme,
Bequest of Katherine S. Dreier

37 **Bird in Space**
1930s
Polished brass
Height 137.7 (53)
Max circumference 35.4 (13 5/8)
Stone base
Height: 17 (6 3/4)
Peggy Guggenheim Collection, Venice
(Solomon R. Guggenheim Foundation, New York)

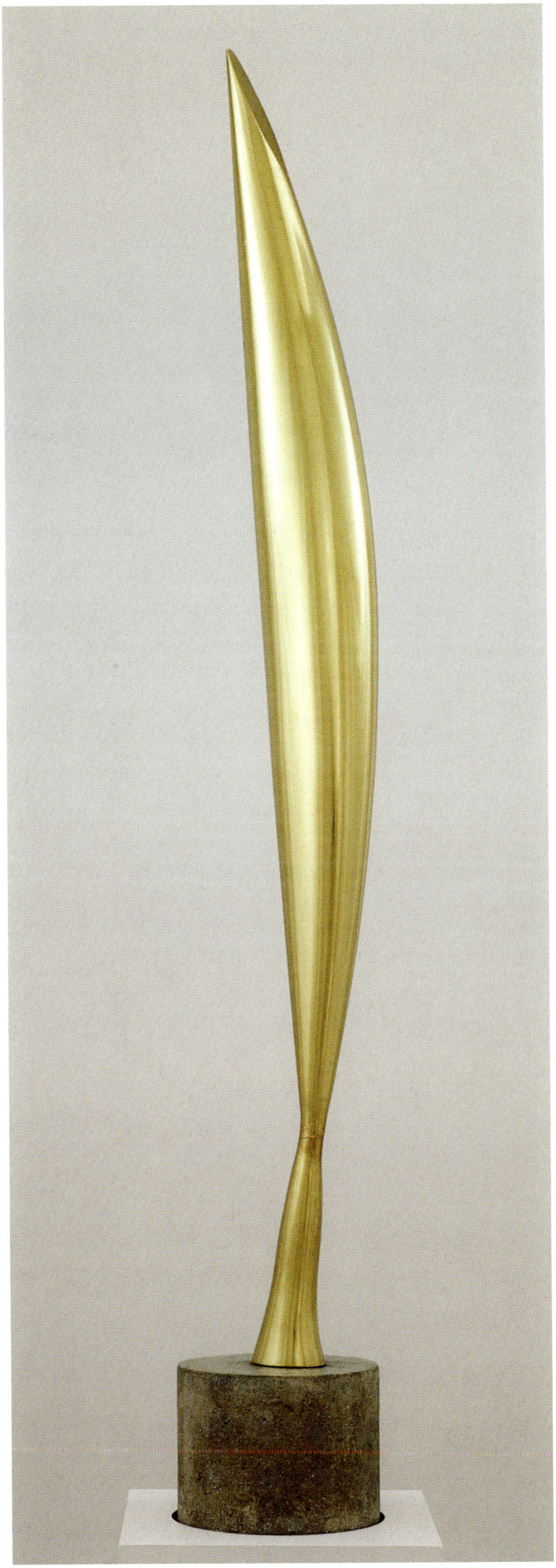
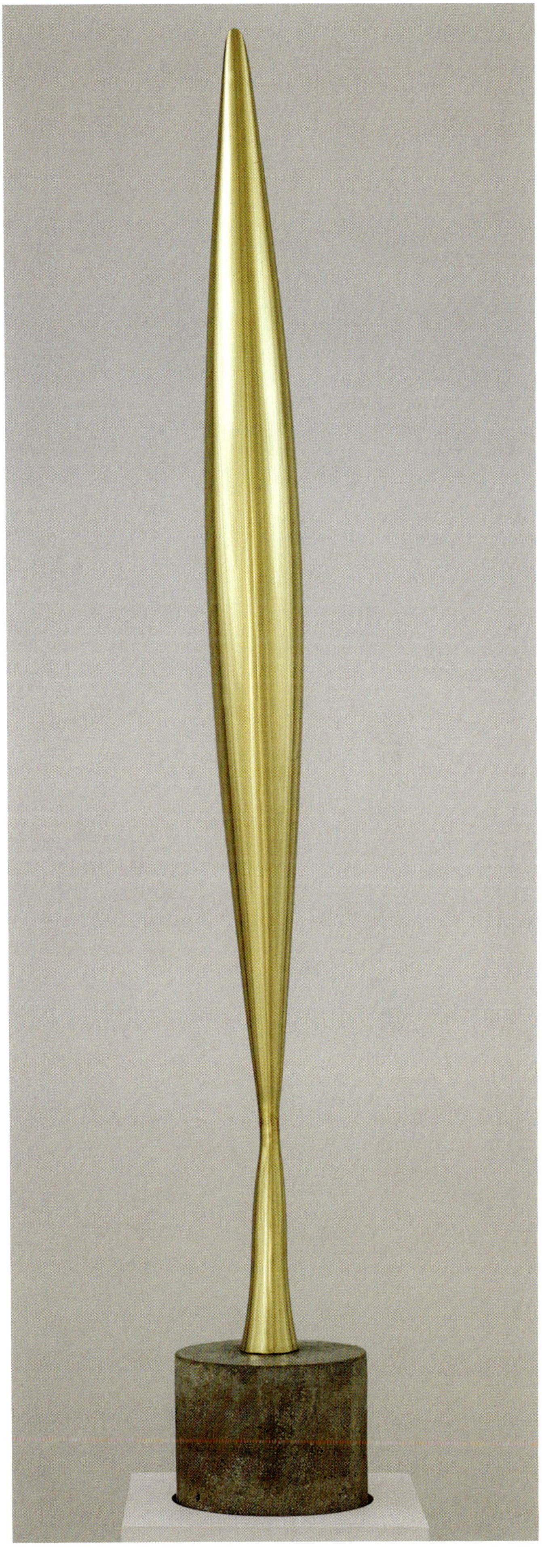

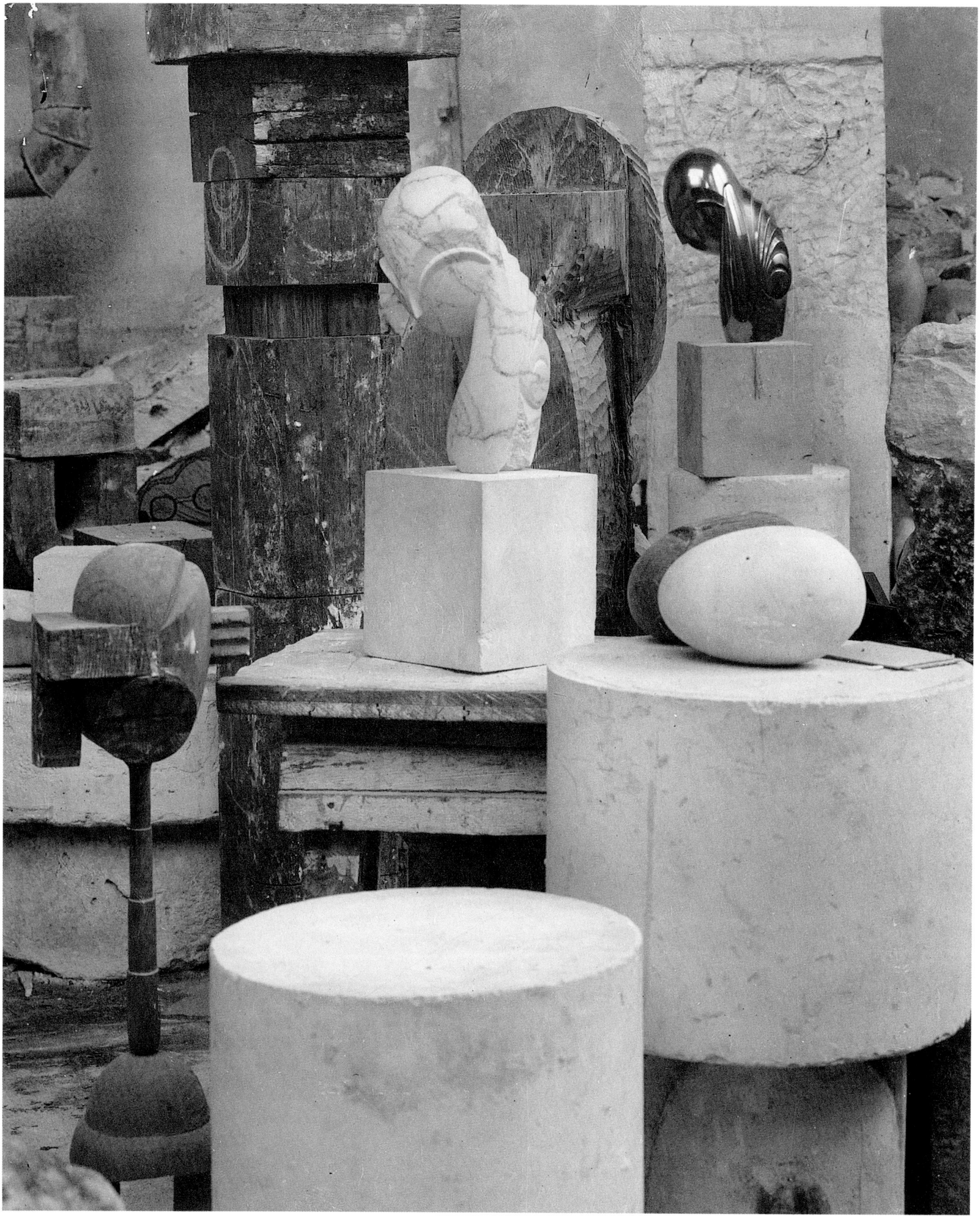

Selected aphorisms

MATTHEW GALE

Brancusi's statements generally take an epigrammatic form. An idea is proposed only for the contrary to be shown to be equally true. In these cases, he tends to favour the former over the latter, with the distinction arising from a division between those people enlightened by experience and those who are still searching. Although this reinforces Brancusi's position and reputation as a 'master', with its overtones of mysticism, he stressed the need for humility.

The aphorisms broadly fall into three categories: those addressing what it means to be an artist, those with more spiritual or philosophical intent, and those of a broadly romantic nature. Such maxims were favoured by many artists, but the direct precursor would appear to be Friedrich Nietzsche. 'A good aphorism,' the German philosopher wrote, 'is too hard for the tooth of time and is not consumed by all millennia, although it serves every time for nourishment: thus it is the great paradox of literature, the intransitory amid the changing.'[1]

It is not certain when Brancusi began committing thoughts to paper, though it may have become a regular activity in the 1920s. A small number were gathered by his friend Irène (Irina) Codreanu and published in 1925.[2] The catalogues of two solo exhibitions in New York in the following year carried English translations of four and seven aphorisms respectively; the latter version opens the present selection.[3] Various small selections were published soon after and many other notes of sayings have survived.[4] Those gathered here are largely concerned with artistic matters.

Fig.40 **Studio view with Mlle Pogany II**, *c.*1921 (AM4002-255(1), PH10A)
Centre Pompidou, Paris

1 Friedrich Nietzsche, 'Mixed Opinions and Maxims' (1879), aphorism 168, in Walter Kaufman (ed.), *Basic Writings of Nietzsche*, New York 1968, p.156.

2 Irène Codreanu, '"Propos" de Brancusi', *This Quarter*, vol.I, no.1, Jan. 1925, pp.235–6

3 Exhibition of Sculpture by Brancusi, Wildenstein Galleries, New York, Feb.–Mar. 1926, and '"Propos" by Brancusi', in *Brancusi*, Brummer Gallery, New York, Nov.–Dec. 1926.

4 Selected manuscript notes were translated in Hulten, Dumitresco and Istrati 1988, pp.103, 269. Transcriptions for many of these, and others, have been gathered in Doïna Lemny, 'Notes autographiques de Brancusi' in Tabart and Lemny 2003; English translations of these are mine. More than 100 were published in Italian by Paola Mola as *Constantin Brancusi Aforismi*, Milan 2001.

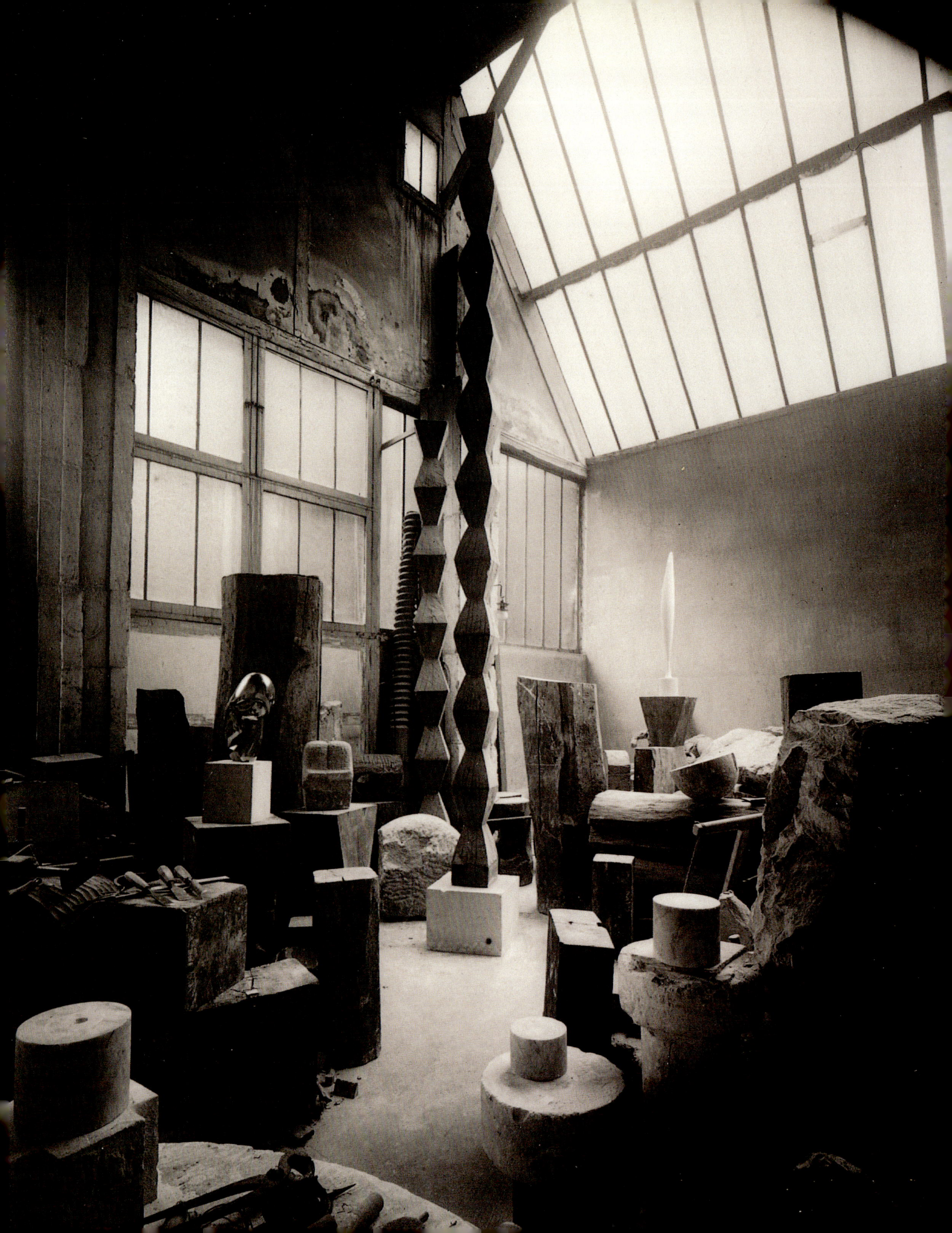

Direct cutting is the true road to sculpture, but also the most dangerous for those who don't know how to walk. And in the end, direct or indirect, cutting means nothing, it is the complete thing that counts.[5]

High polish is a necessity which certain approximately absolute forms demand of some materials. It is not always appropriate, it is even very harmful for certain other forms.[6]

Simplicity is not an end in art, but one arrives at simplicity in spite of oneself, in approaching the real sense of things. Simplicity is complexity itself, and one has to be nourished by its essence in order to understand its value.[7]

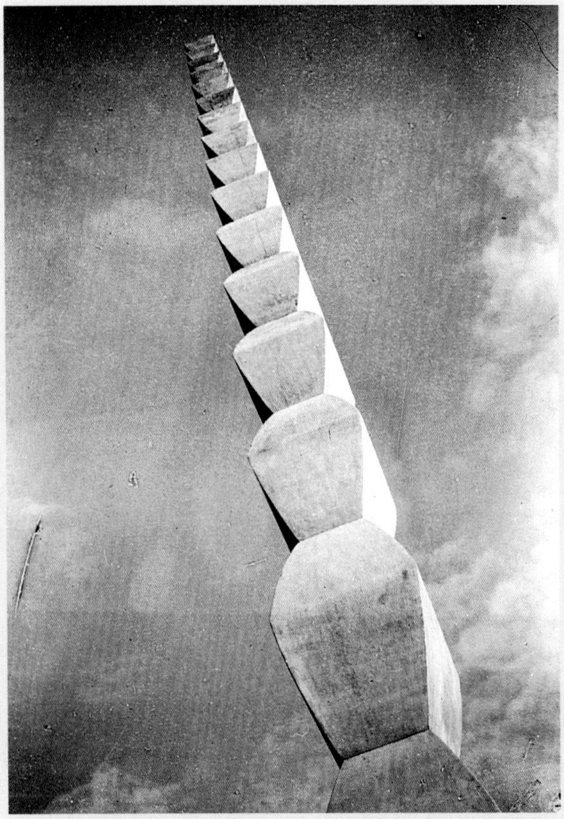

OPPOSITE
Fig.41 **Studio view with Endless Columns and Mlle Pogany**, 1925 (AM4002-298, PH58, modern print)
ABOVE
Fig.42 **Endless Column at Târgu Jiu**, *c.*1938 (AM4002-629, PH585, modern print)
PAGE 131
Fig.43 **Studio view with Large Cocks**, *c.*1940–5 (AM4002-342(2), PH133, modern print)
Including **Flying Turtle**
PAGE 132
Fig.44 **Studio view**, *c.*1930–3 (AM4002-348, PH117, modern print)
Including **Bird in Space**, **Endless Columns** and **Fish**
Centre Pompidou, Paris

5 The seven opening aphorisms are taken from the Brummer Gallery catalogue of late 1926, the first four having already been published in the Wildenstein catalogue. The wording differs slightly. It is notable that 'taille directe' is given literally as 'direct cutting' rather than the (later) more customary 'direct carving'. Notes among the artist's papers indicate that this first aphorism at one time followed the fourth (Tabart and Lemny 2003, p.90) though Brancusi evidently revised the sequence in preparation for publication. His satisfaction with the group is confirmed by their publication again in *De Stijl*, vol.7, 1927, pp.81–2, and, in a slightly different selection, in 'Quelques propos de Brancusi', *Cahiers d'Art*, vol.4, no.8–9, 1929, p.382.
6 These first two aphorisms appear consecutively under the title 'Propos' (literally 'remark') on a manuscript now in the Centre Pompidou (reproduced in Hulten, Dumitresco and Istrati 1988, p.68), on which the artist's spelling has been corrected in another (perhaps Codreanu's) hand.
7 The second sentence was not included in the Wildenstein catalogue.

It is not the things that are difficult to make, but to put ourselves in [a] condition to make them.[8]

When we are no longer children, we are already dead.

To see far, that is one thing; to go there that is another.[9]

It is something to be clever, but being honest is worthwhile.[10]

Beauty is absolute balance.[11]

Theories are nothing but meaningless specimens. It is only actions that count.[12]

Male nudes in sculpture are not even as beautiful as toads.[13]

[On presenting his sculptures]
Do not look for obscure formulae or for mysteries I give you pure joy
Look at them until you see them
Those closest to God have seen them.[14]

The greatest happiness is the contact between our essence and the eternal essence.[15]

In order to make free and universal art one must be a God to create it, a King to control it and a slave to make it.[16]

The good Lord is dead. That's why the world is adrift.[17]

8 As noted above, the artist's papers (see Tabart and Lemny 2003, p.90) indicate that this phrase at one time prefaced the first aphorism. Brancusi subsequently uncoupled the difficulty of creativity from the solution of direct carving.

9 This philosophical message is one of Brancusi's favourites judging by the number of variants, see Tabart and Lemny 2003, pp.90, 91 and 94.

10 This maxim appears in a number of variants, perhaps developed over many years. One version is given as 'Shrewdness has its points – but sincerity's worth the trouble' (Hulten, Dumitresco and Istrati 1988, p.90).

11 This is the first of eight aphorisms published in 'Quelques propos de Brancusi', *Cahiers d'Art*, vol.4, no.8–9, 1929, p.382. Only three of these are grouped here, as the other five repeat (in a different order) those published in the 1926 Brummer catalogue that opens the present selection. They are: 'It is not the things. . .' and 'When we are no longer children. . .' that were placed second and third in *Cahiers d'Art* in 1929, and 'Direct cutting. . .', 'High polish. . .' and 'Simplicity. . .' that formed the final trio. Just as in the Wildenstein version, the aphorism on simplicity was published with the second sentence.

12 This is fourth of the eight aphorisms in *Cahiers d'Art* 1929; an alternative version is given as 'Theories are nothing but colourless equations' (Hulten, Dumitresco and Istrati 1988, p.146).

13 The fifth aphorism in *Cahiers d'Art* 1929, it was followed by those on direct carving, high polish and simplicity. Brancusi objected to the demonstration of musculature in sculpture. He associated it with Rodin and Michelangelo (the tradition in which he was trained), and referred to it dismissively as 'bifteck' (literally beefsteak). In this 1929 sequence he enlarged upon the point by modifying the aphorism on high polish to end: 'It is not always appropriate, it is even very harmful for those who make "bifteck".' It is not clear whether he had a particular artist in mind as his target.

14 Brancusi published this exhortation, in French, in the catalogue of his second exhibition at the Brummer Gallery, New York, Nov.–Dec. 1933; my translation.

15 This phrase is one of those gathered under the title 'A Thought for a Day' by Dodoïca in Hulten, Dumitresco and Istrati 1988, p.103; they note that 'Dodoïca' means 'yours truly' in Romanian.

16 Tabart and Lemny 2003, p.93.

17 Hulten, Dumitresco and Istrati 1988, p.103. This is the most evidently Nietzschean of Brancusi's aphorisms, echoing the philosopher's assertion voiced in the opening pages of *Thus Spoke Zarathustra*, 1885.

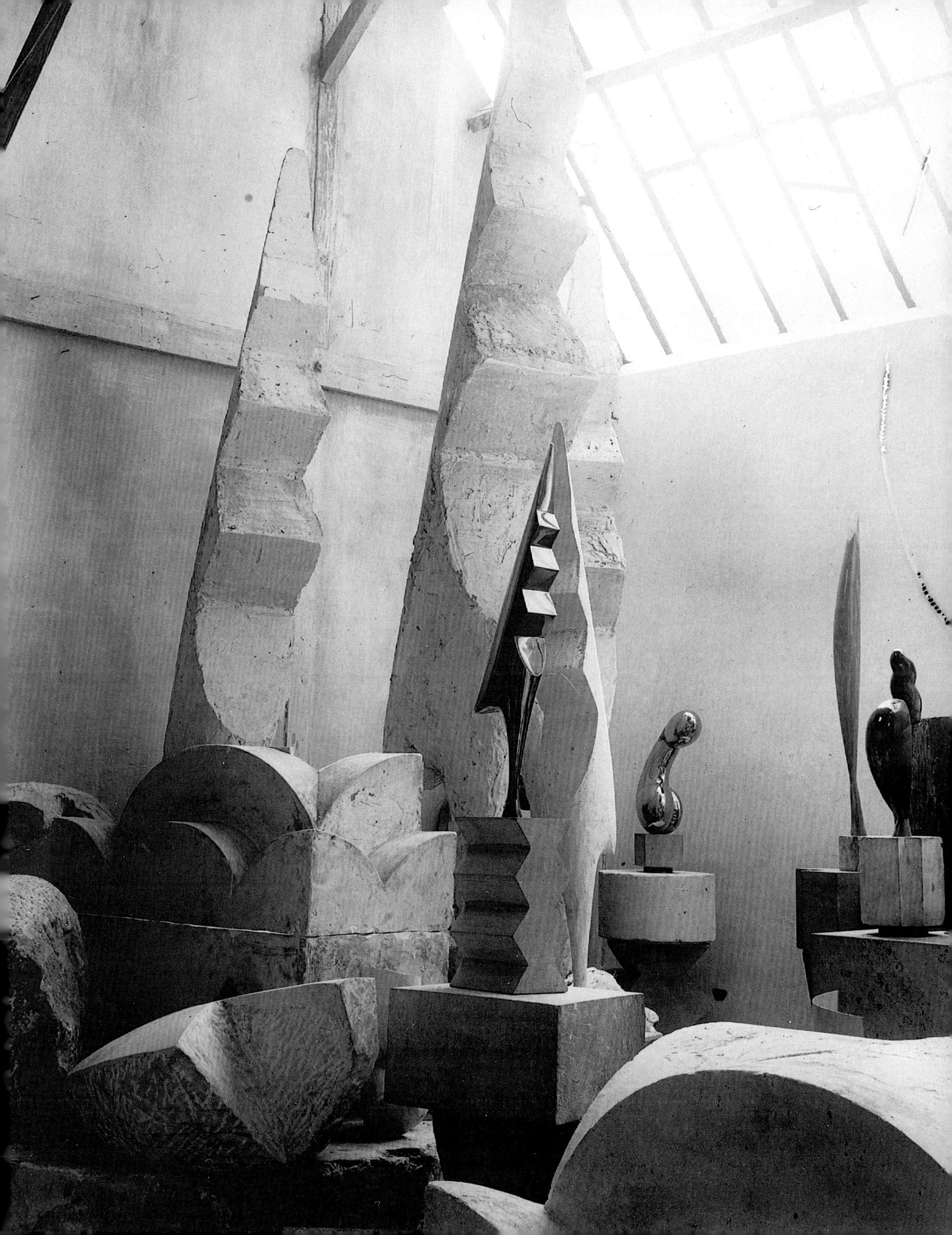

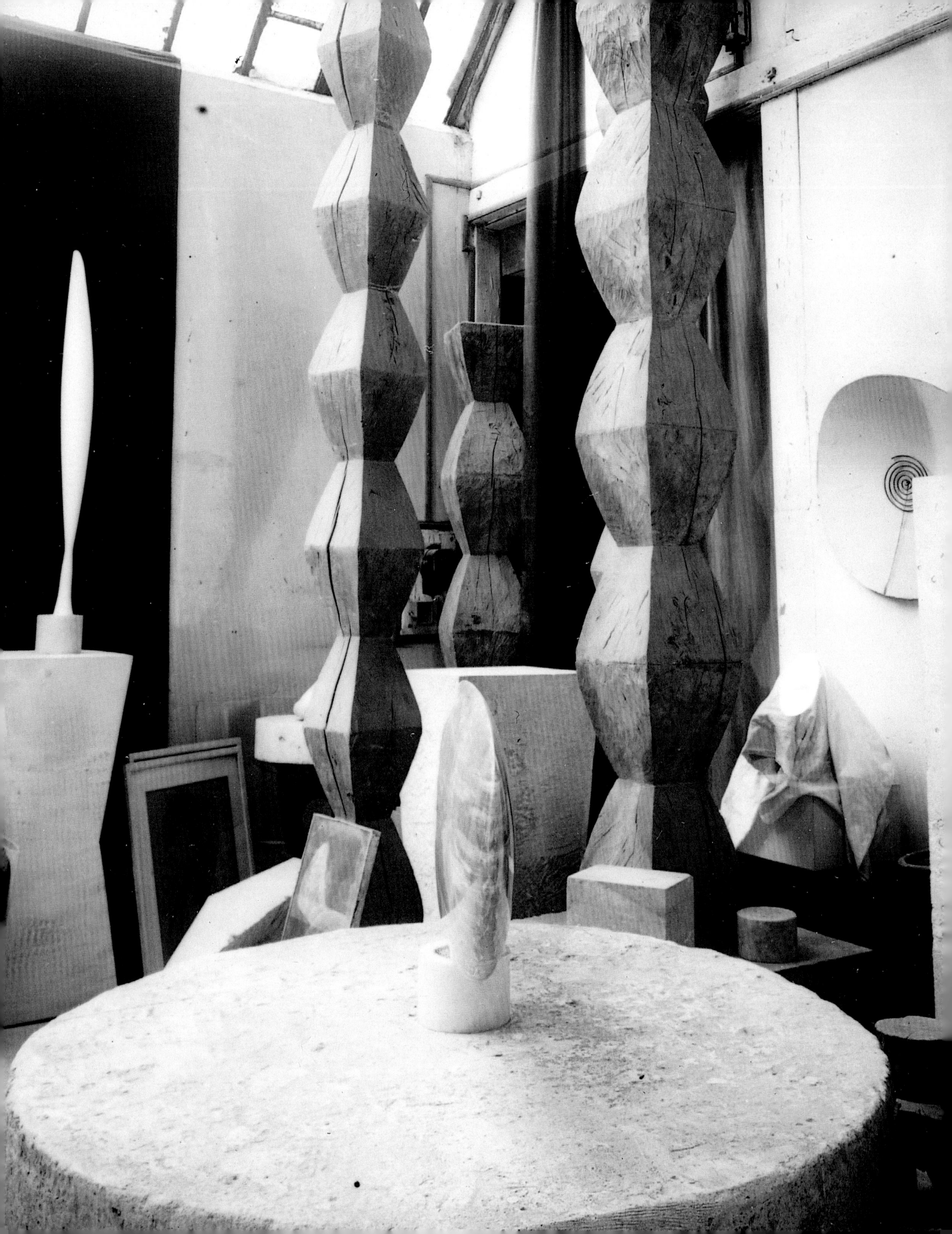

When we choose not to be Master, everything comes our way; when we long to possess, it's nowhere to be found. Such is the forbidden fruit.[18]

Morality is the religion of beauty.
Beauty is the harmony of opposing things.[19]

Exactitude is the confusion of familiar things.
Art is creating things one is unfamiliar with.[20]

An artist: someone who loves things for themselves – not to pocket them.
A true artist makes things despite himself.
A false artist makes things for the glory.
Ever since artists were invented, the arts have vanished.[21]

When one is in the sphere of the beautiful, no explanations are needed.[22]

If we limit ourselves to exact reproduction, we halt the evolution of the spirit.
If the thing we make is not connected to the absolute necessity of evolution, it is useless and harmful.[23]

Is it [possible] that the more difficult it is to reconcile things the greater the beauty?
Works of art are mirrors in which everyone sees his own likeness.[24]

Art gives birth to ideas, it does not represent them. Art comes to life intuitively, devoid of preconceived reasons, because it is the reason itself and cannot be explained *a priori* (beauty is absolute justice).[25]

They are imbeciles who call my work abstract; that which they call abstract is the most realistic, because what is real is not the exterior form but the idea, the essence of things.[26]

18 Translated under 'A Thought for a Day' by Dodoïca in Hulten, Dumitresco and Istrati 1988, p.103.

19 This pairing appears in Tabart and Lemny 2003, p.93, though a different translation of the first phrase alone is offered in Hulten, Dumitresco and Istrati 1988, p.100: 'Ethics is the religion of beauty.'

20 This phrase is translated in Hulten, Dumitresco and Istrati 1988, p.103 and appears coupled with the preceding maxim in Tabart and Lemny 2003, p.94.

21 These thoughts on materialism and ambition are grouped in Tabart and Lemny 2003, p.94. An alternative version of the final phrase is also given by Hulten, Dumitresco and Istrati 1988, p.146 as 'The arts have been beating a retreat ever since artists were invented.'

22 Hulten, Dumitresco and Istrati 1988, p.154; also in Tabart and Lemny 2003, p.92.

23 Tabart and Lemny 2003, p.92. These two phrases are given in reverse order, and a slightly different translation, in Hulten, Dumitresco and Istrati 1988, p.103.

24 The second phrase (from Hulten, Dumitresco and Istrati 1988, p.56) is prefaced by the first in Tabart and Lemny 2003, p.93. The notion of art as a mirror is explored a number of times; an alternative version appears as: 'Art is a mirror in which everyone sees what he likes' (Tabart and Lemny 2003, p.92).

25 Also given as: 'Art generates ideas, it doesn't represent them – which means that a true work of art comes into being intuitively, without preconceived motives, because it is the motive and there can be no accounting for it a priori.' Hulten, Dumitresco and Istrati 1988, p.94.

26 Claire Gilles Guilbert, 'Propos de Brancusi', *Prisme des Arts*, no.12, May 1957, p.6, translated in Herschel B. Chipp, *Theories of Modern Art: A Source Book by Artists and Critics*, Berkeley, Los Angeles and London 1968, p.365.

Chronology

This chronology inevitably draws on material published by others. The major sources among the Brancusi literature are: Brezianu 1976; Bach 1987; Hulten, Dumitresco and Istrati 1988; Bach, Rowell and Temkin 1995; and Tabart and Lemny 1997 (see Selected Reading for abbreviations). The latter, especially, is extremely detailed.

Among the sources covering the period more generally, I have drawn, among others, on: *Paris-Paris: 1937–1957*, exh. cat., Musée nationale d'art moderne, Centre George Pompidou, Paris 1981; Kenneth Silver (ed.), *The Circle of Montparnasse: Jewish Artists in Paris 1905–1945*, exh. cat., Jewish Museum, New York 1985; *Face à l'histoire 1933–1996: L'Artiste moderne devant l'événement historique*, exh. cat., Musée national d'art moderne, Centre Georges Pompidou, Paris 1996; and Sarah Wilson (ed.), *Paris: Capital of the Arts*, exh. cat., Royal Academy, London 2002.

MATTHEW GALE

	BIOGRAPHY	ART WORLD	WORLD EVENTS
1876	Born 19 Feb., Hobița near Peștișani, the second of four children from the marriage of Niculae Brancusi and Maria Deaconescu. His father, who managed the property of the monastery of Tismana, had three children from his first marriage.	Births in 1876 of Raymond Duchamp-Villon and Julio González; of Francis Picabia (1879) and Jacob Epstein (1880); in 1881 of Pablo Picasso and Fernand Léger.	1878: Treaty of Berlin establishes United Principalities of Moldavia and Wallachia as independent Romania; 1881: Prince Carol crowned King.
1883	Said to have first run away (aged seven) to Târgu Jiu, though possibly in 1885, the year his father dies.	Birth in 1884 of Amedeo Modigliani and in 1885 of Henri Laurens. Deaths in 1883 of Edouard Manet, writer Victor Hugo and composer Richard Wagner. Friedrich Nietzsche finishes *Thus Spoke Zarathustra*, 1885; poet Jean Moréas publishes *Manifesto of Symbolism*, 1886.	1885: Daimler and Benz make first motor car, Mannheim.
1887–8	Works in Târgu Jiu and Slatina, moving to Craiova.	Births in 1887 of Jean Arp, Marcel Duchamp and Alexander Archipenko	
1889–93	Works as waiter in Craiova, and in Ion Zamfirescu's grocery shop. Returns to Slatina 1892–3.	Births of Naum Gabo and Ossip Zadkine (1889); in 1891 of Henri Gaudier-Brezska and Jacques Lipchitz. Sculptor Adolf von Hildebrand, publishes *Problem of Form*, 1893.	1889: Eiffel Tower completed for Paris *Exposition Universelle.*
1894–8	Enters Craiova School of Crafts, sponsored by Zamfirescu and others. In second year enters sculpture studio with Madona Dudu church foundation scholarship. Visits Vienna in 1896 or 1897.	Birth in 1894 of Marcel Janco. Death of William Morris. 1895: First Venice Biennale exhibition. Lumière brothers' cinematograph.	1896: Ethiopia defeats invading Italians at Adova; British invade Sudan and establish military presence on Suez Canal.
1898–1902	Sept. graduates (aged 22) from Craiova and enters Bucharest School of Fine Arts; studies with Wladimir Hegel. He assigns his property to his brother and works at Café Oswald; Madona Dudu grant doubled in 1899 and secures scholarship from the Departmental Council of the Prefecture of Gorj. *Ecorché* awarded bronze medal 1901; plaster completed with advice from Dr Dimitrie Gerota. Graduates Sept. 1902.	Births in 1898 of Alexander Calder and Henry Moore; in 1901 of Alberto Giacometti, Marino Marini; in 1902 of Germaine Richier. Death of Romanian sculptor Ion Georgescu (1898); Death of Nietzsche and Oscar Wilde (1900). 1898: First Vienna Secession Exhibition. Auguste Rodin completes *Balzac*, and *Kiss*, 1898; Aristide Maillol completes *Mediterranée*, 1901. 1900: Sigmund Freud, *Interpretation of Dreams*; Paul Gauguin, *Noa-Noa*.	1899: French Presidential pardon for Alfred Dreyfus falsely condemned (in 1894) of selling military secrets to the enemy. 1900: Paris *Exposition Universelle*; Metro inaugurated. 1901: Death of Victoria, Queen since 1837. 1901: Giuseppe Marconi invents radio transmitter.

1903	Some military service; shows *Ecorché* at *Ateneul Roman.*	Birth of Barbara Hepworth. Death of Paul Gauguin. First *Salon d'Automne.* Poet Rainer Maria Rilke publishes *Rodin Book.*	Wright brothers' first flight. Pierre and Marie Curie awarded Nobel Prize for Physics. Henry Ford establishes Ford Motor Company.
1904	May: walks to Budapest, Vienna, Munich and Langres; arrives in Paris 14 July; washes dishes at Brasserie Chartier.	Birth of Isamu Noguchi. *Salon d'Automne*: rooms of works by Puvis de Chavannes and Paul Cézanne. Picasso settles in Paris definitively.	St Louis World Fair. Americans begin work on Panama Canal. Russo-Japanese War.
1905–6	Moves to 16 place Dauphine, neighbours include painter Theodor Pallady, Otilia Cosmutza and Louis Herbette. May: secures annual Ministry of Education scholarship (until 1908) and enters Antonin Mercié's studio at *Ecole des Beaux-Arts* in June (aged 29). Certificate from Ecole received in Jan. 1906. Shows at *Salon* and *Salon d'Automne.*	Birth of David Smith, 1905. Death of Cézanne, 1905. *Salon des Indépendants*: rooms devoted to Georges Seurat and Vincent Van Gogh. *Salon d'Automne*: rooms dedicated to Gauguin and Russian art; 'Fauve' room groups works by Henri Matisse, André Derain and others. Wassily Kandinsky and Gabrielle Munthe stay in Paris. Einstein, *Special Theory of Relativity.*	1905: *Exposition Coloniale*, Marseille. Kaiser's visit to Morocco sparks diplomatic crisis. 1905: Revolution in Russia follows defeat in Russo-Japanese War. First parliamentary elections called (1906). Completion of Trans-Siberian Railway, 1906. 1906: Retrial of Dreyfus in Paris clears his name.
1907	March–April: works as Rodin's assistant and meets photographer Edward Steichen. Shows at Paris *Salon* and at *Tinerimea Artistica,* Bucharest. April: signs contract for Stanescu monument in Buzau. Shows at *Abbaye de Creteil.* Moves to 54 rue du Montparnasse by end of November.	*Salon d'Automne*: room of Cézanne. Picasso completes *Les Demoiselles d'Avignon*; Derain *Crouching Figure* (fig.26). Philosopher Henri Bergson publishes *Creative Evolution.*	Triple Entente, alliance between France, Britain and Russia. First flights of Louis Blériot and Henri Farman. Romania peasant protests.
1908	Completes first direct carvings: *Sleep, The Kiss* (fig.24 & cat.1) and *Wisdom of the Earth.* Works at La Ruche studio complex. Meets Amedeo Modigliani through Paul Alexandre, and Fernand Léger. At banquet in honour of Henri Le Douanier Rousseau at Pablo Picasso's studio.	Matisse opens his Academy and publishes *Notes of a Painter*; coins term 'Cubist' for Braque's paintings. Philosopher Wilhelm Worringer publishes *Abstraction and Empathy* and political philosopher Georges Sorel, *Reflections on Violence.*	Wilbur Wright's one-hour flight at Le Mans.
1909	*Torso* (cat.5) raffled to Victor Popp. Shows at *Tinerimea Artistica* and returns to Romania (May) for *Expozitia oficiala de pictura, sculptura si arhitectura.* Ministry of Education buys *Portrait of Darascu*; other collectors include Anastasiu Simu and Alexandre Bodan-Pitesti. Portrait painted by Modigliani.	F.T. Marinetti publishes *Founding and First Manifesto of Futurism.* Kandinsky and others form *Neue Kunstlerveriningen* in Munich. Founding of *Ballets Russes* by Serge Diaghilev. Lipchitz and Zadkine arrive in Paris.	Blériot completes first cross-Channel flight.
1910	Founding member of *L'Association amicable des Roumains de Paris*; member of *Tinerimea Artistica.* Meets Margit Pogany, Renée Frachon and Léonie Ricou who inspire *Mlle Pogany, Sleeping Muse* (cat.20) and *Mme LR* respectively; frequents Paul Fort's soirées with Guillaume Apollinaire, F.T. Marinetti, Modigliani, Léger, Picasso and others. *The Prayer* (for Stanescu monument) shown at *Salon des Indépendants.* Begins *Maiastra.*	Death of Douanier Rousseau. Publication of *Manifesto of Futurist Painters.* German sculptor Wilhelm Lehmbruck stays in Paris. Duchamp-Villon, *Torso of a Young Man.*	May: Halley's Comet visible in Paris.
1911	Montparnasse *Kiss* (fig.25) commissioned by Dr Marbé as monument for Tatiana Rachewsky who committed suicide in Nov. 1910, installed April 1911. Makes *Prometheus* (cat.19). Helps Portugese painter Amedeo de Souza Cardoso organise an exhibition of Modigliani's sculptures.	Kandinsky and Franz Marc form *Blaue Reiter* group in Munich. *Mona Lisa* stolen from Louvre. Cubist room at *Salon d'Automne*, though Picasso and Braque do not participate.	Agadir Incident heightens Franco-German tension. Italy invades Tripoli (present day Libya).

1912	Shows three works at *Salon des Indépendants* and wins first prize at *Salonul Oficial*, Bucharest. Meets Epstein. Rents studio at 47 rue du Montparnasse. Visits *Salon de la Locomotion Aérienne* with Léger and Duchamp.	Epstein working on *Tomb of Oscar Wilde* in Paris. Publications: Kandinsky, *Concerning the Spiritual in Art*, Umberto Boccioni, *Technical Manifesto of Futurist Sculpture*, Albert Gleizes and Jean Metzinger, *Du Cubisme*, Guillaume Apollinaire, *Les Peintres cubistes*. Ballets Russes perform Claude Debussy's *Prelude to 'The Afternoon of a Faun'* to Nijinsky's choreography.	First Balkan War: Greece, Bulgaria, Montenegro and Serbia unite against Ottoman Empire.
1913	*Armory Show*, New York includes five works by Brancusi. Bronze *Maiastra* (cat.34) at *Salon des Indépendants* is bought by Steichen and installed in his garden at Voulangis. Shows as Romanian representative at *Kunstausstellung* Munich. Visits London while showing three works in Allied Artists Association, Royal Albert Hall meets Gaudier-Brzeska.	*Armory Show* of modern art in New York travels to Chicago and Boston. *Erster Deutsche Herbstsalon* modernist exhibition in Cologne. Ballets Russes perform Igor Stravinsky's *Rite of Spring*. Futurist Luigi Russolo publishes *The Art of Noises* manifesto.	Second Balkan War: Greece, Romania, Montenegro and Serbia unite against Bulgarian expansion.
1914	Exhibits in *Vystava Moderniho Umeni* in Prague, organised by Alexandre Mercereau, alongside Duchamp-Villon, Archipenko and others. Shows at *Tinerimea Artistica*. First solo show, Photo Secession Gallery, New York (March–April) includes *Sleeping Muse* (cat.20), *Mlle Pogany*, and bronze *Maiastra*. Brancusi takes up photography. May–June to Romania to install Stanescu monument (fig.22). On outbreak of war spends six months at Steichen's Voulangis house.	Tatlin visits Paris, meets Lipchitz, Picasso and Braque. On outbreak of war many artists are among those mobilised, including Derain, Braque and Duchamp-Villon in France, Marc and Lehmbruck in Germany.	Assassination of Archduke Franz Ferdinand of Austria sparks First World War (August). Germans rout Russians at Tanneberg and invade France through Belgium; Battle of Marne halts advance on Paris.
1915	New York lawyer John Quinn begins to form major collection of his work.	Duchamp, Picabia and others move to New York. Duchamp begins *The Bride Stripped Bare by Her Bachelors, Even (The Large Glass)*.	Italy enters the war against Austria-Hungary, on side of allies. Allied troops, stationed at Salonika, land at Gallipoli.
1916	January: rents 8 impasse Ronsin; March: exhibits at Allied Artists Association in London. Exhibits *Princess X* (cat.16) and other works in New York. Relieved of military service on medical grounds.	Death of Boccioni. Death of Gaudier-Brzeska on the Western front. Romanians Tristan Tzara and Marcel Janco among founders of artistic *Cabaret Voltaire* in Zurich, with Hugo Ball, Emmy Hennings, Richard Huelsenbeck and Arp.	Battles of Somme and Verdun. Zeppelin raids on Paris. August: Romania declares war on Germany; largely overrun by December. Death of Franz Josef of Austria, Emperor since 1848.
1917	Direct correspondence with Quinn. Shows in *Society of Independent Artists* exhibition, New York. Sept.: signs defence of Paul Poiret in *La Renaissance*.	Deaths of Degas and Rodin. *Dada* periodical edited by Tzara in Zurich. Duchamp's *Fountain* rejected by *Society of Independent Artists* exhibition, New York. Jean Cocteau, Satie and Picasso collaborate on ballet *Parade*.	USA enters war on side of Allies after German unrestricted submarine warfare. February Revolution in Russia brings Tsar's abdication; October Revolution established Bolsheviks; Civil War ensues.
1918	Breaks leg during summer holiday in southern France. Attends Apollinaire's funeral in November.	Deaths of Klimt, Hodler, Debussy, Apollinaire and Duchamp-Villon. Huelsenbeck launches Berlin Dada. Tzara publishes *Dada 3*.	November Armistice followed by influenza epidemic. Kaiser and Emperor abdicate, republics established in Germany, Austria and Hungary.
1919	Death of mother, Maria. Friendship with composer Eric Satie; Milita Patrascu begins apprenticeship (to 1923).	Tzara meets Picabia in Zurich and jointly publish *Dada 4–5*. Walter Gropius becomes director of Bauhaus.	Treaty of Versailles establishes Poland, Latvia, Lithuania, Estonia, Czechoslovakia and Yugoslavia. Transylvania becomes part of Romania. Spartakist Revolution suppressed in Germany. Hungarian Soviet suppressed by Romanian invasion.

1920	*Princess X* controversy at *Salon des Indépendants*; attends Festival Dada. March: to Romania for *Arta Română* exhibition. *Little French Girl* (cat.26) shown in Société Anonyme Inc exhibition organised by Katherine S Dreier with Duchamp and Man Ray. Makes *Beginning of the World* (cat.22)	Death of Modigliani. Tzara arrives in Paris to launch Dada (Jan.) in collaboration with Picabia and editors of *Littérature*, André Breton, Louis Aragon and Philippe Soupault. Periodical *L'Esprit Nouveau*. Lipchitz exhibition at Galerie de l'Effort Moderne, Paris.	League of Nations founded in London. Polish army invades Russia in Civil War. Prohibition of alcohol in USA.
1921	Collector Jacques Doucet buys bronze *Danaïde* (cat.13). Meets Quinn, Man Ray and Ezra Pound who writes first substantial appreciation in *Little Review*.	Man Ray arrives in Paris. Duchamp also returns.	Foundation of Irish Free State. Rampant inflation in Germany.
1922	March–April: 22 sculptures included in *Contemporary French Art*, Sculptors' Gallery, New York. Makes costumes for dancer Lizica Codreanu's performance of Satie's *Gymnopédies* in studio. Meets Romanian composer Marcel Mihalovici. Sept.–Oct.: visits Romania with Eileen Lane; proposes monument for Pestisani.	Various art conferences: abandoned *Congrès de Paris*, *Internationalen Kongress fur fortschrittliche Kunst* in Düsseldorf, and *Konstructivisten-Dadaisten Kongress* in Weimar. Musée du Jeu de Paume established to show work of 'foreign' artists.	Germany and Soviet Union sign Treaty of Rapallo. Benito Mussolini seizes power in Italy in Fascists' 'March on Rome'.
1923	Awarded *Steaua Romaniei* medal by King Ferdinand I of Romania.	Léger designs ballet *Creation of the World.*	French occupy Ruhr over German failure to pay war reparations.
1924	Shows two sculptures in Romanian Pavilion at Venice Biennale. Nearly drowns on holiday, but saved by crocodile-shaped driftwood, which he brings back to Paris. Nov.–Dec.: shows 4 sculptures in *Contimporanul* exhibition in Bucharest.	Death of John Quinn. Janco founds *Contimporanul* periodical in Bucharest. Breton publishes *Manifeste du surréalisme* and launches periodical *La Révolution surréaliste.* Satie and Picabia's ballet *Relâche* and, with René Clair, film *Entr'acte.*	Death of Lenin; power struggle ensues in USSR between Trotsky and Stalin. French election victory of the left 'cartel des gauches'.
1925	Subject of special issue of *Contemporanul* periodical; *This Quarter* publishes photographs and aphorisms collected by Irina Codreanu. Shows in *Exhibition of Tri-National Art* in Paris, London and New York (1926).	Death of Satie. Jacques Bacot publishes *The Tibetan Poet Milarepa*, Paris 1925, a work favoured by Brancusi. *Exposition des Arts Décoratifs*, Paris establishes term *Art Deco.*	French withdrawal from Ruhr. Colonial revolt in French-held Morocco.
1926	Jan.–March: to New York for solo exhibition at Wildenstein Galleries. Penguin Club party in his honour. Supports Duchamp's and Henri-Pierre Roché's purchase of Quinn's stock of his work. Installs 10-metre-high *Endless Column* in Steichen's garden at Voulangis (fig.14); project for large *Bird in Space* for Vicomte de Noailles's villa in South of France. Sept.–Dec.: revisits New York for solo exhibition at Brummer Gallery (then Arts Club of Chicago). USA Customs refuse to classify *Bird in Space* as (tax-free) work of art and levy 40% import tariff on purchase price.	Deaths of Monet and Rilke. Christian Zervos launches *Cahiers d'Art*, and begins to compile comprehensive catalogue of Picasso's work.	General Strike in Britain.
1927	*Brancusi vs. United States* court case begins in Oct. with Steichen and Epstein among defence witnesses. Gives deposition at American Consulate in Paris, 22 Nov. Through writer Robert McAlmon, meets Noguchi who becomes his assistant. June: buys land for a studio in rue Sauvageot; floor of 8 impasse Ronsin caves in, so moves to no.11. Moves *Endless Column* from Steichen's garden to studio. Aphorisms published in *De Stijl.*		Breakdown of German economic system.

1928	Shows in *Exhibition of Contemporary French Art* in Moscow organised by Anatole Lunatcharsky. Meets Jean Arp, Arno Breker, Swiss art historian Carola Giedion-Welcker and James Joyce. November: wins customs trial, forcing legal redefinition of art in USA.	Serge Eisenstein's film *Oktober*.	Briand–Kellogg Pact: Renunciation of war as an instrument of national policy. Stalin's Five-Year Plan for industrialisation of USSR.
1929	Represented in Làzló Moholy-Nagy's *Von Material zur Architektur*; appreciations by Roger Vitrac (*Cahiers d'Art*) and Benjamin Fondane (*Cahiers de l'Étoile*).	Death of Diaghilev. Salvador Dalí and Luis Buñuel make film *Un Chien andalou*. Joaquim Torrès-García and Michel Seuphor found *Cerle et Carré* group.	Wall Street Crash and Depression. France begins Maginot Line of eastern defences.
1930	Meets painters Victor Brauner, Julius Bissier, Joan Miró and Jacques Hérold (who becomes assistant to 1931), and composer Darius Milhaud.	Suicide of poet Vladimir Mayakovsky in Moscow. Breton publishes *Seconde manifeste du surréalisme*.	Coronation of King Carol II of Romania. Allied troops withdraw from Rhineland; Adolf Hitler's National Socialists gain ground at poles.
1931	Maharaja of Indore buys bronze *Bird in Space* and commissions white and black marble versions. Awarded *Meitul Cultural pentru Arta Plastica* by King Carol II of Romania.	*Exposition Coloniale*, Paris. Van Doesburg, Mondrian and others found international *Abstraction-Création* group.	German crisis deepens with 5.7 million unemployed. Establishment of Spanish Republic.
1932			Roosevelt elected President of USA; Hindenburg elected President in Germany; President Paul Doumer of France and Prime Minister Ion Duca of Romania assassinated.
1933	Visited by Barbara Hepworth and Ben Nicholson. To New York for solo exhibition at Brummer Gallery, Nov.–Jan. 1934.	Léger joins anti-Fascist *Association des écrivains et artistes révolutionnaires* (AEAR). Kandinsky moves to Paris.	Hitler becomes German Chancellor; Reichstag fire and Nazi repression. Roosevelt's 'New Deal'. Romanian Communists and Fascist Iron Guard are outlawed for political violence.
1934	Film script *The Next 120 Years*. Vera Moore gives birth to their child John.	Artists and architects, including Gropius and Marcel Breuer, are among those fleeing Nazi repression and moving to London.	French General Strike. On death of President Hindenberg, Hitler amalgamates top offices as *Reichsführer*. Moscow Show-Trials follow murder of Kirov.
1935	War memorial for Târgu Jiu commissioned by National Women's League of Gorj.		Italy invades Abyssinia. Obligatory military service in Germany.
1936	Contributes to *Cubism and Abstract Art* at Museum of Modern Art, New York and *International Surrealist Exhibition* in London. Completes *Birds in Space* for Maharaja of Indore.	Debates around realism in art, stimulated by left-wing desire for engagement.	Left-wing Popular Front government in France. Popular Front victory in Spain sparks General Franco's mutiny and Spanish Civil War. Abdication crisis in Britain.
1937	Cuts element of Târgu Jiu *Endless Column* for casting and specifies metal must be 'yellow'. At Târgu Jiu (Oct.–Nov.) visits quarries and begins work on *Gate of the Kiss*; *Table of Silence* put in place and *Endless Column* assembled (figs.15, 17 & 18). Dec.: to Bombay.	Nazis seize modernist art in public collections for display in *Degenerate Art* exhibition, Munich. Exodus of artists. Picasso makes *Guernica* for Spanish Republican Pavilion at Paris *Exposition Internationale*. Lipchitz makes *Prometheus Strangling the Vulture* (fig.16).	Japanese invasion continues with fall of Peking (Beijing) and Shanghai. Political violence in Romania with swing to Right.
1938	In Indore (Jan.) but Maharaja absent and 'temple' never built to house *Birds in Space*; returns via Egypt. June-July to Târgu Jiu: *Gate of the Kiss* and metalling of *Endless Column* completed. Larger version to *Table of Silence* ordered. In Paris by time of inauguration. Never returns to Romania.	*Twentieth Century German Art* exhibition in London shows works of 'degenerate' artists. *Exposition Internationale du Surréalisme*, Paris.	Nazi annexation of Austria (Anschluss); Daladier and Chamberlain meet Hitler at Munich and accept annexation of Sudetenland from Czechoslovakia. *Kristallnacht* Nazi assault on Jews and Jewish property in Germany. Carol II enforces authoritarian direct rule in Romania; arrest and murder of Iron Guard leadership.

1939	To New York for *Art in Our Time* exhibition at Museum of Modern Art; travels to Philadelphia, Washington and Chicago where 400-metre *Endless Column* is projected. Returns to Paris in May.	1000 works of 'degenerate art' are burnt in Berlin. New York World Fair.	Barcelona falls to Franco; refugee influx into France. German invasion of Czechoslovakia; Italian invasion of Albania. Nazi-Soviet pact divides Poland and Baltic states; German invasion of Poland sparks French and British declaration of Second World War. So-called 'phoney war', without hostilities, until 1940.
1940–4	Spends years of Occupation in seclusion in Paris; young Chilean artist Juana Muller is assistant.	Peggy Guggenheim, protected by American neutrality, purchases bronze *Bird in Space* (cat.37). Artists and writers, including Léger, Zadkine, Breton and Duchamp, go into exile in USA. Death of Mondrian in New York (1944). Picasso spends most of Occupation in Paris. Associated artists and writers, including Tzara, Aragon and Paul Eluard, are clandestine members of the Resistance. Senior artists, including Matisse, Bonnard and Picabia, live in seclusion in South of France. Nazi sculptor Arno Breker's exhibition at Musée de l'Orangerie. Nazis invite artists, including Derain and Vlaminck, to visit Germany. Nazi seizure of art in all occupied lands.	Germany seizes Denmark, Norway, Luxembourg, the Netherlands, Belgium and France. Paris falls in June 1940. Vichy Republic established in south. General Antonescu seizes power in Romania and, with Hungary and Slovakia, joins tripartite alliance of Germany, Italy and Japan. Soviet invasion of Baltic states. 1941: Germans occupy Yugoslavia and Greece and attack Soviet Union; USA enters war after Pearl Harbour attack by Japan (Dec.) Battles of El Alamein (1942) and Stalingrad (1942–3) halt German advances. Allied landings in Italy (1943) and Normandy (1944). Liberation of Paris and Rome (1944). King Michael of Romania deposes Antonescu on eve of Russian invasion.
1945	Emerges from seclusion.	Picasso publicly joins Communist Party and heads committee judging artists' collaboration with Nazis.	Fall of Berlin and revelation of the Nazi Death Camps. Armistice in Europe; Hiroshima and Nagasaki end Pacific war.
1946–7	Meets virologist Pascu Atanasiu who becomes executor. 1947: V.G. Paleolog publishes first monograph.	*Art et Résistance* exhibition at Musée National d'Art Moderne, Paris 1946.	Nuremburg trials. 1946: Communist coup in Hungary. 1947: Michael I abdicates and goes into exile.
1948–9	Romanian artists Alexandre Istrati and Natalia Dumitresco occupy the studio at impasse Ronsin formerly taken by Capellaro (a sculptor of funerary monuments) *Large Cock* probably last work (fig.39).	Christian Dotremont launches international *Cobra* group. Auguste Herbin defends abstraction against Social Realism in *Premier Manifeste du Salon des Réalités Nouvelles.*	1948: Communists declare Romanian Republic. Communist coup in Czechoslovakia (1948). Federal German Republic in West Germany (1949). Berlin Blockade and foundation of NATO.
1950–4	Requests French citizenship – granted 1952. Charges Duchamp and Roché with preserving his studio after his death. Max Ernst (in 1952–4) and Jean Tinguely (from 1954) occupy studios at impasse Ronsin.	Picasso shows *Massacre in Korea* at Salon de Mai 1951. 1953: *Unknown Political Prisoner*, international sculpture competition organised at Institute of Contemporary Art, London. Zadkine completes commemorative monument *To a Destroyed City* for Rotterdam.	Korean War. Death of Stalin (1953).
1955–6	Breaks hip, Jan.–May in hospital. First retrospective, Solomon R. Guggenheim Museum, New York (Oct.–Jan. 1956) and Philadelphia Museum of Art (Jan.–Feb. 1956).		Formation of USSR-led Warsaw Pact. Hungarian Uprising crushed by Soviet Union. Suez Crisis as Egypt repells French and British invasion of Canal zone. Algerian War.
1957	Dies 16 March; interred in Montparnasse Cemetery. *Cahiers d'Art* publishes special posthumous issue.		Treaty of Rome forms European Economic Community.

Selected reading

The major publications are listed chronologically, with abbreviations given for those cited most frequently in the texts.

David Lewis, *Constantin Brancusi*, London 1957

Carola Giedion-Welcker, *Constantin Brancusi*, Neuchâtel 1958, translated by Maria Jolas and Anne Leroy, New York 1959

Ionel Jianou, *Brancusi*, London and New York 1963

Petru Comarnescu, Mircea Eliade and Ionel Jianou, *Témoignages sur Brancusi*, Paris 1967

Geist 1968/1983: Sidney Geist, *Brancusi: A Study of the Sculpture*, New York 1968, revised New York 1983

Sidney Geist, *Constantin Brancusi, 1876–1957: A Retrospective Exhibition*, exh. cat., Philadelphia Museum of Art, Solomon R. Guggenheim Museum, New York and Art Institute of Chicago, 1969–70

Athena T. Spear, *Brancusi's Birds*, New York 1969

Geist 1975: Sidney Geist, *Brancusi: The Sculpture and Drawings*, New York 1975

Brezianu 1976: Barbu Brezianu, *Opera lui Constantin Brancusi in Romania*, Bucharest 1974, revised and translated by Delia Razdolescu and Ilie Marcu, as *Brancusi in Romania*, Bucharest 1976

Marielle Tabart and Isabelle Monod-Fontaine, *Brancusi photographe*, Paris 1977

Geist 1978: Sidney Geist, *Brancusi / The Kiss*, New York, Hagerstown, San Francisco and London 1978

Dan Grigorescu, *Brancusi and the Romanian Roots of his Art*, Bucharest 1984

Qu'est-ce que la sculpture moderne? exh. cat., Centre Georges Pompidou, Paris 1986

Radu Varia, *Brancusi*, translated by Mary Vaudoyer, New York 1986

Bach 1987: Friedrich Teja Bach, *Constantin Brancusi: Metamorphosen plastischer Form*, Cologne 1987

Hulten, Dumitresco and Istrati 1988: Pontus Hulten, Natalia Dumitresco and Alexandre Istrati, *Brancusi*, Paris 1986, English edition Patricia Egan (ed.), London and Boston 1988

Eric Shanes, *Constantin Brancusi*, New York 1989

Chave 1993: Anna C. Chave, *Constantin Brancusi: Shifting the Bases of Art*, New Haven and London 1993

Ina Klein, *Brancusi: Natur, Struktur, Skulptur, Architektur*, Cologne 1994, vol.2

Bach, Rowell and Temkin 1995: Friedrich Teja Bach, Margit Rowell and Ann Temkin, *Constantin Brancusi, 1876–1957*, exh. cat., Centre Georges Pompidou, Paris and Philadelphia Museum of Art 1995

Miller 1995: Sanda Miller, *Constantin Brancusi: A Survey of his Work*, Oxford 1995

Marielle Tabart, *Brancusi: L'Inventeur de la sculpture moderne*, Paris 1995

Tabart and Lemny 1997: Marielle Tabart and Doïna Lemny, *L'Atelier Brancusi: La collection*, Paris 1997

Brezianu 1998: Barbu Brezianu, *Brancusi en Romanie*, Bucharest 1998

Marielle Tabart (ed.), *Les carnets de l'Atelier Brancusi: Le Colonne sans fin*, Paris 1998

Marielle Tabart (ed.), *Les carnets de l'Atelier Brancusi: Leda*, Paris 1998

Sidney Geist, Barbu Brezianu and S.L.F., *Les carnets de l'Atelier Brancusi: Le Baiser*, Paris 1999

Marielle Tabart (ed.), *Les carnets de l'Atelier Brancusi: Princesse X*, Paris 1999

Brancusi vs. United States: The Historic Trial, 1928, Paris 1999

Paola Mola, *Studi su Brancusi*, Milan 2000

Alex Potts, *The Sculptural Imagination: Figurative, Modernism, Minimalist*, New Haven and London 2000

Marielle Tabart (ed.), *Les carnets de l'Atelier Brancusi: Brancusi & Duchamp*, Paris 2000

Marielle Tabart (ed.), *Les carnets de l'Atelier Brancusi: L'Oiseau dans l'espace*, Paris 2001

Timothy O. Benson (ed.), *Central European Avant-gardes: Exchange and Transformation, 1910–1930*, exhibition catalogue, Los Angeles County Museum of Art 2002

Timothy O. Benson and Eva Forgás (eds.), *Between Worlds: A Sourcebook of Central European Avant-gardes, 1910–1930*, Cambridge (Mass.) and London 2002

Marielle Tabart (ed.), *Les carnets de l'Atelier Brancusi: Le Portrait?*, Paris 2002

Pierre Cabanne, *Constantin Brancusi*, Paris 2002

Tabart and Lemny 2003: Marielle Tabart and Doïna Lemny, *La dation Brancusi; Dessins et archives*, exh. cat., Centre Pompidou, Paris 2003

List of works

In addition to the sculptures illustrated in the Catalogue, the following photographs are included in the exhibition.

All are silver gelatine prints lent by Centre Georges Pompidou, Paris. The vintage prints derive from the Constantin Brancusi Bequest 1957; those marked with an asterisk (*) are modern prints from Brancusi's negatives. For purposes of identification Centre Pompidou inventory numbers are given in parentheses; references are given for those illustrated in this catalogue.

Studio view with Sorceress, 1916
29.7 × 23.8 (11 5/8 × 9 3/8)
AM4002-935, PH622

Studio view with Portrait of Mme L.R., 1920
22.5 × 16.8 (8 7/8 × 6 5/8)
AM4002-257(1), PH12A, reproduced p.18, fig.9

Studio view with Mlle Pogany II, *c.*1921
23.8 × 18 (9 3/8 × 7 1/8)
AM4002-255(1), PH10A, reproduced p.126, fig.40

Studio view with marble Bird, *c.*1922–3
39.9 × 29.6 (15 3/4 × 11 5/8)
AM4002-276(1), PH31A

Studio view, *c.*1923–4
29.7 × 23.8 (11 3/4 × 9 3/8)
AM4002-281(1), reproduced p.25, fig.12

Sorceress, 1924
39.8 × 30 (15 5/8 × 11 3/4)
AM4002-293 (1)

Studio view with Sorceress, 1924–5
60 × 44 (23 5/8 × 17 3/8)
PH51* reproduced p.17, fig.8

Studio view with Crocodile, 1925
18 × 13 (7 1/8 × 5 1/8)
PH64* reproduced p.13, fig.1

Studio view with Endless Columns and Mlle Pogany, 1925
24 × 18 (9 1/2 × 7 1/8)
PH58* reproduced p.128, fig.41

Studio view with Endless Columns and Crocodile, 1926
38.2 × 25.2 (15 × 9 7/8)
AM4002-310(1) PH71A

Endless Column at Voulangis, 1926
39.7 × 29.8 (15 5/8 × 11 3/4)
AM4002-901, PH535

Endless Column at Voulangis, 1926
14 × 9 (5 1/2 × 3 1/2)
PH539* reproduced p.27, fig.14

Endless Column at Voulangis, 1926
39 × 29.4 (15 3/8 × 11 5/8)
PH542*

Studio view, *c.*1930–3
18 × 13 (7 1/8 × 5 1/8)
PH117* reproduced p.132, fig.44

Endless Column at Târgu Jiu, 1937
23.9 × 17.9 (9 3/8 × 7)
PH561*

The Table of Silence at Târgu Jiu, *c.*1938
8.7 × 13.5 (3 3/8 × 5 3/8)
AM4002-926, reproduced p.32, fig.17

Endless Column at Târgu Jiu, *c.*1938
17.9 × 23.9 (7 × 9 3/8)
AM4002-618 (1)

Endless Column at Târgu Jiu, *c.*1938
23.9 × 17.9 (9 3/8 × 7)
AM4002-628 (1)

Endless Column at Târgu Jiu, *c.*1938
23.9 × 17.9 (9 3/8 × 7)
AM4002-914, PH570

Endless Column at Târgu Jiu, *c.*1938
39.8 × 29.7 (15 5/8 × 11 3/4)
AM4002-917, PH573

Endless Column at Târgu Jiu, *c.*1938
39.8 × 29.9 (15 5/8 × 11 3/4)
AM4002-922, PH581, reproduced p.28, fig.15

Endless Column at Târgu Jiu, *c.*1938
39.8 × 29.8 (15 5/8 × 11 3/4)
AM4002-923, PH582

Endless Column at Târgu Jiu, 1938
9 × 6.5 (3 1/2 × 2 1/2)
PH585* reproduced p.129, fig.42

The Gate of the Kiss, 1938
17.8 × 22.7 (7 × 8 1/4)
AM4002-803, PH229

The Gate of the Kiss, 1938
29.8 × 39.8 (11 3/4 × 15 5/8)
AM4002-805, PH231, reproduced p.33, fig.18

Studio view with Large Cocks, *c.*1940–5
24 × 18 (9 3/8 × 7 1/8)
PH133* reproduced p.131, fig.43

Studio view, c.1943–6
24.9 × 17.8 (9 3/4 × 7)
AM4002-768, PH144

Studio view with Cocks and King of Kings, *c.*1945–6
18 × 13 (7 1/8 × 5 1/8)
PH140* reproduced p.70, fig.39

List of lenders

Public collections

Basel
Fondation Beyeler, Riehen: 35

Bucharest
Muzeul National de Artă al României: 12

Cambridge, Mass.
The Fogg Art Museum, Harvard University Art Museums: 6, 28

Craiova
Muzeul de Artă: 1, 4

Dallas
Dallas Museum of Art: 22

Lincoln, Nebraska
Sheldon Memorial Art Gallery and Sculpture Garden, University of Nebraska: 16

London
Tate: 13, 25, 34

New Haven
Yale University Art Gallery, Collection of the Société Anonyme: 36

New York
Museum of Modern Art: 30

Solomon R. Guggenheim Museum: 15, 26, 27, 29, 31, 32, 33

Paris
Centre Pompidou: 8, 10, 11, 18, 23, all photographs

Philadelphia
Philadelphia Museum of Art: 3, 7, 19, 21

Stockholm
Moderna Museet: 24

Stuttgart
Staatsgalerie: 5

Venice
Peggy Guggenheim Collection: 37

Washington, D.C.
Hirshhorn Museum and Sculpture Garden, Smithsonian Institution: 20

Private collections

2, 9, 14, 17

Credits

Copyright credits

Photographic credits

Junius Beebe cat.6

Robert Bayer, LAC AG cat.35

Martin Bühler fig.29

© Photo CNAC/MNAM Dist. RMN (Jacques Fajour) figs.1, 40, 9, 43

© Photo CNAC/MNAM Dist. RMN (Philippe Migeat) figs.7–10, 12–15, 17, 18, 32, 34, 36, 37, 39, 41, 42, 44

© Photo CNAC/MNAM figs.35, 38

David Heal © The Solomon R. Guggenheim Foundation, New York cat.15, 26, 27, 29, 31, 32, 33

Frank Hovat figs.4, 5

© Volker Naumann Fotographie cat.5

Michael A. Nedzweski fig.30

© Mihai Oroveanu, Artexpo figs.19–25

© 2004 The Museum of Modern Art, New York cat.30

Adam Rzepka © MNAC cat.12

Adam Rzepka cat.8, 10, 18, 23

Bruce Schwarz cat.2

Tate Archive fig.6

Tate Photography figs.11, 27, 28; cat.13

Tate Photography/Andrew Dunkley cat.34

Tate Photography/Gill Selby cat.25

Graydon Wood, 1988 cat.19

Graydon Wood, 1994 cat.7, 21

Index